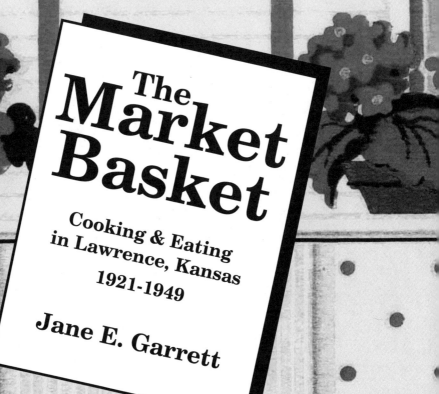

The Market Basket

Cooking & Eating in Lawrence, Kansas

1921-1949

Jane E. Garrett

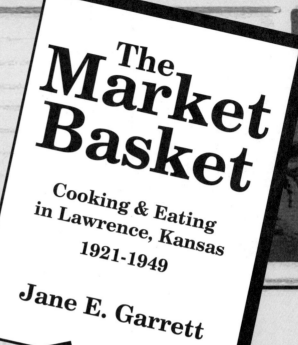

The Market Basket

Cooking & Eating
in Lawrence, Kansas
1921-1949

Jane E. Garrett

Over 600
prize-winning recipes
from residents
of Lawrence
and
surrounding
communities
awarded
by the
Lawrence
Journal-World

Printed in the United States of America.

ISBN: 978-1-59571-138-0

Library of Congress Control Number: 2006927454

Word Association Publishers
205 5th Avenue
Tarentum, Pennsylvania 15084

www.wordassociation.com

1-800-827-7903

This book is dedicated to all the women of Lawrence who overcame the hardships of an economic depression and a world war by bringing good and wholesome food to the table.

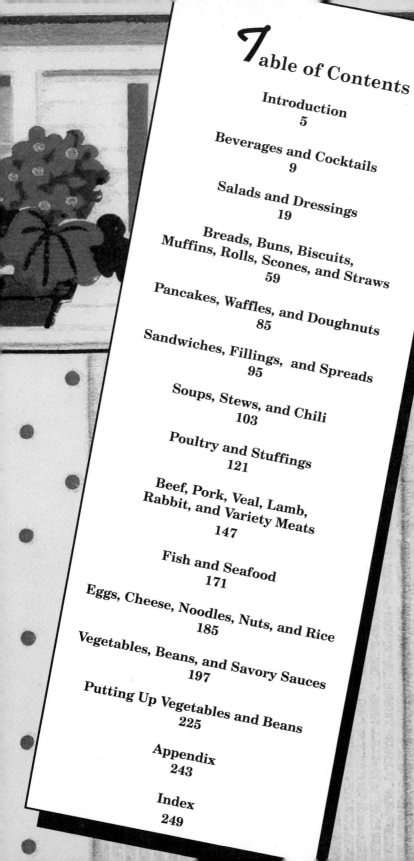

𝒯able of Contents

*I*ntroduction

Nine years ago, I was in the basement of the Lawrence Public Library reading articles from a 1933 issue of the *Lawrence Journal-World*. I was amusing myself at the microfilm reader–not looking for anything in particular—when I spotted, in the supermarket ads section, a recipe for Mrs. George J. Shultz's apple butter and the announcement that it was the week's "Market Basket" prize-winner. Beneath the recipe was the announcement that the following week's prize would be awarded to the one submitting the best recipe for putting up blue plums. It was as if I'd been handed a nice, old piece of china and with it a challenge to collect the entire set. What I didn't know was that it would take me a year and a half to dig up 1,400 recipes, each one a prize-winner in a contest sponsored by the *Lawrence Journal-World* that would begin in July, 1921 and end in November, 1949. Nearly a thousand local and area residents (all but three of them women) were awarded two dollars for their winning entry in a category selected by the *Journal-World* Market Basket judges, and announced every Friday.

On Sept. 1, 1923, the following item appeared in the *Lawrence Journal-World*:

The Market Basket Judges Are Flooded With Good Recipes

Locating Mr. Jones in New York City with a telephone directory as the only aid may sound like a hopeless task. At any rate, it is by no means one that can be accomplished quickly. Yet, that is a comparatively easy one compared to the selection of the best recipe among seventy three, so said the judges in the Market Basket contest this week, when they attempted to decide on one when there were seventy two others clamoring for first place.

The judges are highly gratified however by the interest taken in the contest and welcome all new members, though sorry there can be but one winner when many good recipes are received. They have let fall the hint that their work might be made more pleasant were there now and then a sample of the article accompanying its description, for reading about good things to eat does not encourage a desire to fast, you know. However, such good luck could scarcely be expected.

Like the Market Basket judges, I only *read* about the good things to eat. I did not test the recipes contained in this (and the forthcoming) volume; nor was it ever my intention to do so. Whether or not a recipe resulted in a dish "fit for a king" was not as important to me as it was to have a record of what was being cooked and how. It was a time when cooking "from scratch" meant cooking from the ground up. Backyard gardens were common and so were berry patches, fruit and nut trees, and even chicken coops. It's gruesome to imagine having to start my day by going out to the chicken coop, selecting a fat hen, wringing its neck, hacking off its head and feet, eviscerating it, and plucking out all of its feathers. (On page 142, Mrs. Jesse Carson tells how she used hot, melted paraffin to rid her wild duck of pin feathers.) I would prefer to imagine myself sneaking past the backyard chicken coop and running straight to the corner butcher to purchase an already-cleaned and dressed bird. But, then again, money was scarce.

In 1921, according to a report on the wages and hours of Kansas labor, a woman living in Lawrence earned thirty-nine cents an hour. A dressed hen in 1921 could be had at a local market for thirty-eight cents a pound. It would take a half-day's wages, then, for that Lawrence woman to afford a four-pound dressed hen. Pound for pound, beef, veal, pork, and lamb were significantly cheaper than poultry back then (and why I've yet to understand), ranging in cost from veal breast (ten cents) to spare ribs and lamb forequarters (fifteen cents) to beef rib roast (twenty cents). In 1921, a Lawrence woman's full-day's pay would just barely cover the cost of a five-pound pot roast, three cans of soup, a broom, a Sunday dinner at Wiedemann's Tea Room, and a trip to the movies. A Lawrence man (earning an average of fifty cents an hour) could afford three more trips to the movies than his female counterpart.

By 1939, as a world war was being fought in Europe, Americans continued to pay dearly for food. According to a 1939 U.S. government report, 34.5% of the average family income was spent on clothing, transportation, medical care, personal care, amusement, education, church and gifts; 32% went toward shelter and household operation; and a whopping 33.5% was spent on food alone.

Three years later, American consumers were issued U.S. government war ration stamp books, limiting purchases of meats, processed fruits and vegetables, coffee and sugar, among a number of other foods and commodities. A "Heard In Lawrence" item in the February 13, 1942 issue of the *Lawrence Journal-World* warned: "Rumor has it that no one will be given a sugar rationing stamp book without swearing that the family has no more than two pounds on hand for each member of the family. And for those who don't tell the truth, it's a matter of up to 10 years or $10,000."

A wartime supplement, which appeared in the 1943 *Good Housekeeping Cook Book,* helped its readers adjust to a strained larder by offering advice in meal planning. Butter, for example, could be doubled in amount by combining it with unflavored gelatine and evaporated milk. Alternatives to butter included margarine, salad oil, lard, bacon and sausage drippings, and rendered chicken fat. Coffee could be stretched by adding roasted chicory, cereals and legumes to the coffee before brewing. Less familiar cuts of meat–such as lamb shanks, pork hocks, kidneys, pig knuckles, heart and oxtail–could be substituted for the better cuts–the ones that were feeding our armed forces and allies. Cereals, such as oatmeal and cornflakes, were cited as good meat stretchers. Sugar could be saved in cake and pie baking by substituting corn syrup or honey. Canning fruits and vegetables was not only a symbol of patriotism, it was a necessity. "Gardening and canning were never so important to our family and national welfare as today"–so said the Bernardin company in its 1943 home canning guide.

My former next-door neighbor, Kathe (White) Alkoudsi, 1344 Massachusetts St., relates a story about her mother canning tomatoes on August 20, 1943–the day Kathe was born. The White family resided at 2108 Barker Ave., on a double deep lot. Green beans, peas, potatoes, onions, corn, and tomatoes grew in the Victory Garden behind the home–a garden that was plowed every spring by "Shorty," a man who was a town fixture, well-known for his diminutive stature and for the pencils he sold downtown. Until he was able to purchase a tractor, Shorty plowed the White family garden with a team of horses.

On August 20, 1943, while Kathe's father, Harold, was away at work as a maintenance engineer at the Bowersock Power Plant, Kathe's mother, Wilma, went about her business at hand–canning tomatoes. As she was working, her next door neighbor, Bertha White (no relation to Wilma and Harold), popped into Wilma's kitchen to see how her pregnant friend was doing. Wilma responded, "Well, I think I've gone into labor."

"What are you doing *here?*" Bertha wanted to know, to which Wilma responded, "I can't leave. I have to finish canning these tomatoes." Bertha's reply was "Go call a taxi. I'll finish the tomatoes."

Dr. Fred Isaacs delivered baby Kathe at 2:30 p.m. at Lawrence Memorial Hospital, just minutes after Wilma had left her tomatoes.

✦

Of the 1,400 prize-winning recipes I collected, I eliminated about 100–mostly because of duplications. And though not every recipe from the contest will appear in this and Volume II (many women won multiple prizes), I made sure that every person who entered and won is represented.

I am very grateful to Dolph Simons Jr., chairman of the World Company, and editor of the *Lawrence Journal-World*, for allowing me to reprint this collection. I'm grateful, too, to the *Journal-World* editorial staff of the 1920s, '30s, and '40s who introduced and sustained the contest so that I might one day find it and give it back to the community. And for the authors of these recipes, who put good food on the table during some very difficult times, I have deep respect.

I'm thankful to the employees of the Lawrence Public Library, who assisted me during the "digging" time, and to my friend, Paula Courtney, who advised me in all matters of word processing. And, for their many words of encouragement–ones that always inspired me to keep working–I am grateful to Katie Armitage, Dodie Coker, and Bruce Scoular.

Citations contained within the text include the following:

LJW: *Lawrence Journal-World*
DCR: *Douglas County Republican*
TO: *The Outlook (DCR's* successor)

An appendix–clarifying cooking terms–appears at the back of the book, as well as an index of persons, businesses, organizations, and enterprises.

Jane E. Garrett, 2008

Beverages
and
Cocktails

Andy's Thimble Tea Room Opens

It is not necessary to go to some large city to visit a tea room with the French air and Oriental setting. For Andy has achieved that result in her "Thimble Tea Room" in the McCurdy Building in the 1000 block on Mass. The pastel shades of cream, rose, blue and green have been used to make very attractive rooms. The draperies and tapestries have been imported from Belgium, Persia, India and Japan. Wrought iron lamps are hung from the ceiling. Dainty table lamps of delicate pastel shades are used on the tables. The costumes of the girls who serve are smocks also of delicate pastel shades. In keeping with the general atmosphere and color scheme Andy has purchased dishes of the French Bordeaux pattern, so that all blend and harmonize into a perfect reproduction of an elite French tea room. It is Andy's desire to make the Thimble Tea Room the friendly tea room of Lawrence, where courtesy, service, and quality are the predominating factors in her business. It is not necessary to have reservations. The tea room is always open for luncheon and for dinner in the evening to the general public. Reservations are necessary for parties, banquets, special dinners, etc. [DCR, 9-16-26]

Ice To Return To Fountains

The two-day embargo on ice deliveries to drug stores and restaurants for use in iced drinks was lifted this morning as the first step in restoring normal ice service to Lawrence consumers.

H. C. Thornton, manager of the ice plant, said the cooler weather over the week end and today reduced the heavy demand for ice and that continued cool weather will enable the company to deliver larger quantities of ice to home refrigerators within a few days.

The company allotted 50 pounds to each home consumer today, while drug stores and restaurants are allowed 50 per cent of their normal consumption of ice for use in iced fountain drinks.

This was the first cheerful note in the nearly two-weeks-long ice shortage, and Thornton expressed belief that three or four cool days will enable the company to remove all limits on deliveries for any purpose. But until that time, Thornton declared, the embargo will remain on ice for drinking fountains and soft drink machines. [LJW, 8-12-46]

Mrs. *F*isher's Fruit-Mint Punch

Put in a punch bowl one cup of granulated sugar. Add juice of six lemons. Stir well. Add three lemons, sliced thin. Put on ice. When needed, add twelve sprays of fresh mint and one quart of pounded ice. Stir well and pour from a height 3 bottles of imported ginger ale.

–Mrs. W. C. Fisher, 646 Kentucky St., Jan. 6, 1922.

Hattie *L*ackey's Cream Raspberryade

Wash and look over carefully 3 boxes of raspberries; place in saucepan, and add 1 pound of sugar. Crush well, using either a large spoon or a potato masher. Heat slowly to boiling point and cook for five minutes. Now turn into a piece of cheesecloth and let drip. When cool, press the pulp of the berries through to remove the seeds. Place syrup in fruit jar and store in the refrigerator. To use, place 1 ½ cups of the raspberry syrup in pitcher and add 1 quart of ice water, 2 cups of crushed ice, ½ cup of whipped cream or ½ cup of marshmallow whip thinned with ½ cup of the raspberryade. Whip up and serve.

–Hattie R. Lackey, 838 Illinois St., June 16, 1922.

Mrs. *F*ish's Southern Mint Cordial

Gather the fresh spearmint, wash well and dry in a towel. Cut a generous pint into tiny bits, put this in a crock and bruise with a potato masher. Add to the mint the rind of one lemon, juice of four lemons and two oranges. Let this stand for half hour. Boil without stirring two cups of water and two and a half cups of sugar for five minutes. Pour this over the mint and fruit juices and let it stand for twenty minutes or longer. Strain the entire mixture through cheesecloth. Color a light green with fruit coloring. Serve in tiny glasses over crushed ice.

–Mrs. W. G. Fish, 510 W. 6th St., Apr. 20, 1923.

Mrs. *H*ouk's Pineapple Lemonade

"This makes two quarts, costs thirty cents and takes about thirty minutes to make."

Thinly peeled rind of 2 lemons, 1 1/3 cups sugar, 2 cups boiling water, juice of 4 lemons, 1 can shredded pineapple, 1 quart plain or carbonated water, crushed ice. Cook together for 5 minutes lemon rind, sugar and boiling water. Strain and cool, then add lemon juice and pineapple. Just before serving, add plain or carbonated water and pour into a punch bowl in which has been placed a block of ice, or serve in tall glasses, partly filled with crushed ice.

–Mrs. Harry Houk, 1618 Rhode Island St., July 24, 1925.

Mrs. *S*herfy's Pineapple Ade

One large can grated pineapple, 3 lemons, 3 oranges, 1 cup sugar. Put pineapple in large crock or jar. Squeeze juice from lemons and oranges. Slice rinds of 1 lemon, and 1 orange fine, and add with sugar to the pineapple. Add 1 gallon of water (or more or less) to suit taste. Stir well; set in refrigerator for 2 or 3 hours, if possible, before serving as it is better to blend. Strain before serving. If you wish, it can be made and served at once with ice, but is not so well-flavored. This will serve 20 people.

–Mrs. Luella C. Sherfy, 725 Missouri St., Aug. 6, 1926.

Dr. *B*umgardner's Summer Drink

Juice of 4 lemons, juice of 4 oranges, 1 cup of pineapple juice, 3 cups of sugar, 1 quart of crushed ice. Stir until sugar is thoroughly dissolved, then put in a lump of ice the size of a pint cup and add enough fresh, cool water to make 3 quarts. Cherry juice may be substituted for the pineapple juice and will produce an attractive color.

–Dr. Edward Bumgardner, 1026 Ohio St., July 13, 1928.

Miss *B*ailey's Fruit Punch

Boil together one cup sugar and one cup water for three minutes after sugar is dissolved. Add three cloves, one small stick cinnamon, one teaspoon ground ginger and let stand until cool. Add the juice of four lemons and four oranges and a small can of grated pineapple. Dilute with six cups of water. Mix thoroughly and add cracked ice before serving.

–Miss Margaret Bailey, 742 Ohio St., Aug. 9, 1929.

Mrs. *S*chehrer's "Queen of the May" Cocktail

Shake together the contents of two 15-ounce cans of strained tomato juice, one tablespoon sugar, one tablespoon lemon juice, one teaspoon salt, one-fourth teaspoon Worcestershire sauce and four teaspoons chopped parsley. Chill. Serve in tall glasses.

–Mrs. H. A. Schehrer, 946 Missouri St., Apr. 25, 1930.

**When the sun beats down and the day is hot,
And by the seashore you are not,
When you need cooling off with a drink or two,
A Muehlebach drink is the thing for you.**

LJW, 8-9-23

12

Mrs. *M*iller's Currant Punch

Two cups currant jelly (if desired, plum or grape jelly may be used instead), 1 ½ cups strong hot tea, juice of 3 lemons, juice of 3 oranges. Add the currant jelly to the hot tea, and stir until the jelly is all dissolved. Add the fruit juices, chill thoroughly and serve with chopped ice. No sugar is needed with this drink as the jelly supplies all the necessary sweetness. Makes 4 large glasses.

–*Mrs. H. H. Miller,* 1205 Rhode Island St., July 18, 1930.

Mrs. *C*lark's Fruit Cup

Combine carefully in desired number of glasses equal portions of chilled, sweetened and drained strawberries and cubed fresh pineapple, with cubes of lime gelatine. Pour a small amount of strawberry and pineapple juice over each serving. The lime gelatine is made by dissolving one package of lime gelatine in one cup of boiling water, adding ¾ cup cold water, and let harden in a shallow pan.

–*Mrs. J. W. Clark,* 1929 Massachusetts St., May 8, 1931.

DRINK

Green River

IN BOTTLES OR AT FOUNTAINS

Bottled in Lawrence by McNish Bottling Works.

Tel. 198.   836 Vermont.

LJW, 6-21-21

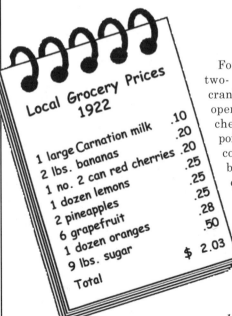

Local Grocery Prices
1922

1 large Carnation milk	.10
2 lbs. bananas	.20
1 no. 2 can red cherries	.20
1 dozen lemons	.25
2 pineapples	.25
6 grapefruit	.25
1 dozen oranges	.28
9 lbs. sugar	.50
Total	$ 2.03

Mrs. *F*letcher's Cranberry Juice Cocktail

Four cups cranberries, four cups water, two- thirds cup granulated sugar. Cook cranberries and water until all skins pop open (about 5 minutes). Strain through cheesecloth. Bring the juice to boiling point, add sugar and boil 2 minutes. Serve cold. For future use, put in sterilized bottles, well-corked and sealed. For large quantity use: 20 pounds cranberries, 5 gallons water, 8 ½ pounds sugar; cook as above.

–*Mrs. Donald Fletcher,* 129 Park St., Nov. 23, 1934.

Mrs. McDonald's Fresh Pineapple
"Try this for breakfast or cocktail."

Two oranges, peeled and diced; 1 grapefruit, peeled and diced; 1 fresh pineapple, peeled and diced; ½ cup sugar. Mix all together. Put in quart jar in ice box; will keep a week. An easy way to peel pineapple: wash and cut around, then peel each slice, then dice or use as wanted.

–Mrs. F. J. McDonald, 845 Tennessee St., June 21, 1935.

Miss Bartz's Black Raspberry Juice
"This juice can be used for making jelly, or if a little
sugar is added after opening the jar, it can be used
as a delightful drink in the summer time."

Select sound, ripe fruit; crush and heat slowly to a simmering point. Strain through a double thickness of cheesecloth. Let stand a few hours in a cool place to allow the sediment to settle to bottom. Carefully pour off the juice from dregs. Pour juice into clean hot jars, partly seal as for canning, and process for 30 minutes in a water bath at simmering temperature. Remove from canner; seal immediately.

–Miss Elizabeth Bartz, Route 1, June 26, 1936.

Mrs. Houk's Royal Punch

Six bananas, 1 dozen lemons, 1 dozen oranges, 1 cup shredded pineapple, 1 cup cherries and juice (canned or fresh), 3 pints gingerale, 1 pint sugar syrup, 2 to 3 quarts of water. Slice bananas thin, add lemon and orange juice and grated rind of 3 oranges. Let stand 5 minutes. Add pineapple, syrup, cherries and gingerale. Mix and add water. Pour over block of ice and crushed mint in punch bowl or other container. This recipe can be divided in any way, according to the number to be served.

–Mrs. Harry Houk, 1618 Rhode Island St., July 10, 1936.

Mrs. *W*ise's Summer Beverage

One and one-half cups orange juice, 1 cup lemon juice, 1 cup gingerale, 2 cups water, 1½ cups grapefruit juice, 1 cup weak tea, 2½ cups sugar. Make a syrup of water and sugar. Cool. Add strained fruit juice. Add tea, gingerale, and enough water to thin to taste. Add slices of oranges, lemons, fresh strawberries or sprig of mint for decoration. Cool with ice.

–Mrs. George Wise, 730 Arkansas St., Aug. 19, 1938.

Mrs. *C*arter's Grape Iceberg
"This is our favorite pick-up on a hot day."

One pint grape juice, 1¾ cups water, ¾ cup sugar, 1 ½ cups orange juice, ½ cup lemon juice, 1 quart dry gingerale. Freeze grape juice cubes in automatic refrigerator tray by releasing half tray of ice cubes and filling with grape juice. Make syrup of water and sugar; cool. Add fruit juices and gingerale. Pour over grape juice cubes. Makes two quarts.

–Mrs. Blanche W. Carter, Route 2, July 14, 1939.

Mrs. *B*anks's Fruit Cocktail for New Year's Dinner

Combine about equal parts grapefruit sections, seedless or seeded white or red grapes, and sliced canned pears to measure 3 cups. Add ¼ cup strained honey, 1 drop spearmint flavoring; cover and chill. Serve in sherbet glasses, sprinkled with pomegranate seeds. One average pomegranate has sufficient seeds for nearly 25 servings. Remove only a portion of the seeds and reserve the rest for another time, keeping them wrapped in waxed paper. If the pomegranates are not available, one can substitute cherries or a small scoop of cranberry ice to each serving, adding a colorful touch in flavor and appearance.

–Mrs. Luella Banks,
Route 6, Dec. 29, 1939.

Heard In Lawrence

The recent removal of every other chair at the Eldridge Coffee Shop counter has resulted in much speculation and facetious comment. Some claim that this change was made necessary in order to eliminate scuffling and unseemly conduct at the counter. The most logical reason seems to be that it was a hot weather remedy for the discomfort of some of the more sturdy and portly customers who found it difficult to wedge themselves up to the counter, such as Pete Reedy, Steve Hinshaw, Mike Getto, et al. [LJW, 7-17-37]

Mrs. *C*omer's Orange Juice Cocktail

Cut a thin slice from tops of perfect oranges. This recipe calls for 6 oranges. Remove pulp and juice, add 1 cup of cut strawberries and 1 cup of crushed pineapple, also a few grains salt, lemon juice and sugar to taste. Put in refrigerator pan–chilling unit–and leave until liquid becomes mushy, stirring occasionally. Serve in orange skins or in glasses surrounded with crushed ice.

–Mrs. H. M. Comer,
1608 Edgehill Rd.,
May 10, 1940.

Mrs. *L*aird's Fruit Flip

Two cups orange juice, 2 cups lemon juice, 2 cups cherry juice, 2 cups pineapple juice, 3 cups sugar, 9 cups of water, 9 mint leaves, 4 cups tea. Combine water and mint leaves. Simmer 5 minutes. Strain. Add sugar and cook 5 minutes. Cool. Combine the syrup, tea, and fruit juices. Mix thoroughly and allow to stand 1 hour. Chill. Serve in tall glasses with plenty of cracked ice. Makes 42 large servings.

–Mrs. John R. Laird,
428 Forest Ave.,
Aug. 9, 1940.

Miss *S*chopper's Three-In-One Milk Shake

One-half cup orange juice, 1 tablespoon lemon juice, ⅛ teaspoon salt, 2 cups fresh milk, ¼ cup grapefruit juice, 3 tablespoons honey, ⅛ teaspoon almond extract. Combine the fruit juices, add honey, flavoring and salt. Add to milk. Beat until well blended. Chill and serve. If honey is not available, a sugar syrup may be made by boiling 1 cup of sugar and ½ cup of water for 5 minutes. Chill and use 4 tablespoons to every 3 of honey in recipe.

–Miss Frances Schopper, Eudora, July 30, 1943.

Mrs. *C*ross's Summer Beverage

Mix two cups each of canned grapefruit, orange, apricot and pineapple juices; add 15 small white mint candies, one-half cup lemon juice and one-third cup chopped red cherries. Chill. Pour into tall frosted glasses, half-filled with chopped ice. Let stand several minutes to frost. Add a few fresh mint leaves and some canned red cherries with the stems on.

–Mrs. Anna Rankin Cross, 921 Illinois St., Sept. 7, 1945.

Most Refreshing

What better way to start the hot weather than by picking out the best fountain in town and the finest drink in that fountain and make it your daily ally against Old Man Heat?

Rankin's Drug Store

1101 Mass. St. Phone 678

DCR, 6-5-30

Mrs. *S*mith's Mint Punch

One and one-half cups strained orange juice, ¾ cup strained lemon juice, 1 cup sugar, 2 quarts water. Make syrup of sugar and water. While still hot, pour over 1 dozen small sprigs of mint, and crush the mint. When cool, add fruit juices. Pour over crushed ice in glasses and put a sprig of mint in the top of glass or freeze sprigs of mint in ice cubes. Serves 15.

–Mrs. R. A. Smith Jr., 1011 Illinois St., Aug. 1, 1947.

Miss *P*arsons's Fruit Cocktail

One grapefruit, segments, diced; 2 oranges, segments, diced; 1 banana, diced (2 bananas, if small); 2 slices pineapple, diced. The rest depends upon what you have: a few canned peaches, pears, apricots, diced, a few strawberries, diced. It is an excellent way to use left-over fruits–canned peaches and pears are especially good. Add sugar to taste, about one third cupful. Prepare ahead of time and put into the refrigerator to chill.

–Miss Margaret W. Parsons, 1108 Ohio St., June 4, 1948.

Miss *B*artz's Fruit Cocktail

One teaspoon gelatine, 2 tablespoons cold water, 2 cups grapefruit pulp, ½ cup orange pulp, ½ cup crushed pineapple (canned), ½ cup fresh strawberries (cut into small pieces), 1 cup sugar, few grains of salt. Soak gelatine in cold water 5 minutes and dissolve over boiling water. When dissolved, add fruit pulp and sugar. Chill in refrigerator trays, but do not freeze. Stir occasionally. Serve in glasses and garnish with mint or pieces of fruit. Serves 6.

–Miss Elizabeth Bartz,
645 Rhode Island St.,
May 20, 1949.

COOLING REFRESHING DRINKS AT OUR FOUNTAIN...

Limeade	5c
Orangeade	10c
Double Dip Cone	5c
Brick Ice Cream, qt.	39c
Coffee Ice Cream Soda	15c
Coco-Cola, bottled, 6 for	25c
Cold Meat Plate Lunch	25c
Fruit Plate Lunch	25c
Ham Salad with Toast	15c

Round Corner Drug Store
LJW, 7-22-37

Mrs. *C*ooke's Spiced Fruit Drink

One cup sugar, 1½ cups water, 2 sticks cinnamon, 12 whole cloves, 4 cups pineapple juice, 1 cup orange juice, ½ cup lemon juice, crushed ice. Boil first four ingredients. Strain and add to fruit juices. Mix and pour over crushed ice. Amount serves eight.

–Mrs. Byron F. Cooke, 1508 Vermont St.,
July 15, 1949.

REDY-PAK ICE
TASTE FREE-CRYSTAL CLEAR

Parties
Picnics
Beverages

Ice Cream
Iced Drinks
Fishing Trips

HOME USE

American Service Co.
Call 48   616 Vermont

Nov., 1949, City Directory

18

Salads
and
Dressings

Mr. and Mrs. King
Grow King-Size Tomatoes

Lawrence people who know their town don't tell their children about Jack and his bean stalk when they want to tell a vegetarian bedtime story—they tell about Mr. King, 1336 Rhode Island Street and his tomatoes. For the past twelve years Mr. and Mrs. King have been raising tomatoes and, what started as a hobby, has become a science. They train a single vine from the plant along a pole and keep it tied to its support. When the plant is about five feet in height, it begins to bear, and the tomatoes keep appearing at each joint as the vine grows taller. By the time frost catches up with the game, the vines are often 15 to 18 feet high. The tomatoes are as large in proportion as the vine, weighing from one to three pounds. We have Mrs. King's word for it that the ripened tomatoes are of excellent quality and taste.

The Kings have an irrigating system of their own to protect their plants from the drought. One pound coffee tins are buried near the plant. Nail holes in the bottom of the tins feed the water out to the roots of the plant. Each evening these cans are filled with water. The tomatoes are kept from sunburning by fastening paper sacks over them. King's "Little Wonders" are, in reality, big wonders. [DCR, 8-8-29]

Mrs. *C*onway's Frozen Combination Vegetable Salad

"This makes a most delicious, as well as very attractive vegetable salad."

Take the contents of a quart can of tomatoes (or same amount in fresh cooked ones), sweeten with three tablespoonfuls of sugar, and season to taste with salt and cayenne pepper or paprika. A teaspoonful of onion juice improves the flavor, but may be omitted if preferred.

Rub this through a sieve, add chopped celery and grated cucumbers. If desired, minced green peppers or pimientos can be added. Turn this mixture into baking-powder cans, and cover tightly. Pack into equal parts of salt and ice, and let stand three hours before serving. When removed from the molds, serve on crisp lettuce leaves, with mayonnaise dressing, which has been modified with whipped cream. Pile the dressing on each dish of salad, and crown all with either crushed nut meats, or grated cheese, leaving a few of the nuts uncrushed for the center.

–Mrs. Robert Conway, 633 Indiana St., Aug. 5, 1921.

Mrs. *W*hitelaw's Oyster Salad

One can cove or one quart fresh oysters, three soda crackers, four eggs, one-half cup of butter, one-half cup sweet thick cream, one cup of vinegar, one teaspoon dry mustard, salt, pepper, sugar and celery seed (or fresh celery) to taste. Roll crackers fine and mix well with the oysters. If fresh oysters are used, steam them until plump and cut in halves.

Mayonnaise Dressing: Beat the eggs well and add the sugar, salt, pepper, mustard and butter; then add slowly, to prevent curdling, the vinegar. Cook over steam till thick. When cold, add the cream (if you have it) and celery seed. If you use the fresh celery, chop in small bits, and use instead of seeds.

–Mrs. John Whitelaw, DeSoto, Dec. 9, 1921.

Mildred *L*ackey's Thousand Island Salad Dressing

"This dressing is delicious to serve on salad at luncheon."

One and one-half cups of mayonnaise; 1 beet, cut very fine; 1 onion, cut very fine; 1 green pepper, cut very fine; small amount of parsley and 1 cup of celery, cut very fine; ½ cup of chili pepper sauce; 1 egg, boiled hard and cut in small pieces; 1½ cups of chili sauce; 1 small bottle of stuffed olives; 1 cup of whipped cream. Put cream in just before serving.

–Mildred Lackey, Route 1, Feb. 10, 1922.

Mrs. *A*llison's Favorite Vegetable Salad

One small crisp head of cabbage, 3 medium-sized green sweet peppers, 2 or 3 small onions, 2 medium-sized cucumbers. Chop together and sprinkle with just a pinch of salt and a small teaspoon of sugar. Now rim out 6 or 8 solid, ripe tomatoes, sprinkle each with a little salt, lay each one on a lettuce leaf and fill with chopped mixture. Serve cold with French or Mayonnaise dressing.

–Mrs. Mabel Allison, Route 3, Lecompton, May 26, 1922.

Mrs. *W*ilcox's Tomato Surprise

Four medium-size tomatoes, 2 cucumbers, ½ cup black walnut meats, ½ cup shredded lettuce. Peel tomatoes and hollow out; place in ice box to chill thoroughly. Dice the cucumbers and nut meats, and add shredded lettuce; salt to taste. Just before serving, fill tomatoes with this mixture. Add one tablespoonful of mayonnaise to top serving. Place tomatoes on large lettuce leaves. Serve with crisp salad wafers.

–Mrs. Roy A. Wilcox, 946½ Alabama St., July 14, 1922.

Miss *L*own's Pineapple Salad
"This is very pretty as well as a delicious dish."

Put slice of pineapple on crisp lettuce. On this, place a dice-shaped piece of gelatine, which has been previously prepared. Over this, sprinkle finely chopped celery. Over this, put a tablespoon of mayonnaise which has been mixed with whipped cream. Over all, sprinkle chopped nuts.

–Miss Etta Lown, 315 Johnson Ave., July 21, 1922.

Mrs. *W*ilson's Fruit Salad

Yolks of 4 eggs, beaten light. Stir in juice of 1 lemon very slowly. Add ¼ teaspoon dry mustard, and ½ cup warm sweet milk. Stir all together and let boil. (This makes the dressing.) One pound marshmallows, quartered; 2 lbs. white grapes, cut in halves and seeded; ¼ lb. pecan nuts; and 1 qt. pineapple. Drain juice off pineapple and cut in half-inch squares. One pint cream, whipped. Stir all together with dressing and let stand over night. When ready to serve, arrange on lettuce leaf with teaspoon of whipped cream on top of each serving.

–Mrs. Eli Wilson, 323 Illinois St., Feb. 23, 1923.

Mrs. *B*ryant's Dandelion Greens

Gather greens, enough to fill a gallon measure, well packed. Pick all dry leaves from them, and wash in cold water until thoroughly cleansed from all particles of dirt. Place in a covered vessel with enough water to half cover greens, with ¼ teaspoon salt and ½ teaspoon baking soda. Cook until tender. Remove from stove, drain off water; season with 4 tablespoons bacon drippings; let stand a few minutes. Place crisp lettuce leaves on a shallow dish; place greens on lettuce. Have ready two hard-boiled eggs; slice and place on top of greens.

–Mrs. J. C. Bryant, 714 Alabama St., Apr. 27, 1923.

Heard In Lawrence

Bill Boardman, public relations man for the Kansas Electric Power Co., is bragging about the fresh strawberries that he enjoyed out of his own garden this week. He says he picked almost a quart and a half of berries; more than half of them, he claims, did not have green knots on them. Here is the real story back of the berries. Last year Bill bought some ever-bearing plants–the variety even the super-gardener could not spell. The cost was in proportion to the name, plenty big. Then Bill discovered that if the plants bore fruit all the time they would have to have plenty of water. So he dug a well that cost $125. Pumping water and using a sprinkling can every evening got old so he built a power line and perfected an irrigating system. So far the berries have not cost him more than $9.87 each. He likes 'em good. [TO, 7-31-41]

Mrs. Smith's Mock Chicken Salad

Three cups boiled lean fresh pork, 3 medium-sized sweet pickles, 2 hard-boiled eggs, ½ cup English walnuts. To prepare: Chop meat, pickles and eggs; cut nut meats fine, and add. Mix well and sprinkle over all a bit of Hungarian paprika. Add enough mayonnaise to hold ingredients together. Mix, chill and serve as chicken salad.

–*Mrs. Gilbert L. Smith,* 547½ Indiana St., July 7, 1923.

Mrs. Dickerson's Fruit Cup

One cup white grapes; 1 cup orange sections; 1 cup pineapple, diced; ½ cup orange juce; ½ cup pineapple syrup; sugar, and a few grains of salt. Remove skins and seeds from grapes, and membrane from orange sections. Mix fruit, orange juice and pineapple syrup (or fresh pineapple juice), salt, and sugar to sweeten. Put in freezer, pack in ice and salt, and stir occasionally, until juice begins to freeze. Serve in tulip cups, made by cutting tops from oranges, and removing pulp. Cut orange peel into four segments. Shape and bend outward a little, to simulate a tulip. Fill and place in long-stemmed sherbet glasses; garnish with fresh green leaves and top with maraschino cherries, or if preferred, may be served in half cantaloupe with edges notched, and garnished with maraschino cherries.

–*Mrs. H. L. Dickerson,* 2118 Tennessee St., Aug. 3, 1923.

Mrs. Mack's Cottage Cheese and Fruit Salad

Arrange three lettuce leaves with stems meeting in center. On one leaf pile small balls of cottage cheese rolled in chopped nuts. On another leaf place sections of orange free from membrane. On the other leaf place cubed pineapple. Make a nest in the center with heart leaves and fill with salad dressing made as follows: Mix and add ½ cup sugar, 1 teaspoon salt, 1 cup sour cream, ¾ cup vinegar, 1 teaspoon mustard, 1 tablespoon flour, 1 cup sweet milk or water, yolks of four eggs. Cook in a double boiler. This makes a little over a pint of dressing. Add whipped cream if desired.

–*Mrs. H. H. Mack,* 833 Missouri St., May 2, 1924.

Mrs. *A*lexander's Egg Salad For A Picnic Lunch

Six eggs, 2 teaspoons chopped pimientoes, mayonnaise dressing, ½ cup cream cheese, lettuce. Drop eggs in boiling water, and cover. Turn fire out, let stand for twenty minutes. Remove from hot water and place in cold water. Peel and divide each egg into halves lengthwise. Remove the yolk and mash. Mix the mashed yolk, chopped pimientos, cheese, and enough mayonnaise to form a paste. Roll into balls and return to egg white. Brush the edges of egg white with a little raw egg white and put halves together. Make a nest of shredded lettuce and place eggs in center.

–Mrs. J. W. Alexander, 2015 New Hampshire St., June 19, 1925.

Miss *D*olbee's White Salad
"A twenty-four hour salad."

Make a dressing of four egg yolks, the juice of one lemon, one-fourth cup of cream, and a pinch of salt, cooked until thick in a double boiler. Add one-half pint of whipped cream when the mixture is cold. Mix with one can of diced pineapple, one can of seeded white cherries, one box (one-half pound) marshmallows cut in small pieces, one-fourth pound of pecans or almonds cut in small pieces. Let stand from twelve to twenty-four hours and serve on lettuce leaves. White grapes may be substituted for the white cherries. The recipe makes a large salad, but if it is not all needed at one time, it will keep well for later serving. It is at its best from twenty-four to forty-eight hours after making.

–Miss Cora Dolbee, 1301 Rhode Island St., Aug. 1, 1924.

Mrs. *H*edberg's Easter Lily Salad

Six hard-boiled eggs, 1 cup seasoned mashed potatoes, mayonnaise dressing, shredded lettuce. Mold mashed potatoes, while still warm, into balls about three-quarters of an inch in diameter (1 cup makes about sixteen). Let stand until cold. Arrange bed of shredded lettuce on four salad plates. Cut eggs in quarters lengthwise, leaving the quartered yolk lying in the quartered white. Place eggs petal-wise on lettuce. Six petals to the plate. Put four or more potato balls in center and heap on these stiff mayonnaise dressing.

–Mrs. Z. D. Hedberg, 1725 Ohio St., Apr. 3, 1925.

Mrs. $\mathcal{E}$nlow's Chicken Salad

One quart cold boiled chicken, cut into small cubes; 1 pint finely cut celery; 1 teaspoon salt; 2 teaspoons pepper; 2 hard-boiled eggs; 2 cups mayonnaise dressing; 6 olives; French dressing. Mix chicken, which should be very tender, with celery, seasoning and one egg cut into small pieces. Marinate with a little French dressing and let stand in a cold place one hour. Serve on lettuce leaves and spread mayonnaise over top. Garnish with olives and remaining egg cut into slices. Dust with paprika.

–Mrs. A. Enlow, 1304 Massachusetts St., Jan. 1, 1926.

Mrs. $\mathcal{G}$reen's Pineapple Salad

Three-fourths of a fresh pineapple, cut into dice-shaped pieces; 3 cups of fresh cabbage, cut medium fine; 10 cents worth of marshmallows, cut into dice-shaped pieces. Pour pineapple juice over all, dissolving into it 3 tablespoonfuls sugar. Makes a fine salad, and enough to serve 6 or 8 people.

–Mrs. N. Green, 1211 E. 13th St., June 24, 1927.

Mrs. $\mathcal{K}$rum's Combination Vegetable Salad

Three tomatoes (ripe, but firm), 1 large cucumber (or 2 small ones), 1 large onion, 1 green pepper, 1 head lettuce. Pare the cucumber and slice. Sprinkle with salt and let stand at least half an hour to draw out the green juice. Take out seeds of pepper and cut the pepper into small pieces. Sprinkle with a little salt and let stand half an hour. Cut onion into small pieces and place in diluted vinegar (about half water). Drain the cucumbers and peppers and rinse off the salt. Shred the lettuce. Cut tomatoes into small pieces. Mix the tomatoes, cucumbers, onions, peppers and lettuce together and add Thousand Island Dressing or French Dressing. Serve cold. This makes six liberal servings. Shredded cabbage, also radishes, may be added if desired. The ingredients may be prepared as above and kept in a jar of well-diluted vinegar (about ⅔ water) in the refrigerator for a few hours until ready to serve, when the dressing should be added.

–Mrs. Lillian Krum, 432 Elm St., Aug. 12, 1927.

Local Grocery Prices
1935

2 mangoes	.05
1 bunch carrots	.05
1 cucumber	.05
1 no. 2 can pears	.10
3 lbs. cabbage	.10
4 bunches radishes	.10
1 no. 2 1/2 can peaches	.12
1 lb. marshmallows	.15
2 bunches asparagus	.15
4 pints cherries	.25
2 lbs. cottage cheese	.25
1 qt. salad dressing	.30
1 jar stuffed olives	.35
Total	$ 2.02

25

Miss *M*arshall's Chicken Salad

Two tablespoons gelatine, ½ cup cold chicken stock, 1½ cups heavy cream, ¾ cup of hot chicken stock, 3 cups cold cooked chicken, 1 cup of nuts, ½ cup celery. Soften the gelatine in the stock. Cool some and add the chicken, nuts, celery, cut fine, and season with salt, pepper, lemon juice and onion juice if preferred. Fold in the heavy cream, beaten until stiff. Chill, cut into blocks and serve on crisp lettuce leaves with mayonnaise dressing.

–Miss Mary Marshall, 1637 New Hampshire St., Nov. 25, 1927.

Mrs. *S*chultz's Pineapple Salad

Cut the following ingredients together fine: 1 quart can of pineapple, ¼ pound pecan meats, 1 pound marshmallows, 1½ pounds white grapes. Dressing: yolks of 4 eggs, ½ cup milk, ¼ teaspoon mustard. Heat the milk. Stir in yolks of eggs, mustard, and the juice of 1 lemon; then cook. When almost cool, mix dressing with fruit and let stand 24 hours. Before serving, stir in one pint of whipped cream.

–Mrs. George J. Schultz, 746 Indiana St., Feb. 17, 1928.

Miss *C*rowder's Tuna Fish Salad

Two cups tuna fish, one-half cup chopped celery, two teaspoons chopped onions, one-fourth cup chopped green olives, one-half teaspoon salt, one-eighth teaspoon paprika. Flake the fish with a fork. Add celery, olives, salt, paprika, onions and 1 cup mayonnaise dressing. Mix thoroughly and serve in nests of crisp lettuce, garnished with bits of pimiento and celery curls.

–Miss Nettie Crowder, Route 5, July 20, 1928.

Mrs. *V*an Deusen's Moulded Vegetable Salad

Two tablespoons of gelatine, ½ cupful of cold water, ½ cupful liquor from canned peas, 1 teaspoonful of salt, ½ teaspoon of paprika, 1 cupful of canned peas, 1 cupful of cooked carrots, 1½ tablespoonfuls of chopped mint, ¼ cupful of vinegar. Soften the gelatine in cold water and then dissolve it in the hot liquor of the canned peas, which are boiled five minutes before being used. Add the salt and paprika. Heat the mint in the vinegar and add to the peas and carrots. The carrots should be cut finely. Pour into wet molds and serve, when firm, on lettuce leaves with salad dressing accompanying. Garnish with sliced stuffed olives or strips of pimiento.

–Mrs. C. A. Van Deusen, 1624 Tennessee St., July 27, 1928.

LJW, 10-14-48

Mrs. *M*ueller's Fruit Salad

Make a custard of one-half cup milk, one egg, one tablespoon of flour; cook and cool. One pound marshmallows, one and one-half pounds of white grapes (or a can of white cherries, or both grapes and cherries), juice of one lemon, one can sliced pineapple, one pint of cream to whip. Prepare fruit. Be sure to seed and skin the grapes. If cherries are used, seed them. Dice pineapple. Quarter the marshmallows, using scissors to cut. Whip cream and add to custard. Add lemon juice last. Mix and let stand a few hours in a cool place, and it will be thick. This makes one gallon.

–Mrs. R. G. Mueller, 1140 Rhode Island St., Aug. 3, 1928.

Miss *P*rice's Pineapple-Cabbage Salad

Three cups shredded cabbage, one-fourth lb. almonds, four slices of pineapple, one cup salad dressing. Quarter the head of cabbage (have a firm one; slice or shred). Soak in ice water one hour. Drain and dry. Blanch almonds by pouring boiling water over them and letting them stand two minutes. Drain and put in cold water. Rub between fingers to take off skin. Dry with towels. Drain pineapple and cut with scissors in ¼-inch pieces. Mix cabbage, almonds and pineapple with dressing. Serve on lettuce or cabbage leaf with garnish of green pepper or red cherry. Salad Dressing: one-third cup orange juice, 1½ tablespoons lemon juice, 1 egg, ½ cup sugar, ½ pint double cream, few grains salt. Mix fruit juices, add egg (slightly beaten) and sugar, and cook in double boiler ten minutes. Cool and fold in cream, beaten stiff, then add salt. Serves four.

–Miss Frances T. Price, 1523 Tennessee St., Mar. 22, 1929.

Mrs. *W*hitelaw's Egg and Pepper Salad for Easter

Dissolve a tablespoonful of gelatine in a pint of boiling water. Cut off the ends of three sweet green peppers, and after removing the seeds, place in each pepper a peeled, hard-boiled egg. Fill in around the egg with the cooled gelatine liquid and set away to harden. Cut in slices with a sharp knife. Serve on a lettuce leaf with a red cross, cut from pimiento, placed on the center, which will be on the egg yolk. Pass mayonnaise dressing with the salad.

–Mrs. Bertha Whitelaw, DeSoto, Mar. 29, 1929.

Mrs. $\mathcal{S}$chuman's Tuna and Cucumber Salad

One pound can tuna fish, one cup diced cucumber, one cup diced celery, one pimiento, two ripe tomatoes, one-third cup French dressing. Peel and cut cucumber into small dice and let soak in ice water. Dice celery. Slice tomatoes into three slices, rejecting the ends. Flake the fish, add celery, drained cucumbers, and dressing. Heap onto the sliced tomatoes and garnish with the sliced pimiento. French Dressing: Six tablespoonfuls of salad oil, two tablespoonfuls of vinegar or lemon juice, one-third teaspoonful of salt, a few shakes of pepper. Stir well. Paprika may be added if desired.

–Mrs. M. A. Schuman, 1229 Haskell Ave., Apr. 26, 1929.

Mrs. $\mathcal{B}$eguelin's Molded Tomato and Asparagus Salad

Put one cup of tomato sauce into a sauce pan, add one cup hot water or soup stock, a tiny bit of bay leaf, one-half teaspoon salt, one-half onion (sliced), and one clove. Simmer 15 minutes. Then add two tablespoons gelatine, which has been soaked in cold water five minutes. Stir until gelatine is dissolved, then strain; set aside to cool and thicken. When about the consistency of cream, add one and one-half cups cooked asparagus tips, which have been cut into one-inch pieces. Turn into individual molds or custard cups, and chill until firm. Unmold on lettuce leaves and garnish with asparagus tips and thick mayonnaise.

–Mrs. H. E. Beguelin, 1312 New Hampshire St., May 3, 1929.

Mrs. $\mathcal{H}$oward's White Fruit Salad

Salad: 1 large can sliced pineapple, 1 large can white cherries, 1 lb. white grapes, 1 lb. marshmallows, ¼ lb. salted almonds. Dressing: 4 egg yolks, 1 cup milk, ¼ tsp. mustard, 1 lemon, 1 pint whipping cream. Seed fruit and cut all ingredients into small pieces except almonds, which should be only split. For dressing, beat egg yolks until light, then add milk and mustard. Cook until like thin custard. Remove from fire and add strained lemon juice. Cool. Stir in one pint stiffly whipped cream. Mix with other ingredients and place in ice box overnight. Serve garnished with whipped cream and a red or green cherry.

–Mrs. Fred Howard, 1613 Rhode Island St., Aug. 2, 1929.

Mrs. $\mathcal{E}$ndacott's Cranberry Salad

One quart cranberries, 1 cup of chopped nut meats, 1 package of lemon gelatine powder, 1 cup of marshmallows (cut in small pieces), ½ pint of whipping cream. Dissolve powder in one pint of boiling water and pour into pan about 8 x 12 inches. While still hot, add marshmallows. Let cool. Whip cream. Wash cranberries and grind through medium-fine food chopper. When the gelatine begins to set, add cranberries, nuts and one-half of the whipped cream, and blend thoroughly. Place in the refrigerator until thoroughly chilled. Serve on crisp lettuce leaf with remaining whipped cream on top, and top all with a small quantity of mayonnaise dressing. This quantity will serve about twelve.

–Mrs. F. C. Endacott, 943 Ohio St., Dec. 20, 1929.

LJW, 10-30-31

Miss *Z*wick's Tomato Gelatine Salad

Two cups strained canned tomatoes, 2 tablespoons gelatine, ¼ teaspoon salt, ⅛ teaspoon pepper, ⅛ teaspoon celery salt, 3 or 4 drops onion juice (if desired), 6 slices cucumber, 1 small can peas, head lettuce. Soak gelatine in one cup of tomato juice. Heat remainder of juice; add seasonings, and add to gelatine mixture, stirring until dissolved. Rinse six cups or molds in cold water. Place a slice of cucumber (or of hard-boiled egg) in the bottom of each cup; add a little of gelatine-tomato mixture and chill. When ready to serve, place each mold on a leaf of head lettuce and surround with about two tablespoons of peas. Serve with boiled dressing. Serves six.

–Miss Alice Zwick, 1236 Connecticut St., Apr. 4, 1930.

Mrs. *H*ouk's Raw Vegetable Salad

One package lemon gelatine powder; 1 pint boiling water; 2 tablespoons vinegar; ½ teaspoon salt; dash of cayenne; ¾ cup raw carrots, chopped finely; 1 cup raw cabbage, shredded; 4 tablespoons green pepper, finely chopped. Dissolve powder in boiling water; add vinegar, salt and cayenne. Chill. When slightly thickened, fold in vegetables. Turn into individual molds. Chill until firm. Unmold on crisp lettuce and garnish with mayonnaise. Serves 6.

–Mrs. H. A. Houk, 1618 Rhode Island St., July 4, 1930.

Mrs. *O*lson's Cranberry Whipped Cream Salad

One pint heavy whipping cream, 2½ cups finely diced celery, 2½ cups cranberry jelly, ¼ cup white cherries (measured after pitted and cut into halves), ½ cup chopped English walnuts or pecans. Drain cherries well. Whip the cream, add celery, cherries, cranberry jelly and nuts. Serve on a pretty tuft of lettuce.

–Mrs. Vic Olson, 1208 Connecticut St., Dec. 26, 1930.

Mrs. White's Grapefruit Salad

One package lemon gelatine powder; 1 cup boiling water; 2 grapefruit, sections free from membrane and cut in pieces; 2 tablespoons sugar; 1 cup grapefruit juice and cold water. Dissolve gelatine in boiling water. Sprinkle grapefruit with sugar and drain thoroughly. Add grapefruit juice and water to gelatine. Turn into shallow pan; chill until firm, and cut in cubes. Combine cubes and grapefruit on crisp lettuce, and serve with mayonnaise. Serves 8.

–Mrs. T. H. White, 1016 Ohio St., Mar. 6, 1931.

Mrs. Norris's Shrimp Salad

Two cups shrimps; 1 cup diced celery; 1 cup diced cucumbers; 2 hard-boiled eggs, chopped; 1 teaspoon salt; ¼ teaspoon paprika; 2 tablespoons chopped pimientos; 1 cup stiff mayonnaise; ½ cup whipped cream. Mix mayonnaise and cream; mix and chill other ingredients. Use half mayonnaise mixture with shrimp mixture. Serve on lettuce with a small portion of mayonnaise on top. A garnish of diced eggs and sprigs of parsley may be added. Makes eight servings.

–Mrs. M. E. Norris, Route 6, Mar. 27, 1931.

Mrs. Griffis's Tuna Salad

One package lemon gelatine powder; 1 teaspoon onion juice; 1 pint boiling water; ½ teaspoon salt; ½ cup celery, finely chopped; dash of cayenne; 2 pimientos, finely chopped; 2 teaspoons horseradish, drained; ½ green pepper, finely chopped; 2 cups tuna fish, flaked; crisp lettuce. Dissolve gelatine in boiling water. Pour thin layer into loaf pan. Chill until firm. Combine celery, pimientos, green pepper, onion juice, salt, cayenne and horseradish. Add half of vegetables to loaf pan and cover with another layer of gelatine. Chill. When firm, add fish and another layer of gelatine. Chill again. When firm, add the remaining vegetables and remaining gelatine. Chill until firm. Unmold. Serve in ¾-inch slices on lettuce. Garnish with mayonnaise. Serves 8.

–Mrs. Fred Griffis, Vinland, July 3, 1931.

Miss $\mathcal{E}$nlow's Potato Salad

Two cups diced potatoes (cold), ½ cup diced celery, 2 tablespoons chopped parsley, 2 tablespoons chopped green peppers, 2 tablespoons chopped onion, 2 tablespoons cucumber pickle, 2 hard-boiled eggs. Mix potatoes, celery, peppers, onion, cucumber and egg (saving one yolk to grate over the top). Mix with enough mayonnaise to moisten thoroughly. Serve on lettuce leaves, and sprinkle with the grated egg yolk, parsley, and a dash of red pepper.

–Miss Dorothy Enlow, 1304 Massachusetts St., Aug. 7, 1931.

Mrs. $\mathcal{B}$ahnmaier's Combination Vegetable Salad

One cup shredded cabbage, ½ cup diced carrots, ¼ cup diced green peppers, 1 cup diced celery, ¼ cup diced pimiento, 2 tablespoons minced parsley, salt to taste. Mix ingredients and moisten with cream salad dressing made with ½ cup thick cream, 3 tablespoons vinegar, ¼ teaspoon salt, dash of paprika, 2 teaspoons sugar. Add salt, sugar and paprika to vinegar. Add this mixture slowly to cream and beat until thoroughly blended. Serve salad on lettuce leaves, and top with more dressing if desired.

–Mrs. E. M. Bahnmaier, Route 2, Lecompton, Dec. 4, 1931.

Mrs. $\mathcal{D}$unigan's Grapefruit Salad

Two cups diced grapefruit, 2 cups diced pineapple, 2 cups diced pears, ½ cup sugar, 1 cup fruit juices, 2 tablespoons lemon juice, ½ cup red cherries. Boil sugar and fruit juices two minutes. Cool. Add rest of ingredients and chill. Serve on crisp lettuce leaves. Serves eight.

–Mrs. Charlotte E. Dunigan, Route 6, Feb. 26, 1932.

Mrs. $\mathcal{D}$ickey's Under-the-Sea Salad
"Suitable for St. Patrick's Day."

One package lemon gelatine, 2 cups boiling water, 1 cup pink salmon (flaked), ½ cup celery (chopped), ½ cup sweet pickles (chopped), 1 tablespoon green pepper (chopped), 1 tablespoon pimientos (chopped). Add boiling water to the gelatine and stir. When nearly set, add the rest of the ingredients and chill. When this has become entirely set, pour over it a lime gelatine made with one package of lime-flavored gelatine dissolved in 2 cups boiling water, which must be cool enough that it will not soften the first mixture. Serve on beds of lettuce and top with a salad dressing, stiff enough to shape the outline of a boat, which may float an Irish flag. The salad may be molded in shamrock molds or in a flat pan and cut out with a shamrock cutter.

–Mrs. R. O. Dickey, Route 1, Mar. 11, 1932.

Mrs. *J*ohnson's Potato Salad

Six cold boiled potatoes, 2 hard-boiled eggs, 1 small Bermuda onion, 1 sweet pepper, 1 cucumber. Peel cucumber and soak in salt water for one hour. Dice cucumber, potatoes and eggs. Mince onion and shred the pepper. Mix thoroughly with the following dressing: 1 cup vinegar, 2 tablespoonfuls flour, 1 tablespoonful sugar, ½ teaspoon salt, red and black pepper to taste, 1 teaspoonful celery seed, 1 egg, 1 teaspoonful prepared mustard, ½ cup sour cream. Mix dry ingredients to a smooth paste with a little of the vinegar. Add rest, and the celery seed, and boil until thick, stirring to prevent lumping. Beat the egg thoroughly and add the vinegar mixture, whipping with an egg beater. Add mustard and cream. Beat until smooth. Chill thoroughly before serving.

–Mrs. Dan Johnson, 800 Illinois St., July 29, 1932.

Mrs. *N*isely's Tuna Fish Salad

One small can white tuna, 4 small apples, 1½ cups diced celery, 1 head lettuce, 2 tablespoons lemon juice, double-whipped mayonnaise. Shred tuna fish with fork, after pouring off the oil. Add to diced apples, lemon juice and diced celery. Chill. Arrange lettuce on salad dish and place salad on lettuce. Garnish with strip of pimiento and serve. Individual dishes may be used if desired.

–Mrs. Floyd Nisely, Route 6, Sept. 16, 1932.

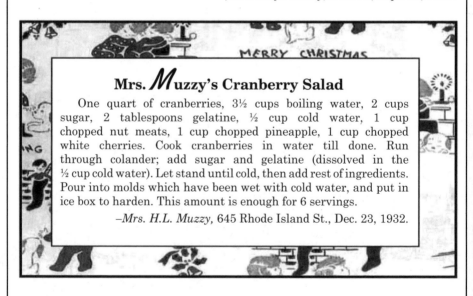

MERRY CHRISTMAS

Mrs. *M*uzzy's Cranberry Salad

One quart of cranberries, 3½ cups boiling water, 2 cups sugar, 2 tablespoons gelatine, ½ cup cold water, 1 cup chopped nut meats, 1 cup chopped pineapple, 1 cup chopped white cherries. Cook cranberries in water till done. Run through colander; add sugar and gelatine (dissolved in the ½ cup cold water). Let stand until cold, then add rest of ingredients. Pour into molds which have been wet with cold water, and put in ice box to harden. This amount is enough for 6 servings.

–Mrs. H.L. Muzzy, 645 Rhode Island St., Dec. 23, 1932.

Mrs. *F*letcher's Jellied Vegetable Macedoine in Tomatoes

Eight medium-sized firm tomatoes, 1 package lemon gelatine, 1 pint boiling strained tomato juice or tomato juice and water, ½ teaspoon salt, 2 cups mixed cooked vegetables (carrots, string beans, peas and celery). Wash tomatoes, remove a thin slice from top, and scoop out centers. Place tomato cases upside down on plate and set in cool place until ready to fill. Dissolve gelatine in boiling tomato juice; add salt and chill.When slightly thickened, fold in vegetables, and fill tomatoes with mixture. Chill until firm. When ready to serve, cut each tomato in quarters, arrange on crisp lettuce leaf and garnish with mayonnaise. Serves 8.

–Mrs. Donald Fletcher, 129 Park St., Mar. 10, 1933.

Mrs. *R*egier's Halloween Salad

One dozen seedless oranges, 6 lbs. large prunes, 18 ounces cream cheese, 2 cups nut meats, ⅓ to ½ cup cream, 1½ teaspoons salt, lettuce leaves, French dressing. Soak prunes and bring to boil. Cool, drain and remove stones. Combine cheese, cream, salt and nuts, and stuff prunes. Arrange three prunes and three orange sections on a lettuce leaf and add a tablespoonful of French dressing. This recipe is enough to serve 25.

–Mrs. A. J. Regier, 1016 Alabama St., Oct. 27, 1933.

Mrs. *H*elwig's Frozen Cottage Cheese Salad

One and a half cups cottage cheese, ½ cup chopped nut meats, 2 minced small green onions, ½ cup mayonnaise dressing, ½ cup whipped cream, 2 tablespoons salad oil, ½ tablespoon lemon juice, 1 teaspoon salt, ¼ teaspoon paprika. Combine all ingredients and fold in the whipped cream. Pack the mixture into fancy molds or refrigerator trays until salad is firm. Serve on crisp lettuce leaves with chilled French dressing.

–Mrs. Earl Helwig, 1120 Pennsylvania St., Apr. 7, 1933.

Mrs. *V*iets's Asparagus en Gelee

One and a half tablespoons gelatine, ¼ cup cold water, 1 cup hot asparagus juice, 2 tablespoons lemon juice, 1 package cream cheese, ¼ cup mayonnaise, 1½ cups coarsely chopped cooked asparagus, ½ cup chopped celery, 2 tablespoons chopped green pepper, 1 teaspoon Worcestershire sauce, salt and pepper. Soak gelatine in cold water; add hot asparagus juice and stir until dissolved. Add lemon juice and cool. Cream the cheese with the mayonnaise and add to cooled gelatine. When it begins to set, add asparagus, celery and green pepper–with Worcestershire and seasonings to taste. Pour into a mold. When firm, unmold on a platter and surround with crisp lettuce. Serve with mayonnaise.

–Mrs. I. D. Viets, 716 Arkansas St., May 12, 1933.

Miss *M*iller's Stuffed Apple Salad for Christmas

Take an apple for each service, pare and remove all the seed cavities from the center. For six apples, make a syrup of one cup of sugar and one cup and one-half of water; add a speck of red color paste and the juice and grated rind of a lemon or an orange; in this syrup cook the apples until tender, turning as needed to keep whole; let cool in the liquid. To serve, set in nests of heart leaves of lettuce or on a bed of shredded lettuce. Fill the centers with the salad dressing [recipe follows], mixed with one-half a cup of fine-cut pecan nut meats, six halves of pears cut in small pieces and one-half a cup of diced celery.

Salad Dressing for Stuffed Apple Salad: Mix two teaspoonfuls of flour with one-fourth a cup of sugar and one-fourth a teaspoonful of salt; when thoroughly blended, gradually stir into it one tablespoonful of vinegar and the juice of one lemon made hot over boiling water. When smooth and thoroughly cooked, stir in one egg, beaten light. Stir and cook until the egg is cooked and the mixture thick. When cool, gradually beat in one-half a cup of cream cheese (pressed through a sieve), then fold in one-half to two-thirds a cup of cream, beaten firm.

–Miss Alberta Miller, 2146 Massachusetts St., Dec. 22, 1933.

The Waffle Shoppe

SATURDAY MENU
35¢
Fried Chicken
(Country Style)
Mashed Potatoes
and Gravy
Buttered Lima Beans
Lettuce and Tomato Salad
Home Baked Parker House Rolls
Coffee Milk Ice Tea
Buttermilk
Marshmallow Whip

Dickinson Theater Building
LJW, 8-12-32

Mrs. *S*chooler's Shrimp Salad

Two cups cooked shrimps, three hard-cooked eggs, one cup diced celery, one-half cup shredded lettuce, one cup mayonnaise, one-half teaspoon paprika, two tablespoons rich cream. Break up shrimp into small pieces. Slice eggs fine. Add diced celery and shredded lettuce. Mix together lightly with a fork and add mayonnaise to which has been added the cream and paprika. Serve in tomato cups with dash of mayonnaise on top, or in cup-shaped lettuce leaves. Tomato cups are made by cutting top from tomatoes, hollowing out the inside and replacing the top after salad has been filled into cup.

–Mrs. Frances Schooler, 901 Maine St., Mar. 9, 1934.

Mrs. *W*oodruff's Tomato Jelly

Two cups tomatoes and water, 1 teaspoon salt, 1 teaspoon powdered sugar, 1 tablespoon gelatine dissolved in ⅓ cup cold water, 1 slice onion, 1 teaspoon celery salt, speck cayenne, 1 hard-boiled egg. Cook the tomatoes and seasonings together until soft. Press through strainer. Add dissolved gelatine. Cut egg in slices crosswise and place in bottom of the mold. Fill with gelatine mixture and chill. Serve on lettuce with mayonnaise.

–Mrs. Roy Woodruff, Route 3, July 20, 1934.

Mrs. *M*artin's Poinsettia Christmas Salad
"This makes a decorative, as well as tasty salad
for the Christmas table, and is easy to make."

Place a lettuce leaf on a salad plate, then a slice of pineapple. Fill the center of pineapple with cream cheese, then place a stuffed olive in center of cheese. Cut strips of pimiento to resemble poinsettia petals, and lay around top of pineapple slice. Serve with a spoonful of mayonnaise, which may be put over the cheese before inserting stuffed olive.

–Mrs. Jessie Martin, Route 4, Dec. 21, 1934.

Miss *E*vans's Stuffed Artichoke Salad
"I have found this stuffed artichoke salad very delicious,
and as it is a meal in itself, quite suitable for luncheon or supper."

Four medium-sized artichokes, 3/8 cup well-seasoned French dressing, 3/4 teaspoon salt, 2 1/4 cups whole canned shrimp, 1 1/8 cups chopped celery, 2 1/2 tablespoons green peppers, 1 1/8 cups mayonnaise. Cut off the stem end of the artichoke so it will stand. Boil for about 45 minutes in water to cover, to which the French dressing and salt have been added. When done, remove from water and drain upside down. Let cool; stand the artichokes on their bases. Spread the leaves outward and lift out the tight center leaves. With a teaspoon, scoop out the mass of thorny leaves and fuzzy substance in the center–until you come to the firm bottom. While the artichokes are cooking, combine the cleaned shrimp, celery, green pepper, and 2/3 cup of the mayonnaise. Fill each artichoke with this salad and place a tablespoon of mayonnaise on top. As the outer leaves are detached for eating, they can be dipped into the mayonnaise on top, then the salad and artichoke bottom can be eaten with a fork.

–Miss Mary Louise Evans,
1208 E. 13th St.,
Mar. 22, 1935.

Saturday Menu
Old Fashioned Chicken Pie
Snowflake Potatoes
Chicken Giblet Gravy
Buttered Peas and Carrots
Fruit Jello Salad
Hot Rolls
Coffee, Milk
or Buttermilk

25¢

Crown
Drug

LJW, 11-3-38

Nick Douvas and Nick Chrones

*A*nnounce

The Grand Opening

of

The Liberty Cafe

Lawrence's Newest and Finest Restaurant

at

719 Massachusetts Street

in the building formerly occupied by the Kansas Electric Power Company

Saturday and Sunday, Nov. 7-8

Music at Meal Times Saturday and Sunday

by Grey's Orchestra of Kansas City, Missouri

A Souvenier Will Be Given to Every Guest

Beautiful Fixtures   Delicious Well Cooked Food   Excellent Service
Home Made American and French Pastry   Coffee that Calls for More

After the Theatre
Supper Service
All Night, Starting at 8 p.m.

A Special Menu Will Be
Served, Including Salads,
Toasted Sandwiches and
French Pastries

Reservations can be made
for special parties by calling 372

LJW, 11-6-25

36

Miss *H*ird's Shrimp Salad

Two tablespoons butter, 1 can shrimps, 1 cup celery (cut fine), 1 cup tart apple cubes, 1 cup nuts, salt and pepper to taste, 1 cup whipped cream, ½ cup thick cream, 1 lemon, 4 tablespoons vinegar, 2 tablespoons water, 4 eggs, 1 teaspoon ground mustard, 1 teaspoon salt, 1 teaspoon sugar. Break shrimps into pieces in bowl, moisten with a little melted butter, season with vinegar, salt and pepper. Put apple cubes in small dish and sprinkle lightly with lemon juice, then put in celery with a little more lemon juice and toss together. Cover and set aside. Heat vinegar and water in double boiler. Beat eggs, and gradually add to the vinegar, stirring constantly. Add butter and cook slowly, still stirring. Remove from fire and beat till cold, then add mustard, salt, sugar and pepper. Add thick cream just before serving. When ready to serve, toss nuts, celery, apples and shrimps together and a little dressing. Heap on crisp lettuce leaves on individual plates and pour over each salad a heaping spoon of dressing and top with spoon of unsweetened whipped cream.

–Miss Mildred Hird, Route 3, Baldwin, Mar. 29, 1935.

Mrs. *B*ahnmaier's Potato Salad with Cheese Mask

"Delicious to serve for picnics, accompanying fried chicken."

Boil potatoes tender without paring. Peel and dice enough to make 1 quart. Season with salt and pepper. Add: 1 cup diced celery, 2 hard-boiled eggs (diced), 1 cup diced fresh cucumbers, 2 tablespoons diced green pepper, 2 tablespoons of diced onion. Mix with just enough boiled salad dressing to moisten well. Season well with pepper and salt. Set away to chill for several hours. When ready to serve, cover the mound of salad with the cheese mask made as follows: ¼ pound American cheese, cut fine; 2 tablespoons diced pimientos; ¼ cup thin cream; ½ cup mayonnaise. Put cheese into double boiler; add cream and stir until cheese melts. Remove from fire and whip with Dover beater until smooth. When cool, fold in rest of ingredients.

–Mrs. George F. Bahnmaier, Route 1, Lecompton, July 26, 1935.

Mrs. *S*chott's Tomato Salad

Soak 1¼ tablespoons gelatine in ¼ cup of cold tomato juice. Add 1 cup of tomato juice, boiling hot. Stir well to dissolve gelatine. When gelatine is dissolved, add ¾ cup cold tomato juice, 2 teaspoons lemon juice, 1 teaspoon Worcestershire sauce, 1 teaspoon sugar, and 1 teaspoon salt. Chill until gelatine is slightly thickened, then add ½ cup bread and butter pickles, chopped, and 1 cup celery or crisp cabbage, chopped. Pour into oiled mold and chill until firm; unmold on bed of lettuce and serve with mayonnaise. This serves six. When using cabbage without celery, 1 teaspoon grated onion can be added for seasoning.

–Mrs. Victor Schott, Route 1, Lone Star, Apr. 3, 1936.

Mrs. *K*ey's Easter Lily Salad

Six hard-cooked eggs, ¼ cup grated cheese, mayonnaise dressing, 1 cup seasoned mashed potatoes, shredded lettuce. Mix cheese and mashed potatoes together. Mold mashed potatoes while still warm into small balls. Arrange bed of shredded lettuce on four salad plates. Cut eggs in quarters lengthwise, leaving the quartered yolk lying in the quartered white. Place eggs petal-like on lettuce. Use six petals on each plate. Put four potato balls in center and heap on these very stiff mayonnaise dressing.

–Mrs. Richard Key, 311 Missouri St., Apr. 10, 1936.

Mrs. *A*lbrecht's Asparagus Bouquet Salad

Four small rings cut from green peppers; 8 three-inch strips cucumber; 8 three-inch strips tender celery; 8 asparagus tips, cooked; 2½ cups shredded lettuce; paprika French dressing. Wash the peppers and cut crosswise to form four small rings. Allow two strips each of cucumbers, celery, and two asparagus tips for each person. Place in the pepper rings and stand upright in lettuce nests arranged individually. Pour paprika French dressing over.

–Mrs. R. M. Albrecht, 425 Maine St., May 8, 1936.

Mrs. *L*indsey's Cottage Cheese Salad

One quart dry cottage cheese, ½ teaspoon salt, 1 cup heavy cream, 2 teaspoons gelatine. Dissolve gelatine in small amount of water. Combine with the above and add any favorite salad mixture or combination, such as: ½ cup chopped sweet pickles, ½ cup chopped olives, 1 tablespoon chopped parsley. Fill large sweet pepper cups with the mixture and place in ice box to harden. When firm, slice one inch thick and place on lettuce leaves, and serve with your favorite salad dressing. Other combinations are: ½ cup finely chopped green onion and ½ cup chopped pimiento; ½ cup chopped nuts and ½ cup chopped tender celery; ¼ cup chopped dates and ¼ cup chopped raisins. Note: the gelatine need not be added if the salad is to be served at once and not molded.

–Mrs. L. Lindsey, Lawrence, June 5, 1936.

Mrs. *W*ilderson's Sardine Surprise Salad

Three tomatoes; ¼ cup chopped, stuffed olives; 1 can sardines; 1 hard-cooked egg, chopped fine. Put the tomatoes in boiling water for a moment to loosen skins. Peel and put in ice box to chill. Drain oil from sardines. Remove skin and backbone, if necessary. Mash to a paste and add the olives. Moisten slightly with mayonnaise dressing and spread mixture on thick slices of tomatoes. Sprinkle with the chopped egg. Arrange each slice on a lettuce leaf and serve with Piquant dressing made as follows: 1 teaspoon salt, 1 teaspoon sugar, ¼ teaspoon paprika, ½ teaspoon mustard, ⅛ teaspoon Worcestershire sauce, 3 tablespoons pure vinegar, ¾ cup olive oil, ½ teaspoon onion juice, 2 drops Tabasco sauce. Mix thoroughly.

–Mrs. Mary Wilderson,
1117 Connecticut St.,
July 17, 1936.

Mrs. *B*eal's Chicken Supreme Salad

One and one-half cups cold chicken, ¾ cup crushed pineapple, 6 tablespoons pecans, pinch of salt, 1 cup whipping cream, 1 cup mayonnaise. Cut chicken into small cubes, drain pineapple and chop the nut meats fine. Add salt to chicken and combine first four ingredients. Whip cream and blend with mayonnaise. Fold two mixtures together. Place in tray of refrigerator and freeze. Cut in squares and serve on lettuce, garnished with mayonnaise and a slice of tomato. Serves ten.

–Mrs. Mary Beal, 828 Mississippi St., Aug. 28, 1936.

Mrs. *G*lenn's Shamrock Salad

Cut 3-inch circles of stiffer-than-usual lime gelatine. Lay on lettuce in threes to form a shamrock. On this place a slice of canned pineapple. Cut tiny gelatine circles with a thimble, place in groups of 3 on the pineapple to make little shamrocks. With a pastry tube, pipe on green-colored cream cheese stems. Pass dainty green-colored mayonnaise.

–Mrs. V. H. Glenn, Route 1, Lecompton, Mar. 12, 1937.

Mrs. *O*wen's Boiled Salad Dressing

One teaspoon salt, 1 teaspoon mustard, 2 teaspoons sugar, dash of cayenne, 2 tablespoons melted butter or oil, ¾ cup scalded milk, ½ cup hot vinegar, 2½ tablespoons flour, yolks of 2 eggs, or 1 whole egg. Mix salt, mustard, oil, sugar and cayenne, add yolks of eggs and mix thoroughly. Stir flour with 1 tablespoon cold water until smooth. Add a little of the scalded milk; stir, then pour it into the scalded milk. Cook in a double boiler, and continue stirring until thickened. Pour it into the yolk mixture, return to double boiler, add the hot vinegar, stirring constantly until mixture thickens. Cool before using. If cooked too long, it will curdle.

–Mrs. Leslie Owen, 2101 Kentucky St., July 9, 1937.

Mrs. *G*regory's Fruit Salad in Orange Jack-o-Lanterns

Cut tops from six oranges. Scoop out pulp. Cut eyes, nose and mouth on side of each orange and refill with fruit salad made by mixing together the scooped-out orange, one-half cup diced pineapple, one sliced banana, one cup seedless grapes, and one diced apple. Serve with French dressing. The recipe may be increased by keeping the proportions the same. French Dressing: ½ teaspoon salt, ⅛ teaspoon white pepper, ⅛ teaspoon paprika, ½ teaspoon powdered sugar, pinch of mustard, 1 tablespoon lemon juice, 1 tablespoon vinegar, 4 tablespoons olive oil. Mix dry ingredients, add oil and stir until thoroughly mixed; then add vinegar and lemon juice, a few drops at a time, and beat until an emulsion is formed. Or ingredients may all be placed in a bottle and shaken vigorously together to form an emulsion. One-fourth cup of whipped cream added to the above quantity of French dressing improves the dressing for fruit salads.

–Mrs. Howard Gregory, Route 1, Oct. 29, 1937.

Mrs. *H*unter's Valentine Fruit Salad

Blend two packages of cream cheese with one-half cup of mayonnaise. Add one-half cup of chopped nuts, one cup of drained pitted cherries and one-half cup chopped celery. Soften one and one-half tablespoons plain gelatine in one-fourth cup cold water. Dissolve over hot water; cool and add to mixture. Fold in one cup heavy whipping cream, whipped, dash of salt and red food coloring to tint delicate pink. Mold in heart-shaped mold.

–Mrs. Alfred Hunter, Williamstown, Feb. 3, 1939.

Mrs. *P*ayne's Cranberry Fruit Salad

Chop 1 quart cranberries and 2 large red apples; add 1½ cups of sugar, and let stand overnight. Next morning, dissolve 1 package raspberry gelatine powder in 1 pint boiling water, and add to mixture. When chilled, but not set, add ½ cup chopped celery and ½ cup nut meats. Put into molds and chill. When ready to serve, garnish with celery tips and mayonnaise.

–Mrs. Raymond Payne, 1109 Connecticut St., Dec. 16, 1938.

Mrs. *O*'Neill's Poinsettia Salad for New Year's Supper
"This makes a beautiful as well as tasty salad."

One envelope plain gelatine, ½ cup cold water, ¾ cup boiling water, juice of one lemon, 3 tablespoonfuls sugar, 1 pimiento pepper, 1 hard-boiled egg, ¾ cup finely shredded cabbage, 8 or 10 marshmallows (cut into small pieces), a few nut meats. Cut pimiento into small pieces, ½ to ¾ inches long, to represent poinsettia petals. Arrange in the bottom of a shallow pan, about 5 by 8 inches, or individual molds if preferred. In the center of each flower, place a piece of hard boiled egg yolk. Sprinkle a small amount of shredded cabbage over this. Next, soak 1 envelope of gelatine at least five minutes. Add boiling water, sugar, and lemon juice. Set aside to cool. When cool, pour a little of the gelatine over the pimiento and cabbage arranged in the pan. Set in the refrigerator to congeal. Add all the other ingredients, cabbage, marshmallows, and nuts to the remainder of the gelatine. Add this to the already congealed gelatine in the pan and set in the refrigerator. To unmold, set in pan of warm water a few seconds until loosened. Cut between each flower. Serve on lettuce leaves with any preferred salad dressing. Serves six.

–Mrs. James O'Neill, 1410 New York St., Dec. 30, 1938.

Mrs. *M*iller's Cottage Cheese Salad

One envelope unsweetened gelatine (¼ pkg.), ¼ cup cold water, 1 cup hot water, ¼ tsp. salt, ¼ cup mild vinegar, ¼ cup cream (whipped), 1½ cups cottage cheese, ⅓ cup stuffed olives (chopped), ½ cup celery (chopped), ¼ cup green pepper (chopped). Soften gelatine in cold water and add hot water. Stir until dissolved. Add salt and vinegar. When the above begins to thicken, fold in cheese, olives, celery, pepper and whipped cream. Turn into mold that has been rinsed in cold water, and chill. Unmold on lettuce; serve with salad dressing. Serves 6.

–Mrs. George E. Miller, Route 1, Mar. 31, 1939.

Mrs. *A*ul's Pineapple in the Shell

Cut a fresh pineapple in halves or fourths. Remove the pineapple and mix with any desired fruits, such as strawberries or bananas. Add quartered marshmallows and any desired salad dressing or whipped cream. Fill the pineapple shell and garnish with maraschino cherries and nuts.

–Mrs. C. P. Aul, 1420 New York St., May 19, 1939.

Miss *B*roers's Potato Salad

Peel 4 medium-sized cold (cooked) potatoes; cut in small cubes. Combine 2 tablespoons vinegar, 2 tablespoons lemon juice, 2 teaspoons grated onion, 2 teaspoons chopped parsley, and 1 cup thick sour cream. Salt to taste, and add a dash of paprika. Add 2 tablespoons chopped pimiento, ½ cup chopped dill pickle, and ¼ cup crisp fried bacon to the potatoes. Toss together with the sour cream mixture and chill before serving.

–Miss Dorothy Broers, Route 2, June 30, 1939.

Mrs. *D*ick's Tuna Fish Salad

Two cups of tuna; 1 cucumber, chopped; 1 cup celery, chopped; 4 sweet pickles, chopped; 4 hard-cooked eggs, chopped; ¼ teaspoon salt; ⅛ teaspoon paprika; ⅛ teaspoon black pepper; juice of one lemon. Combine ingredients; chill and serve on crisp lettuce. Garnish with mayonnaise, and surround with stuffed olives. Serves six.

–Mrs. Stella Dick, 718 Kentucky St., July 28, 1939.

LJW, 6-6-29

Mrs. $\mathcal{E}$vans's Pineapple Peach Salad

One and one-half cups diced pineapple, 1½ cups diced canned peaches, ½ tablespoon lemon juice, 1 cup gingerale, ½ cup sliced maraschino cherries, 4 bananas (diced), 1 pkg. sweetened lemon gelatine, 1 cup boiling water. Dissolve gelatine in boiling water. Cool. Add gingerale and lemon juice. Mix thoroughly. Cool until partially set. Arrange fruit in a mold. Cover with gelatine mixture. Chill until firm. Serve with fruit salad dressing. If desired, 1 cup of chopped nuts may be added. Fruit Salad Dressing: ½ cup syrup from canned peaches, 1 tablespoon sugar, ⅛ teaspoon paprika, 2 egg yolks (well beaten), ⅛ teaspoon salt, 1½ teaspoons lemon juice. Heat peach syrup. Combine egg yolks, sugar, salt and paprika. Add peach syrup slowly, stirring constantly. Cook over hot water until thick and smooth. Remove from stove. Add lemon juice slowly. Mix thoroughly. Chill.

–Mrs. Clara Evans, 928 Vermont St., Sept. 1, 1939.

Mrs. $\mathcal{H}$umphries's Special Halloween Salad

Take half peaches and fill cavity with cream cheese. Turn peach open side down and make face, using cloves for eyes, and almond for nose; make a slit with sharp knife for mouth. Fill this slit with softened cream cheese. Mold lemon gelatine in square or round molds. Invert on lettuce. Set head (or peach) on gelatine molds.

–Mrs. Clyde Humphries, Perry, Oct. 27, 1939.

Mrs. $\mathcal{C}$otton's Raw Cranberry Salad

Part I. One package lemon gelatine. Dissolve gelatine in 1 cup boiling water, ½ cup pineapple juice, and ½ cup orange juice. Part II. Combine one cup ground cranberries and 1 cup sugar. Let stand one hour. Add 2 cups diced celery, 1 cup diced pineapple, 1 cup diced apple (do not peel), 1 cup nut meats. Mix parts I and II. Place in icebox until ready to serve.

–Mrs. Corlett Cotton, 704 W. 12th St., Nov. 28, 1939.

Mrs. $\mathcal{P}$eterson's Cottage Cheese Salad

Dissolve one package each of lime and lemon gelatine powder in two cupfuls of hot water. Add 1 small can of crushed pineapple and let stand until slightly congealed. Mix together 1 cup milk, 1 cup salad dressing, 2 tablespoons horseradish and 1 pound of cottage cheese, and stir into the gelatine mixture. Pour into a square cake pan and set in a cool place until it becomes firm. Cut in squares and serve on lettuce leaves. The salad may be topped with whipped cream if desired.

–Mrs. Oliver Peterson, 1108 Kentucky St., May 3, 1940.

Fritzel Dairy Products, LJW, 3-17-39

Mrs. *L*aCoss's Crabmeat Salad

Four teaspoons lemon juice, 1 teaspoon salt, 4 tablespoons salad oil, 2 cups crabmeat, 1 cup diced celery, 1 ½ cups diced and pared tart apples, 3 hard-cooked eggs, ¼ cup mayonnaise, lettuce, stuffed olives. Combine the lemon juice, salt and salad oil. Mix the crabmeat, celery and apple, and let stand in the salad oil mixture for 20 minutes in the refrigerator. Then add the eggs, coarsely chopped, and the mayonnaise. Serve on 8 individual beds of lettuce garnished with stuffed olives or green pepper strips.

–Mrs. William LaCoss, 1301 Kentucky St., July 19, 1940.

Mrs. *H*ird's Cranberry Salad

One quart raw cranberries, 1 cup cold water, 2 oranges, 1 cup diced celery, 2 cups sugar, 1 cup chopped nuts, 2 tablespoons gelatine, 1 head lettuce, 1 cup of crushed pineapple. Grate yellow rind from orange and peel off white membrane. Put berries and orange through food chopper. Add sugar and boil 2 minutes. Dissolve the gelatine in 1 cup cold water; add to the hot mixture. Cool slightly and add celery and nuts. Mold and serve on lettuce leaf or on shredded lettuce with or without salad dressing. A half-cup of chopped apples may be added.

–Mrs. I. T. Hird, Route 3, Baldwin, Dec. 27, 1940.

Mrs. *B*each's St. Patrick Salad

Six green peppers, ¾ cup crushed pineapple, 2 tablespoons pineapple juice, 2 tablespoons chopped nuts, salt and paprika, 1 (3 oz.) package cream cheese, 2 tablespoons minced pimiento, 1 teaspoon gelatine, mayonnaise. Cut a slice from top of each green pepper. Remove seeds and membrane. Soften gelatine in pineapple juice. Dissolve over boiling water. Combine cheese, pineapple, nuts, pimiento, and gelatine. Season with salt and paprika. Fill pepper cases. Place in refrigerator until filling is firm. Slice with a sharp knife. Arrange green pepper slices in the shape of four leaf clovers, with the stem cut from slice first taken off the top. Serve on lettuce with mayonnaise.

–Mrs. M. P. Beach, 1809 Mississippi St., Mar. 14, 1941.

Mrs. *E*wing's Molded Grapefruit Salad

One package sweetened lemon-flavored gelatine, 1½ cups water, ¼ cup sugar, 2 cups grapefruit sections (fresh or canned), 8 maraschino cherries, ½ cup grapefruit juice. Dissolve gelatine in water. Follow directions on package for temperature of water. Add sugar. Stir until dissolved. Cool. Add grapefruit juice. Chill until partially set. Pour into mold. Add grapefruit sections. Chill until firm. Serve with mayonnaise on crisp salad greens. Garnish with cherries. 8 servings.

–Mrs. M. T. Ewing, 1209 Haskell Ave., May 16, 1941.

Mrs. $\mathcal{S}$ terling's Grapefruit Salad

To prepare the grapefruit, pour boiling water over it and let it stand in the hot water until the skin is heated through (about five or ten minutes); then cool thoroughly. The rind will then come off easily and completely. Remove the bitter skins from the separate sections, keeping the sections whole. Peel a ripe avocado and slice lengthwise in strips about half as thick as the grapefruit sections. Arrange grapefruit sections and strips of avocado on head lettuce leaf cups and garnish with a teaspoon of salad dressing (recipe follows) in the center.

Thousand Island Dressing: Sift together several times the following dry ingredients: ½ cup flour, ½ cup sugar, 1 level teaspoon salt, ½ level teaspoon dry mustard, ½ level teaspoon paprika. Moisten with ½ cup vinegar and ½ cup water, beaten with 2 egg yolks. Pour on a cup of boiling water and cook until thick as starch, stirring constantly. It will take about five minutes. Cool thoroughly. Then add 1 pint whipping cream, whipped stiff; 1 small can pimientos; 1 dozen sweet pickles, both of which have been put through the food grinder. This salad dressing will keep in a fruit jar in the refrigerator for a week or more. If making the Thousand Island Dressing seems too much work, any of the commercial dressings will do.

–Mrs. M. W. Sterling,
1129 Louisiana St.,
Feb. 20, 1942.

Mrs. $\mathcal{R}$ oberts's Hawaiian Queen Salad

"This salad, while very simple, is so appealing to the palate, as well as festive in appearance, that you'll be serving it to the family as well as to company."

On a nest of endive, place a slice of pineapple cut in half with the curved edges together in the middle of the plate. Peel avocado, and cut through the center so as to make a round slice. Place ¼-inch slice on top of pineapple. Top avocado with slice of peeled orange and three slices of banana. Dress with strawberry mayonnaise made by combining ¼ cup sliced strawberries, 1 tablespoon mashed strawberries, 1 tablespoon lemon juice, 2 tablespoons sugar, and ½ cup mayonnaise. Garnish with whole strawberries dipped in powdered sugar. Directions are for individual salads with dressing for 8 servings.

–Mrs. Byron Roberts, 1226 Almira St., May 2, 1941.

Mrs. *P*fleger's Easter Bunny Salad

"This is enjoyed by the grown-ups, as well as the kiddies,
and is delicious as well as pretty."

Shred lettuce on individual plates. Place one slice of pineapple on plate. On this put one half of a pear, rounded side up. Make a rabbit by using cloves for the eyes, nose and mouth; blanched almonds for the ears; and a piece of marshmallow cut for a tail. Spread mayonnaise on the pineapple around rabbit for a nest. Scatter tiny Easter eggs on dressing.

–Mrs. Hanna Pfleger, Linwood, Mar. 27, 1942.

Mrs. *G*riffeth's Potato Salad

Six potatoes, cooked in jackets, to make 4 cups diced; 1 small onion; 3 hard-cooked eggs, sliced; 1 cup chopped celery; 1 cup grated carrot; 1 cucumber, diced; 1½ teaspoons salt; ¼ teaspoon paprika; 1 teaspoon celery seed; ¼ cup French dressing; mayonnaise. Combine ingredients, except mayonnaise dressing. Chill and marinate in French dressing 4 to 6 hours. Just before serving, add mayonnaise and mix carefully. Serves 10.

–Mrs. Ida Griffeth, 1033 New Jersey St., July 3, 1942.

Mrs. *B*unn's Summer Fruit Plate with Dressing

For each plate, prepare 5 lettuce leaves with tips dipped in paprika; 1 slice cantaloupe, rind removed; ¼ cup seedless grapes; ½ pear marinated in lemon juice; 5 ripe olives; ripe peach slices around a center of cottage cheese. Arrange lettuce on plate, and place cantaloupe slice in center. Slice pear in narrow strips, and alternate pear and peach slices with grapes and olives outside the melon rind. Place cheese in center of cantaloupe. Serve with the following dressing: ½ cup orange juice, 3 tablespoons lemon juice, ¼ teaspoon salt, ¼ teaspoon paprika, a few grains nutmeg. Shake or stir well before serving.

–Mrs. E. E. Bunn, 1809 Massachusetts St., July 31, 1942.

Mrs. *K*irchhoff's Potato Salad

Twelve medium-sized potatoes, 4 hard-boiled eggs, 1 large- or 2 medium-sized cucumbers, 2 medium-sized onions, ¾ cup mayonnaise (or salad dressing), salt and pepper to taste. Boil unpeeled potatoes until tender. Hard boil the eggs. Cool both. When cool, combine diced potatoes with diced eggs. Add diced onions and diced cucumber. Add mayonnaise, and salt and pepper. Mix lightly with fork until well-blended. Place in lettuce-lined salad bowl. Set in refrigerator and serve cold.

–Mrs. G. G. Kirchhoff, 1014 Vermont St., July 2, 1943.

Mrs. *W*oodard's Chicken Salad

One chicken, ½ stalk medium-sized celery, 2 tablespoons salad oil, 1 tablespoon vinegar. Cook chicken until tender and season before it is done. Cool in liquor. When cold, cut in ½-inch pieces. Marinate with oil and vinegar or use lemon juice without the oil. Let stand 2 hours. Cut celery in very small pieces, and put a little French dressing or lemon juice over celery. When ready to serve, drain chicken and celery. Mix together and pour over a good cooked dressing, blending well. Serve in lettuce cups with a spoonful of mayonnaise. Almonds and olives make a nice garnish.

–Mrs. Emery Woodard, 1216 Rhode Island St., July 16, 1943.

Mrs. *G*uffin's
Stuffed Tomato and Cucumber-Cheese Salad

Dip firm, ripe tomatoes (one for each serving) into boiling water and peel carefully. Chill. Cucumber and cheese stuffing: 1 teaspoon salt for tomatoes, ⅔ cup chopped fresh cucumber, ¼ cup chopped celery, ½ teaspoon salt, ⅔ cup cottage cheese, ⅓ cup mayonnaise, ⅛ teaspoon paprika, lettuce. Mix cucumber, celery, ½ teaspoon salt and cottage cheese with mayonnaise and fill tomato cups with this mixture. Sprinkle with paprika and serve on crisp lettuce leaves. Makes 4 servings.

–Mrs. L. A. Guffin, 2124 Learnard Ave., Aug. 13, 1943.

Mrs. *B*rockman's Cranberry Salad

One package cherry-flavored gelatine; 1¾ cups boiling water; ½ cup sugar; 1½ cups cranberries, chopped; 1½ cups apples, chopped; ¼ cup orange juice; ½ cup chopped nuts; 12 marshmallows (optional). Dissolve gelatine in boiling water; set aside to cool. Core apples, but do not peel. Chop both apples and cranberries with medium-to-coarse blade of food chopper. Cut marshmallows into fourths. Chop nuts coarsely. When gelatine has begun to thicken, mix all ingredients and pour into mold.

–Mrs. H. C. Brockman, 243 N. 4th St., Jan. 7, 1944.

Mrs. *T*aylor's Grapefruit Salad

Add one and one-half cups of boiling water to one package of lemon gelatine. Stir well and chill. When it first begins to harden, add 2 cups of fresh grapefruit picked to pieces; also one cup of diced oranges, one-half cup pecans, ¼ cup sugar, and one-half cup diced celery. Turn onto lettuce leaves and serve with a lemon dressing made of one egg yolk, three tablespoons of sugar, and three tablespoons of lemon juice. Beat thoroughly; cook until thick, and add whipped cream.

–Mrs. Bessie Taylor, 907 Rhode Island St., Mar. 24, 1944.

Mrs. *E*llis's Chicken Salad Supreme

Two cups cooked chicken, cubed; 2 tablespoons chopped green olives; ¾ cup chopped celery; ½ cup toasted almonds; 2 tablespoons chopped ripe (black) olives; 2 tablespoons chopped mixed pickles; 2 hard-cooked eggs, sliced; ¾ cup mayonnaise. Combine ingredients and toss lightly. Serve on lettuce. Serves 6.

–Mrs. O. M. Ellis, 2129 New Hampshire St., Aug. 18, 1944.

Mrs. *G*lenn's Norwegian Potato Salad

Three cups diced, cooked potatoes; 1 tablespoon horseradish; 1 teaspoon chopped onion; French dressing; salt and pepper; ¼ cup diced sardines; ½ cup mayonnaise; ¼ cup chopped pickles. Combine potatoes, horseradish and onion. Moisten with French dressing. Season to taste. Chill. Add remaining ingredients. Mix lightly with two forks. Serve on crisp lettuce or salad greens.

–Mrs. Viola Glenn, Lecompton, Aug. 25, 1944.

Mrs. *R*obb's
Individual Grapefruit Salad with Three Fruits Dressing

Remove membrane and seeds from four sections of orange and four sections of grapefruit. Remove skin and center from a calavo (avocado) and cut it into ½-inch slices. Arrange grapefruit sections in a circle on a lettuce leaf. Lay 2 or 3 slices of calavo on top of the grapefruit sections. Arrange the orange sections on the slices of calavo. Add Three Fruits Dressing and top with a maraschino cherry. Three Fruits Dressing: Beat 2 large eggs very lightly. Mix together 1 cup sugar, 2 teaspoons flour and 1 teaspoon dry mustard. Add gradually to the beaten eggs and continue beating until all the dry ingredients have been added. Gradually add ¼ cup lemon juice, ¼ cup orange juice and ¼ cup pineapple juice. Cook over hot water until thick; stir constantly. When cold, add ½ cup whipping cream beaten stiff.

–Mrs. J. E. Robb, 1717 Illinois St., Feb. 16, 1945.

1925 Jayhawker

Miss *K*oerner's Spring Salad

One cup shredded cabbage; 1 cup shredded carrots; 1 cup shredded apples; ½ cup brown sugar; ½ cup raisins; 1 banana, sliced; ¼ teaspoon salt; juice of ½ lemon. Mix salt with cabbage, brown sugar, carrots, lemon juice and raisins. Put all the ingredients together. Serve on lettuce leaves.

–Miss Wilma Koerner, 750 N. 3rd St., Apr. 6, 1945.

Mrs. *H*ird's Chicken Salad

Remove skin and bones from a tender, cooked chicken, and cut into small pieces. Add one half the amount of celery, cut into tiny pieces. Mix together carefully and chill. Dressing: 1 cup weak vinegar, 3 beaten eggs, 1 teaspoon dry mustard, 1 teaspoon flour, 1 teaspoon sugar, ¼ teaspoon salt, ⅛ teaspoon pepper. Mix together and cook over hot water. When thick, add 1 teaspoon butter; beat well, then add 3 teaspoons sweet cream. Chill; use half mixed into salad. Serve on lettuce, topped with 1 teaspoon of dressing. A small amount of diced sweet pickles may be added to celery and chicken.

–Mrs. Carl Hird, Route 1, July 27, 1945.

Mrs. *L*awson's Stuffed Tomato Salad

Select large, ripe tomatoes, one for each person. Peel the tomatoes; cut a round piece from the stem end, and remove enough of the pulp to leave a hollow cup. Season inside with salt, and turn the tomatoes upside down to drain. Then place them in the ice-box until ready to serve. Stuff with a filling made of chopped meat (such as chicken, veal, or tongue); cooked peas; pickle or fresh cucumber, chopped fine; and salad dressing. Mix the ingredients thoroughly so the flavors will be well-blended. Serve on lettuce with salad dressing.

–Mrs. Ruth Lawson, 1202 Rhode Island St., Aug. 3, 1945.

Mrs. *K*nox's Cranberry Salad

Dissolve 1 pkg. of orange gelatine in 1 ¼ cups hot water. Add ½ cup sugar, and stir until well-dissolved. Let cool. Grind in food chopper ½ lb. cranberries and 1 large orange (rind and pulp). To cooled gelatine add cranberries, orange, ½ cup chopped celery, and ½ cup pecan meats. Pour into molds and let set. Serve on lettuce leaf with or without dressing.

–Mrs. William F. Knox, 1238 Tennessee St., Dec. 7, 1945.

Mrs. *J*ones's Frozen Cranberry Salad

The dressing: Beat 6 eggs; add 1 cup sugar and 1 cup vinegar, and cook until thick. Add 1 lb. (or 50 individual) marshmallows that have been previously heated. Makes ½ gallon, and is fine for any fruit salad. The salad: 1 quart cranberries, 1 orange, 1 cup sugar, 1 pint salad dressing, 1 pint cream (whipped). Reserve 1 cup of cranberry mixture. Grind cranberries and whole orange. Mix with sugar and let stand until sweetened. Use dressing above or any dressing which has been made with lemon or canned fruit juice. Mix other ingredients, place in refrigerator tray, and spread top with the reserved cup of cranberry mixture. Freeze.

–Mrs. I. J. Jones, 1328 Ohio St., Dec. 21, 1945.

Mrs. *H*igginbottom's Chop Suey Salad
"A breath of spring"

One cup finely shredded cabbage; 1 cup coarsely diced cucumber; 1 cup thinly sliced red radishes; ½ cup finely chopped green pepper; 4 medium-sized tomatoes; 1 cup chopped spinach; 6 green onions, chopped fine; 4 medium-sized carrots, grated; 1 teaspoon salt; 2 hard-cooked eggs; ¼ teaspoon pepper; ½ cup French dressing, or more, if desired. Combine all vegetables, salt and pepper. Set in refrigerator to chill. Add French dressing and toss lightly to mix. To serve, top with sieved eggs. Serves 6.

–Mrs. E. E. Higginbottom, 812 Tennessee St., May 3, 1946.

Local Grocery Prices 1947

1 pkg. Jello	.10
1 lb. cauliflower	.13
1 lb. celery	.14
1 lb. iceberg lettuce	.15
1 lb. green peppers	.19
2 lbs. apples	.27
1 jar dill pickles	.29
1 pint salad dressing	.33
1 lb. cranberries	.39
Total	$ 1.99

Mrs. *J*ones's Boiled Salad Dressing

One and one-half tablespoons sugar, ¼ teaspoon salt, 1 tablespoon flour, 1 teaspoon dry mustard, 3 egg yolks, ¾ cup cold water, ¼ cup vinegar. Mix salt, sugar, flour and mustard together; beat egg yolks slightly. Add dry ingredients, water, and vinegar, and mix to a smooth paste. Cook over low heat, stirring constantly until thickened. When ready to use, thin with cream to desired consistency, or fold in whipped cream.

–Mrs. C. A. Jones, 734½ Massachusetts St., May 24, 1946.

Mrs. $\mathcal{D}$ick's Easter Lily Salad Plate

Hard cook an egg for each serving; remove shells. Upon a glass plate, make a bed of salad greens, such as shredded lettuce or chopped pickle. Arrange the eggs upon it, standing each firmly upon the large end. Slit carefully downward lengthwise of the egg to form petals like a lily, leaving short uncut space at bottom to hold in shape. Ease the petals down upon the supporting bed of greens. Remove yolks; mash, season with salt, pepper, butter and salad dressing. Make into balls, putting one in the center of each lily.

–Mrs. Ethel Dick, 726 Illinois St., Apr. 12, 1946.

Mrs. $\mathcal{W}$ilson's Cabbage Salad

Two cups shredded cabbage; 1 green or red pepper, cut fine; 1 teaspoon salt; ½ cup salad dressing. Mix shredded cabbage, pepper and salt. Pour dressing over cabbage and mix well. Chill. This serves 6.

–Mrs. Clarence Wilson, 203 Lyons St., Aug. 2, 1946.

Mrs. $\mathcal{M}$inor's Frozen Fruit Holiday Salad

"The colors of the fruit will add an appetizing note to the holiday meal, and the tasty combination of fruit and frozen cream will confirm its delicious appearance."

One teaspoon unflavored gelatine; 2 tablespoons cold water; ¾ cup mayonnaise; 1 teaspoon sugar; 2 cups whipping cream; 2 cups canned fruit cocktail (drained); ⅓ cup maraschino cherries, half red and half green. Soften gelatine in the cold water. Melt it over hot water and beat it into the mayonnaise. Whip the cream and add the sugar, then combine this with the mayonnaise. Cut the cherries in half and add all fruit to the whipped cream mixture. Pour this into refrigerator drawers and freeze at very cold temperature. This requires from 2½ to 3½ hours. The cream mixture should be frozen, but not the fruit. Cut into squares and serve them upside down on lettuce cups. This portion serves eight large pieces or ten medium pieces.

–Mrs. John T. Minor, 1002 W. 6th St., Dec. 27, 1946.

Mrs. *M*cKenzie's Log Cabin Salad

Cut cooked whole carrots in long strips. Arrange these carrots in strips with asparagus stalks in log cabin fashion on a lettuce leaf, using four carrot strips and four stalks of asparagus. Make the cabin two logs high. Fill the center with cole slaw or cabbage salad. Garnish with chopped green peppers.

–Mrs. H. N. McKenzie, Leavenworth, Jan. 31, 1947.

Mrs. *H*ouser's Easter Baskets

"This makes a very attractive salad for the Easter season."

Six pear halves, ½ cup shredded cocoanut, 2 packages Philadelphia cream cheese, ½ cup mayonnaise, 6 long celery curls. Tint the cocoanut green. Divide the cheese into three equal parts and tint one part yellow, one part pink and one part blue. Mold into small egg- shaped portions. This should make 18 small eggs, six of each color. Arrange half a pear on shredded lettuce, cut side up. Spread pear with mayonnaise. Cover with green cocoanut. Arrange the cheese eggs on the cocoanut, using one egg of each color for each pear. Complete the Easter Basket by tucking the celery curls under the pears for the handles. Serves 6.

–Mrs. Winifred Houser, 933 Alabama St., Apr. 4, 1947.

Mrs. *S*kinner's Cabbage Salad

"Rich in Vitamins A and C."

One-half head cabbage (medium size), finely shredded; 2 ripe tomatoes, diced; 1 cup carrots, grated; 1 teaspoon grated onion, or one green onion, chopped; ½ cup celery, chopped; 2 tablespoons green pepper, chopped; ½ cup mayonnaise. Toss chilled vegetables with mayonnaise immediately after preparation to avoid loss of vitamins by air. Serve at once. Serves 6. Note: Do not lose valuable, water-soluble minerals by soaking prepared vegetables in water to freshen. Keep them fresh for use in refrigerator crisper, or wrapped in a damp cloth or wax paper.

–Mrs. Harold Skinner,
227 Mississippi St.,
Apr. 25, 1947.

Miss *L*ongacre's Thanksgiving Salad

One cup shredded cabbage; 1 cup shredded carrots; 1 cup shredded apples; ½ cup brown sugar; ½ cup raisins; 1 banana, sliced; ¼ teaspoon salt; juice of half lemon. Mix salt with cabbage, brown sugar, carrots, lemon juice and raisins. Put all the ingredients together. This salad, put on lettuce leaves and nicely arranged on salad plates, is good served with any roast meat or fowl.

–Miss Olive Longacre, Route 5, Nov. 22, 1946.

Mrs. *B*anks's Picnic Potato Salad

Four cups cooked potatoes (diced), 4 hard-cooked eggs, ½ cup chopped onions, ½ cup chopped cucumber, 1 cup chopped celery, 2 teaspoons salt, ¼ teaspoon pepper, ½ cup sour cream (thick), ¼ cup mayonnaise, 3 tablespoons vinegar, 2 tablespoons prepared mustard. Combine potatoes, eggs, onion, cucumber, celery and salt. Whip sour cream; blend in remaining ingredients. Mix gently with potato mixture. Chill. Garnish with hard-cooked egg slices arranged to imitate a Kansas sunflower, using the yellow of egg for the center, and the white for the petals around it. One-half of a hard-cooked egg yolk, or whole one grated or crumbled, can be used for the center. Serves 6.

DCR, 5-24-28

Doesn't This Look Good To You?

FRESH VEGETABLES

Fresh, Crisp, Tender Vegetables—only a few hours out of the ground! Tasty variety.

Phone 58 **WEBSTER'S GROCERY**

935 Mass.

–*Mrs. Nellie Banks,* Route 6, July 11, 1947.

Mrs. *B*lack's Supper Bean Salad Bowl

One and one-half cups cooked, chilled green string beans; 2 hard-cooked eggs, chopped; 1 small onion, minced; 1 cup mayonnaise or salad dressing; ½ cup pickled beets or sweet pickles, chopped; ½ cup Swiss or American cheese; 1 tomato, diced; ½ teaspoon salt. Toss vegetables, salt, and salad dressing lightly together with a fork and a spoon until well-mixed. Chill and serve from a salad bowl lined with salad greens.

–*Mrs. M. F. Black,* Tonganoxie, July 25, 1947.

Mrs. *W*illiams's Chicken Salad

Three cups cold chicken, diced; 1½ cups celery, cut fine; ¼ cup chopped green pepper or pimientos; 2 hard-boiled eggs; 1½ cups mayonnaise; 1 small head lettuce, shredded. Mix chicken, celery and peppers. Chill. Just before serving, mix with dressing and arrange on lettuce. Garnish with whites and yolks of eggs to look like daisies.

*–Mrs. Leta Williams, 414 W. 12*th *St., Aug. 15, 1947.*

Mrs. *A*vey's Thanksgiving Salad

Put three cups of raw cranberries through a food chopper. Follow these with one apple (core removed), but not peeled, and one orange (seeds removed), but grinding pulp and peeling as with apple. Add ½ cup crushed pineapple, ½ cup ground celery, one-half cup nut meats (black walnut preferred), one and one-half cups sugar, and pinch of salt. Mix well and chill thoroughly (but do not freeze). Heap on lettuce leaf and stand a turkey on each. Turkeys are made by shaping dried, pressed figs into shape of strutting gobbler. Shape a head and press on a tiny scrap of cranberry or red apple peeling to resemble red wattles. Use two tooth picks for feet, leaving long to press deeply into salad, and also well up into shaped fig so it will stand erect. Turkeys are quickly and easily made. Makes 12 to 15 servings.

–Mrs. Charles Avey, 1306 Oak Hill Ave., Nov. 21, 1947.

Mrs. *H*oover's Carrot Salad

One cup crushed pineapple, 1 tablespoon vinegar, 1 package lemon or orange gelatine, 1 cup hot water, 1 cup shredded carrots. Drain pineapple. Dissolve gelatine in hot water; add pineapple juice, vinegar and cold water to make 1 cup. When thickened, add rest of ingredients. One-half cup of nuts may be added if desired.

–Mrs. Elva M. Hoover, Route 6, Mar. 5, 1948.

LJW, 10-14-38

Mrs. $\mathcal{S}$choenlein's Tropical Coleslaw Supreme

Two tablespoons unflavored gelatine, ½ cup cold water, 1 No. 2½ can of sliced pineapple, ½ cup orange juice, ¼ cup lemon juice, 2 tablespoons vinegar, 1½ teaspoons salt, 1 cup finely cut red cabbage, 2 cups finely cut green cabbage, 4 tablespoons chopped green pepper. Soften gelatine in cold water in top of double boiler, then dissolve over hot water. Drain syrup (and reserve) from pineapple. Cut 2 slices in ¼-inch wedges. Combine pineapple syrup, orange juice, vinegar, lemon juice and salt. Stir in dissolved gelatine. Chill until syrupy. In a loaf pan, toss together cabbage, green pepper and pineapple wedges. Pour gelatine mixture over cabbage mixture. Chill for several hours or until firm. Unmold on a large plate and garnish with the remaining pineapple slices and salad greens. Serve with mayonnaise. Serves 6.

–Mrs. Evelyn Schoenlein, Lecompton, Mar. 12, 1948.

Mrs. *B*lack's Picnic Tuna Fish and Potato Salad Platter

Twelve boiled potatoes; 4 hard-boiled eggs; 2 cans tuna fish; ½ cup mayonnaise; 1 cup chopped sweet pickles; 2 cups diced celery; 1 large onion, diced finely; ½ cup melted butter; salt, pepper, and vinegar to taste. Sweet pickle liquor may be used instead of vinegar, and gives a better flavor. Heap the salad in a huge chop-plate. The gayer the color, the better. Flank it on one side with a stack of pimiento cheese sandwiches made of whole wheat and white bread. Pile a stack of potato chips on the other side. Fill in the remaining cavities with sweet pickles and olives.

–*Mrs. M. F. Black,* Route 3, Tonganoxie, June 25, 1948.

Mrs. *Z*illner's Tuna Fish Salad in Tomato Cups

Two cups tuna fish, 1 cup shredded celery, 1 minced green pepper, ⅓ teaspoon salt, ⅓ teaspoon paprika, 3 tablespoons French dressing, ⅔ cup mayonnaise, 6 stuffed olives. Add tuna to celery, minced pepper and seasonings; then pour French dressing over and set aside for ½ hour. Remove tops of tomatoes and scoop out seeds and pulp. Fill with tuna salad and garnish with olives and mayonnaise. Serve on lettuce leaf.

–*Mrs. C. A. Zillner,* 1804 Barker Ave., July 16, 1948.

Mrs. *W*iseman's Fresh Fruit Salad

One-fourth cup lemon juice, 1½ cups diced or sliced fresh fruit or berries, ½ cup diced celery, 1 tablespoon plain gelatine; ⅓ cup sugar, 1 ¼ cups water, ¼ cup orange juice. Combine gelatine, sugar, water, orange and lemon juice in a sauce pan. Bring slowly to boiling over low heat. Stir until sugar and gelatine are dissolved. Chill until slightly thickened. Fold in fruit and celery. Turn into 6 individual custard cups or one large mold. Chill until firm. Unmold on crisp lettuce and garnish with mayonnaise. Note: To serve as dessert, omit celery and add other fruit, and garnish with whipped cream instead of mayonnaise. Makes 6 servings.

–*Mrs. Nadine Wiseman,* Lecompton, July 23, 1948.

Mrs. $\mathcal{S}$tringham's Potato Salad

Four cupfuls cold boiled potatoes (cubed); ½ cupful diced celery; ½ cupful chopped sweet pickle; 1 small onion, grated; 4 chopped hard-cooked eggs. For variation, chopped cucumber, green pepper or parsley may be added; and some may prefer to omit the onion. Mix together lightly, adding a good sprinkle of salt, and 1½ cupsful boiled dressing. Garnish with small lettuce leaves around bowl and slices of boiled egg and sweet pickle over top of salad. Boiled Dressing: 2 tablespoons flour, 1 tablespoon sugar, 1 teaspoon salt, 1 teaspoon dry mustard, ⅛ teaspoon pepper, ⅓ teaspoon paprika. Mix dry ingredients in sauce pan. Add 1 egg and stir until free of lumps. Add ¼ cupful cider vinegar and mix thoroughly. While stirring, pour in ½ cupful boiling water, then put on stove and cook until thick. Add ½ cup top milk or cream and bring to boiling point again. Chill before using. This may be thinned with more cream.

–*Mrs. R. P. Stringham,* 1609 Rhode Island St., July 30, 1948.

Mrs. $\mathcal{H}$ull's 24-Hour Salad

Dressing: one-half lemon, 2 eggs. Beat eggs thoroughly; add lemon juice. Put into a double boiler and cook slowly until thick. Salad: 1 can white cherries (pitted and drained), ½ large can pineapple (grated), ½ lb. marshmallows (cut into pieces). When dressing is cold, fold in ½ pint of cream, which has been whipped, and mix thoroughly with fruit. Let stand 24 hours in refrigerator and serve on lettuce. Serves 6 people.

–*Mrs. Maggie V. Hull,* 406 E. 12th St., Nov. 19, 1948.

Mrs. $\mathcal{L}$anning's Cranberry Salad
"Delicious with turkey or chicken dinner"

Grind 2 cups cranberries and 1 medium-sized peeled orange. Add 1 cup white sugar and grated rind of 1 orange. Mix thoroughly and let stand until sugar is dissolved. Dissolve 1 package orange gelatine in 1 cup hot water. Add ½ cup cold water; let stand until it starts to gel. Add ¼ cup chopped walnut meats to cranberry mixture. Add to gelatine; mix thoroughly and let stand until firm.

–*Mrs. George B. Lanning,* 2022 Kentucky St., Dec. 24, 1948.

56

Mrs. *B*anks's Easter Salad

One-half lb. cottage cheese, ½ teaspoon salt, ¾ cup chopped nuts. Mix the cheese and salt and form into small balls; then roll in chopped nuts. Make nests of shredded lettuce, and put 3 balls in each nest to represent eggs. Garnish with sprays of parsley. Serve with French dressing made as follows: 1 teaspoon salt, 1 teaspoon sugar, ¼ teaspoon paprika, 3 tablespoons vinegar, ¾ cup olive oil. Mix salt, sugar and paprika together; add vinegar and oil and beat thoroughly until thick.

–Mrs. Luella Banks, Route 6, Apr. 15, 1949.

Mrs. *A*nderson's Chicken Salad

Two cups diced, cooked chicken; 2 cups cooked macaroni; 2 cups diced celery; 2 tablespoons chopped green pepper; 1 tablespoon chopped pimiento; 1 tablespoon grated onion; 1 tablespoon capers (if desired). Mix with mayonnaise at least a few hours before serving. Toss lightly and serve on bed of lettuce. May be garnished with sliced stuffed olives or grated egg yolk. One small can of tuna, sprinkled with lemon juice, may be substituted for the chicken.

–Mrs. Ed Anderson, 725 ½ Massachusetts St., June 10, 1949.

Mrs. *D*enham's Crisp Summer Salad

One package lemon gelatine; 1 cup boiling water; 1 cup cold water; 1 teaspoon salt; 1 tablespoon vinegar; 1 cup cucumbers, diced; 1 cup red radishes, sliced; 1 cup tender young onions, sliced thin; crisp lettuce. Dissolve gelatine in boiling water. Add cold water, salt and vinegar. Chill. When slightly thickened, add vegetables. Turn into individual molds. Chill until firm. Unmold on crisp lettuce. Garnish with salad dressing or mayonnaise. Serves 8.

–Mrs. James Denham, Route 2, June 24, 1949.

Mrs. *A*vey's Picnic Fruit Salad

"This is delicious as a dessert, or served at a chicken or steak fry. Will not become soupy in the warmest weather."

Three oranges; 3 bananas; 1 No. 1 can white seedless grapes; 1 No. 2 can cubed peaches; 1 (8-ounce) can, or 1 cup, cubed pineapple; 1 dozen marshmallows; 1 small jar maraschino cherries, red or green, or both; 1 tablespoon each of cornstarch and sugar. Drain juice from all the fruit. Mix juices together–should be about 1 pint of liquid. Add a little water, if necessary, to make one pint. Mix the sugar and cornstarch well; add enough water to make a thin paste, and add to boiling juices, stirring constantly. Cook until smooth. Cool. Add to the mixed fruits. Add bananas and marshmallows, cut into pieces. Makes about 15 servings.

–Mrs. Irven Avey, 1306 Oak Hill St., July 1, 1949.

Mrs. *R*uss's Tomato Salad

For a change, and as vegetable and salad, I use tomatoes with a chopped cabbage filling. Cut off stem end of tomatoes. Take out about one-half of pulp. Chop cabbage. I use a little chopped celery or celery seed with it. Mix with any good prepared or homemade salad dressing, and put into open tomato, using a little dressing on top. Adding a little sugar and salt to the dressing often improves the flavor.

–*Mrs. W. W. Russ,* 732½ Massachusetts St., July 29, 1949.

Mrs. *S*keet's Potato Salad

Boil 4 large potatoes with the peeling on, salting the water. When cool, peel and cut into small pieces. Add 4 hard-boiled eggs, 2 small onions, 6 sweet pickles–all chopped fine. Add a pinch of salt, 2 tablespoons vinegar, 2 tablespoons sugar, ½ cup mayonnaise. Then add cream to suit taste. Mix all together well. Put into a dish and slice 2 hard-boiled eggs to cover salad.

–*Mrs. Anna M. Skeet,* 333 Elm St., Aug. 19, 1949.

Breads, Buns, Biscuits, Muffins, Rolls, Scones,

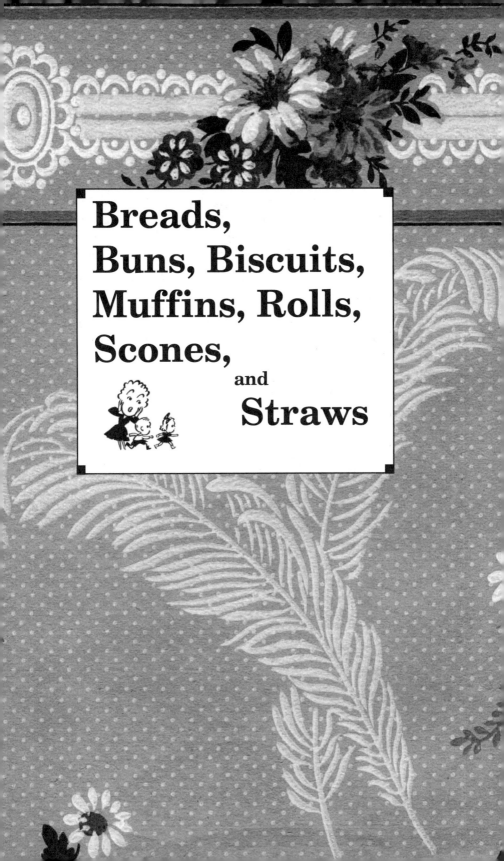

and

Straws

State Bread-baking Champions
Share Roll Recipe

Although 158,000 Kansas people visited the wheat festival train when it toured the state this summer, not all the homemakers of Kansas have been given the recipe for Parker House rolls used on that demonstration train by champion bread baking girls of Kansas, Loretta Pease and Leonice Fisher of Bourbon county.

Extension men from the agricultural college and railroad officials will vouch for the palatability of rolls made according to directions of the champions.

Here's their recipe: 1 cup scalded milk, 2 T. sugar, 2 T. shortening, 1 t. salt, 1 cake of compressed yeast, 2 T. lukewarm water, 1 ½ to 2 cups white flour, 1½ to 2 cups whole wheat flour.

Pour scalded milk over the sugar, salt and fat which have been measured into a mixing bowl. When mixture is lukewarm, add yeast which has been soaking in the lukewarm water. Add flour gradually, beating thoroughly until no more can be worked in with a spoon. Cover tightly and let it rise until three times its bulk. Turn onto a slightly floured board and roll half inch thick. Shape with a round, or oval, floured cutter. Crease in the middle with the handle of a knife. Brush half of each circle with melted fat. Fold each roll over double. Place one inch apart on an oiled pan. Let rise until double in size and bake 15 to 20 minutes in hot oven.

The cinnamon rolls are made from the same dough. Roll the dough until it is half an inch thick. Spread with a thick coating of butter and a mixture of five parts brown sugar and one part cinnamon. Roll as a jelly roll and cut in inch slices. Place on a buttered baking dish and set in a lukewarm place until double in bulk. Bake in a moderate oven for 30 minutes. [DCR, 9-16-26]

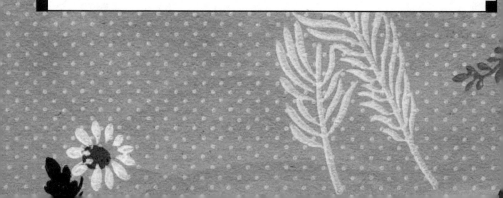

Mrs. *S*choewe's Raisin Bread

Soak one yeast cake in one and one-half cups of potato water. Mix enough flour to make a stiff batter. Let stand until light. (If dry yeast cake is used, let it stand over night.)

Scald two cups of sweet milk into which put one rounded tablespoon butter, 1 tablespoon salt, 3 tablespoons sugar. When the milk is lukewarm, mix with the yeast; add enough flour to make a stiff batter, beat about ten minutes. Set in warm place and let rise until light. Add two cups of seeded raisins and enough flour to make a soft dough. Knead until smooth. Let rise. Knead and make into loaves. Let rise. Bake in moderate oven for one hour. When baked, butter the tops of the loaves to prevent the crusts from becoming hard. (Nuts may be added with the raisins or as a substitute for them.)

–*Mrs. W. H. Schoewe,* 1016 Rhode Island St., Nov. 18, 1921.

Mrs. *L*owman's Virginia Fruit Muffins

Two cups of flour sifted with 1½ cups of white corn meal, 2 tablespoons of sugar, 1 teaspoon of salt, 6 teaspoons of baking powder, 3 tablespoons of melted butter, 2 well-beaten eggs, 2 cups of milk. Beat this all together and while beating, add one cup of chopped seeded raisins. Bake in cup cake forms in a hot oven for 15 minutes.

–*Mrs. Josephine Lowman,* 841 Mississippi St., Dec. 23, 1921.

Mrs. *M*oon's Brown Nut Bread

Beat together 2 eggs, pinch of salt, and 1 cup of sugar. Add 2 cups milk, 3 cups graham flour, ¾ cup English walnuts, chopped and dredged in heaping cupful of flour sieved with 2 teaspoons baking powder. Bake in slow oven for twenty minutes; the last few minutes increase the heat.

–*Mrs. Guy Moon,* 1801 Kentucky St., Mar. 24, 1922.

Mrs. *W*hitelaw's Salt Rising Bread

Stir into two tablespoonfuls boiling milk one heaping tablespoonful cornmeal. Let this stand over night. Make a thick sponge of warm water and flour–a quart bowl full; add to this the corn meal and milk. Stir thoroughly together with 2 tablespoonfuls of salt. Place bowl in a kettle of warm water, not hot; let stand until it rises so that the bowl is full, usually about an hour. Take a pint each of water and milk; stir thick with flour; add to this the sponge in a bowl; let stand one hour in warm place until bowl is full or nearly so. Knead very little; make into loaves and let rise one hour in a warm place. This quantity makes three loaves.

–*Mrs. Bertha Bell Whitelaw,* DeSoto, Apr. 14, 1922.

Mrs. *R*eed's Date Muffins

Two eggs, well beaten; 1 cup milk; 1 teaspoon melted butter; 1½ cups flour; 2 teaspoons baking powder; ½ teaspoon salt; 1 cup finely chopped dates. Add to beaten eggs, the milk, melted fat, and flour which has been sifted with baking powder and salt. Beat well. To this batter add dates and mix thoroughly. Pour batter into well-greased and hot muffin tins. Over each muffin sift a little sugar, and scatter a few chopped English walnuts. Bake quickly and serve hot.

–Mrs. Dan Reed, 730 Kentucky St., Mar. 2, 1923.

Mrs. *F*lory's New England Nut Bread
"This bread is excellent for sandwiches."

One level cupful (6 ounce weight) brown sugar; 1 level cupful (¼ lb.) chopped nut meats; 1 level cupful (¼ lb.) chopped dates, stoned; 2 level cupfuls (10 ounces) graham flour; 2 level cupfuls (½ lb.) white flour; 1 level teaspoon salt; 4 level teaspoonfuls baking powder; 2 cupfuls (1 pint) milk; 1 egg. Put brown sugar into a mixing bowl; add nuts, dates, graham flour, and white flour sifted with baking powder and salt. Add the egg, beaten and mixed with milk. Mix well; place into two greased and floured loaf pans, and set to rise for fifteen minutes in a warm place. Bake in a moderate oven for one hour. Recipe is sufficient for two small loaves.

–Mrs. Roy Flory, Lone Star, Aug. 31, 1923.

Mrs. *B*urnett's Pocket-Book Rolls

Sift 2 quarts of flour, and thoroughly rub into it 2 tablespoons lard or Crisco; 1 pint of cool, boiled milk; 2 tablespoons brown sugar; 1 cake of yeast; and half a teaspoon of salt. Mix and beat. If wanted for breakfast, mix and knead again. Roll half an inch thick; cut out with round cutter. Brush with melted butter. Turn one half over the other, pocketbook style. Put in pan. Let rise fifteen minutes. Brush tops with melted butter. Bake fifteen or twenty minutes in brisk oven.

–Mrs. W. W. Burnett, 909 Missouri St., Oct. 26, 1923.

Mrs. *H*erd's Corn Bread

Three cups corn meal, ½ cup flour, 2¼ cups sweet milk, 2 eggs, 2 tablespoonfuls shortening, 2 teaspoonfuls baking powder, 2 teaspoonfuls sugar, 1 teaspoonful salt. Sift meal, flour, baking powder, sugar and salt together 3 times; then mix shortening thoroughly into the mixture. Add eggs, well-beaten; then add milk and stir well. Bake thirty minutes.

–Mrs. Celia Herd, 922 Tennessee St., Dec. 5, 1924.

Mrs. *H*olt's Crackling Bread

Two eggs, 1½ cups of sweet milk, 2½ teaspoons of baking powder, 1 tablespoon of sugar, ⅔ teaspoon of salt, 3½ cups of corn meal. Sift meal and baking powder together; add salt and sugar–and sift. Beat eggs until light, then add milk, corn meal with salt and baking powder. Then add to the mixture 1½ cups of fresh cracklings. Put in a greased pan and bake 25 to 30 minutes, and serve hot.

–*Mrs. Alberta Holt,* 719 Michigan St., Jan. 9, 1925.

Miss *A*they's Hot Cross Buns

One and one-half cups scalded milk, ⅓ cup sugar, 2 tablespoons butter, 1 teaspoon salt, ½ yeast cake dissolved in 3 tablespoons lukewarm water, 1 teaspoon cinnamon, 2 eggs, ½ cup currants, flour. Mix milk, sugar, butter and salt. When lukewarm, add dissolved yeast cake and 2 ½ cups flour. Beat well. Add cinnamon and eggs, well beaten. Mix well, and add currants and flour to knead. Cover and let rise over night. In morning, shape into small balls. On top of each, cut a deep cross with a sharp knife. Let the buns rise, then bake twenty minutes. When nearly baked, brush buns over with a syrup made of 1 tablespoon of milk and 2 tablespoons of sugar boiled together for one minute. Dredge the cross with granulated sugar and finish baking.

–*Miss Peggy Jane Athey,* 625 Indiana St., Mar. 20, 1925.

Mrs. *R*utherford's Starter for Making Bread

Boil two medium-sized potatoes till well-done. Take out potatoes, mash smooth, and return to water the potatoes were boiled in. Add large tablespoon of salt and a half a cup of sugar. Cover tight, as it will turn dark if left exposed to air. Set aside till just warm, then add one cake compressed yeast. Cover and let stand over night. When weather is cold, wrap and set in warm place. In the morning, add enough warm water to make required sponge. Fill pint jar within an inch of top with this liquid yeast. Seal and set away in cool place. This is starter. Make bread in the usual way, using starter in place of compressed yeast. May be kept in this way two months or longer if care is taken not to scald yeast or starter.

–*Mrs. A. C. Rutherford,* 944 Rhode Island St., Aug. 14, 1925.

Mrs. *W*hitelaw's Boston Brown Bread

One quart sour milk, 1 cup molasses, 1 teaspoon baking powder, 1 teaspoon soda (more if milk is very sour), 2 cups corn meal, 2 cups graham or whole wheat flour, 1 cup ground oats or white flour, 1 teaspoon salt. Combine ingredients, and into it mix well one cup raisins, or ½ cup nut meats may be added, or both. This quantity will fill three tin cans the size of a one pound baking powder can. Fill cans two-thirds full, and punch a few holes in top of can lid as a vent. Steam 3 hours, drying off in oven with lid off. Put on to steam in cold water. Rye flour may be used instead of white flour or ground oats.

–*Mrs. John Whitelaw,* DeSoto, Nov. 27, 1925.

Mrs. *B*eery's Refrigerator Rolls

Scald 1 quart milk. When cool, add: 1 level tablespoon salt, 1 cup sugar, 1 cup mashed potatoes, 1 cup lard, 2 heaping teaspoons baking powder, 1 level teaspoon soda, and 1 cake compressed yeast, which has been dissolved in ½ cup warm water. Stir in flour enough to make a stiff batter. Let stand until light. Add more flour and knead until a soft, smooth dough is obtained. Let rise for three hours, and then place in the refrigerator to be made up not before the next day. When wanted for use, roll dough one-half inch thick. Cut with biscuit cutter; brush with melted butter; fold over half, and place in greased pan. Set in a warm room for two and one-half hours before baking. This dough will keep for several days in the refrigerator.

–*Mrs. Byron B. Beery,* 600 Ohio St., Mar. 19, 1926.

Mrs. *I*nce's Hot Cross Buns
**"A recipe that can be completed in one day,
this one is especially delicious."**

Scald a pint of milk, and add to it, while hot, 3 tablespoons of butter, 1 cup sugar, and one teaspoon salt. Cool to lukewarm, then whip in 3 well- beaten eggs and 1 cup flour. With a rotary egg beater, whip the mixture, adding gradually 3 cups flour. Stir in 1 cake compressed yeast dissolved in ¼ cup tepid water. Beat again with the egg beater. Set mixture aside in a warm place to rise for 3 or 4 hours, or until very light. Beat it down well and add ¼ teaspoon each of cinnamon and mace, and ½ pound currants, dredged with flour. Then stir in as much flour as is necessary to knead the mixture and work it well. Four cups usually is required. Place in greased bowl and stand it in a warm place. As the dough rises and becomes light, push it down with the tips of the fingers, repeating this operation several times. Then make the dough into buns. Place two inches apart in buttered pans and let rise. When twice their original size, mark with a cross, using a sharp pair of shears for the purpose, and cutting rather deeply. Let rise a few minutes longer to round out, and bake in a moderate oven about 20 minutes. Fill the crosses with icing, and cover the rest of the buns with a glaze made by dissolving 2 tablespoons of sugar in 2 tablespoons milk. Sprinkle with sugar and stand in an oven to dry the glaze.

–*Mrs. Mary E. Ince,* 1729 Vermont St., Apr. 2, 1926.

Mrs. *S*tanwix's Brown Nut Sandwich Bread

One-fourth cup brown sugar, ½ cup of molasses, 2 cups of sweet milk, ½ teaspoon salt, 1 teaspoon soda, 1 cup white flour, 2 cups graham flour, 1 cup of chopped nuts. Mix sugar and the molasses (to which soda has been added); add salt, then flour and milk, alternately. Add the nuts last. Bake 45 minutes in moderate oven.

–*Mrs. C. E. Stanwix,* Route 3, Lecompton, Nov. 12, 1926.

Mrs. *L*emon's Boston Brown Bread

Two cups sorghum; 3 teaspoons soda; 6 cups sour milk; 1 tablespoon salt; 2 or 3 eggs; 3 cups corn meal; 3 cups whole wheat flour; 3½ cups white flour, or enough to make stiff; 2 cups raisins or 1 cup raisins and 1 cup chopped dates, figs, and prunes; ½ cup chopped nuts; 5 teaspoons baking powder.

Put sorghum in a mixing bowl; place on stove and, when warm, stir in soda, mixing thoroughly. Add milk, then beat in eggs, baking powder, salt, corn meal, whole wheat flour and white flour. Place raisins in pan with 3 tablespoons water; let come to a boil, then dredge in flour and stir in. If dates, figs and prunes are used, grind them. Last, add the nuts. Put dough in four deep pans, each half full. Steam two hours, then bake one-half hour.

–*Mrs. J. H. Lemon,* 1346 Connecticut St., Mar. 4, 1927.

Mrs. *M*oorman's Hot Cross Buns

Two cakes yeast; 2 cups milk, scalded and cooled; 2 tablespoons sugar; 7½ cups sifted flour; ½ cup butter; ⅔ cup sugar; 2 eggs; ½ cup raisins or currants; ½ tablespoon salt.

Method: Dissolve yeast and 2 tablespoons sugar in lukewarm water. Add 3¼ cups flour to make sponge. Beat until smooth; cover and let rise until light, in warm place–about one hour. Add butter and sugar, creamed; eggs, well-beaten; raisins or currants, which have been floured; remainder of flour, or enough to make a moderately soft dough, and salt. Turn on board, and knead lightly. Place in a greased bowl. Cover and set aside in warm place, until double in bulk, which should be in about 2 hours. Shape with hands into medium-sized round buns. Place in well-greased shallow pans about 2 inches apart. Cover and let rise again, about 1 hour. Glaze with egg diluted with water. With a sharp knife, cut a cross on top of each. Bake 20 minutes in hot oven. Just before removing from oven, brush with sugar moistened with water. While hot, fill crosses with plain frosting.

–*Mrs. F. J. Moorman,* 1901 Learnard Ave., Apr. 1, 1927.

Mrs. *B*igsby's Orange Nut Bread

Grind through food chopper, or chop fine, the peelings from three oranges. Cook until tender in boiling, salted water, using a scant teaspoon salt to 2 cups of water. If the water evaporates before the bits of peeling are tender, add more water. Drain and cook in a syrup made of 1 cup sugar and ⅓ cup of water until quite thick. Cool, and add 3 cups of flour, sifted before measuring, and sifted several times with 3 teaspoons baking powder, ½ teaspoon each of salt and soda. Before stirring, drop into the flour ½ cup of nut meats. Add 1 cup of milk to one well-beaten egg, and stir all the ingredients together until well-blended. Pour into a well-greased loaf pan and let rise about 15 minutes. Bake one hour in a moderate oven (300 degrees F.). Let cool in the pan in which it was baked if intended to be sliced for sandwiches the same day. But it is better the next day, and good as long as it lasts. If ready-mixed flour is used, no baking powder, salt or soda is needed to be added to the flour.

–*Mrs. Guy Bigsby,* Route 1, Dec. 30, 1927.

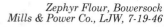

Zephyr Flour, Bowersock Mills & Power Co., LJW, 7-19-46

Mrs. *S*trong's Boston Brown Bread

One and one-half cups brown sugar, ½ cup molasses, 2 cups of sour milk, 2½ cups graham flour, 1½ cups white flour, 1½ cups seeded raisins, two teaspoonsful of soda in milk, 1½ teaspoons salt, two tablespoons of melted butter, two eggs (well-beaten). Mix well and fill baking powder cans little more than half full. Have cans well-greased. Set in kettle filled with hot water to within two inches of top of cans. Steam three hours. Add more water as it boils away.

–*Mrs. C. B. Strong,* 447 Ohio St.,
Apr. 13, 1928.

Mrs. *H*obbs's Ice Box Potato Split Rolls

"This dough may be kept for two or three days and will be just as good as the first day."

Take one cup hot mashed potato, add ½ cup lard, and mix. Add ½ cup sugar and 1 teaspoon of salt; then add alternately 1 cup scalded milk and 1 cup of flour. Beat two eggs light and add to mixture. Also add 1 cake of compressed yeast, dissolved in ½ cup lukewarm water. Let rise for two hours in warm place–out of draft. Whip in 6 cups of flour; let rise 2 hours more. Take the amount you need for hot rolls, and roll ½-inch thick.

Spread with melted butter; double and cut with biscuit cutter. Let rise 1 hour, and bake in quick oven. Place the remaining dough in ice box, and roll out as needed. Always allow 1 hour to rise. Parker House rolls may be made if desired.

–*Mrs. W. F. Hobbs,* 1008 Mississippi St., Nov. 9, 1928.

Mrs. *G*lathart's Orange Bread

"This recipe is said to be a favorite in the household of Secretary and Mrs. Arthur Hyde."

Grind the peel of twelve oranges in food chopper. Put into kettle, cover with cold water, and boil five minutes. Repeat three times, each time adding cold water, and the last time also adding 2½ cups sugar. Let boil until dry. Stir well to keep from burning; then let cool. Mix ¾ cup sugar, 2 eggs, 6 tablespoons butter, 1¼ cups sweet milk, 2 level teaspoons salt, 6 heaping teaspoons baking powder, and 3 cups flour. Add orange peel and bake in slow oven. Makes two loaves.

–*Mrs. A. B. Glathart,* Lineville, Iowa, Oct. 25, 1929.

Mrs. *B*lankenship's Ice Box Rolls

One quart milk, one cup mashed potatoes, one cup sugar, one cup butter, one teaspoon salt. Put in pan and bring to boiling point. Let cool and add two cakes compressed yeast, two teaspoons baking powder, one teaspoon soda, and enough flour to make a stiff batter. Let rise 15 minutes; add flour to make a stiff dough. Knead and put in ice box for twenty-four hours before using. Ice box dough can be kept four weeks. Take from ice box; mould into rolls, and let rise one hour–or one hour and a half if wanted especially light. Bake in a quick oven 10 minutes.

–Mrs. Pearl Blankenship, 510 Ohio St., Nov. 29, 1929.

Mrs. *K*apfer's Boston Brown Bread

One cup whole wheat or graham flour, 1 cup corn meal, 1 cup rye meal or ground rolled oats, 5 teaspoons baking powder, 1 teaspoon salt, ¾ cup dark molasses, 1⅓ cups milk. Mix dry ingredients thoroughly. Add molasses to milk, and add to dry ingredients. Beat thoroughly, and put into greased moulds two-thirds full. Cover tightly and steam three and one-half hours. Remove covers, and bake in moderate oven at 400 degrees F. until top is dry. Makes one large or three small loaves.

–Mrs. George L. Kapfer, 1737 Alabama St., Jan. 2, 1931.

Mrs. *F*etty's Boston Brown Bread

One cup of flour, 1 cup of sweet milk, 1 cup of corn meal, 1 cup of sour milk, 2 cups of graham flour, 1 cup of molasses, 2 teaspoons of baking soda, 2 teaspoons of salt. Steam in four 1-lb. baking powder cans for 3 hours, and then bake in oven 15 minutes.

–Mrs. R. B. Fetty, 619 Lyons St., Jan. 15, 1932.

Mrs. *H*arbeson's Corn Meal Muffins

One cup sour milk, 1 egg, 3 tablespoons melted shortening, 1 cup flour, 1 cup corn meal, ¼ teaspoon salt, 1½ teaspoons baking powder, ¼ teaspoon soda. Mix the dry ingredients, and add to the milk, egg and shortening. Put into oiled pans, and bake in a moderate oven.

–Mrs. Bert Harbeson, 837 Indiana St., Feb. 5, 1932.

Local Grocery Prices 1943

1 pkg. yeast	.03
1 doz. pan rolls	.06
1 loaf whole wheat bread	.10
1 loaf raisin nut bread	.12
8 ozs. vanilla extract	.15
15 ozs. raisins	.15
1 lb. oleo	.24
1 lb. peanut butter	.27
1 lb. marmalade	.29
2 lbs. flour	.29
5 lbs. flour	
Total	$ 1.70

Mrs. *J*ones's Cinnamon Rolls for the Lunch Box

Four cups flour, sifted; 1 cake compressed yeast; 1½ cups milk, scalded and cooled; ½ cup shortening; ⅓ cup sugar; 2 eggs; 1¼ teaspoon salt. Method: Dissolve yeast in lukewarm milk, and stir well. Add sugar, beaten eggs, salt and half the flour; mix well and add the melted shortening. Beat thoroughly; add balance of flour or enough to make a soft dough. Turn out on floured board; knead into smooth dough. Place in well-greased bowl. Knead down and let rise 45 minutes. Shape dough. Let stand 5 minutes. Roll to ½-inch thickness. Spread with melted butter and sprinkle with sugar and cinnamon that have been mixed together in the proportion of ½ teaspoon cinnamon to 2 tablespoons of sugar. Currants or raisins may be added. Roll as for jelly-roll, and press edges firmly together. Cut in pieces ½- to ¾-inch thick. Place in a well-greased pan. Let rise until very light. Bake in a moderate oven (400 degrees F.) for 25 to 30 minutes.

–Mrs. Eli Jones, 633 N. 3rd St., Mar. 25, 1932.

Mrs. *D*rennon's Boston Brown Bread

One cup corn meal, 1 cup rye flour or 1 cup graham flour, ¾ cup molasses, 1 teaspoon salt, ¾ teaspoon soda, 2 cups sour milk, ½ cup raisins (if desired). Sift together dry ingredients; mix well with sour milk and molasses. If mixture is too stiff, thin with a little water. If raisins are used, either add to dry mixture before liquid, or reserve out a little flour. Sift reserved flour well over raisins and stir in last. Grease molds and their covers. Fill one-half full with batter. Steam 3 hours or more, depending on size of molds used. Keep the water boiling all the time during the steaming. Add more water if necessary. Cover the kettle during the steaming, and be careful not to jar it while cooking.

–Mrs. W. M. Drennon, Route 2, Jan. 13, 1933.

Mrs. *B*randhorst's Ice Box Rolls

One cake compressed yeast dissolved in 1 cup lukewarm water (98 degrees F.), ¾ cup sugar, ½ cup fat, 1 cup hot mashed potatoes, 1 cup cold water, 1 teaspoon salt, flour (6 to 6½ cups). Mix fat, sugar and potatoes. When lukewarm, add to yeast cake and water. Let stand 2 hours in warm room. Add cold water, salt, and enough flour to make stiff dough. Let stand covered in refrigerator 24 hours. Shape in any way. Let rise 2 hours before baking. This mixture may be kept in refrigerator several days and baked as needed. Milk may be used for the liquid, but it seems to shorten the keeping period of the dough. If milk is used, it is well to add ½ teaspoon soda to aid in neutralizing acid as it forms. This makes about 30 rolls, medium size. It is desirable to serve rolls hot. To reheat, put in a paper bag or other tight container, then place in a hot oven (400 to 450 degrees F.) until rolls are heated through.

–Mrs. A. E. Brandhorst, 1112 Delaware St., Jan. 27, 1933.

Mrs. *C*hristenson's Real Southern Corn Bread

Two cups cornmeal, ½ teaspoon soda, 2 teaspoons baking powder, 2 teaspoons salt; 2 cups sour milk, 2 eggs, 2 tablespoons melted fat. Use all cornmeal, rather than mixture of white flour and corn meal, if you want to make real southern cornbread; and use water-ground meal if you can get it. Sift the dry ingredients and add the milk. Add the well-beaten egg and the fat. Pour into a very hot, well-greased pan. Bake from 40 to 50 minutes in hot oven.

–*Mrs. Clifford Christenson,* 846 Rhode Island St., Feb. 24, 1933.

Miss *W*ickey's Salt Rising Bread

In the evening, take ¾ cup of fresh, sweet milk, heat to steaming point (not boiling). Stir into this enough white corn meal to make a soft mush. Add a pinch of sugar. Put it in a warm place to rise. In the morning, it should be light and full of little holes. It is ready to make up. This is your yeast. Then take 3 cups of sweet milk, 1 cup of water, and heat until warm. Add enough flour to make a stiff batter, and combine with the mush or yeast. Set in a warm place to rise. It should rise about 3 inches in 1 hour. When light enough, sift 8 pints of flour into mixing bowl. Add to flour ½ teaspoon of soda, ½ cup of sugar, and 1 tablespoon salt. Mix. Add ½ cup of lard and the raised batter. Mix all well and knead for 15 minutes. Keep adding flour till you have used all. Let rise, then make into loaves. Cover closely and leave till it is light. Bake in a steady oven.

–*Miss Anna Wickey,*
Tonganoxie,
Mar. 31, 1933.

Mrs. *M*iller's Hot Cross Buns

Heat 1½ cupfuls of bottled milk (or ¾ cupfuls of evaporated milk diluted with ¾ cupful of water) to scalding. Add ⅓ cupful of sugar, ¼ cupful of butter or other shortening, and ¾ teaspoon of salt. Let stand until the shortening is melted. Cool to lukewarm and add 1 cake of compressed yeast crumbled into bits. Stir until the yeast is dissolved, then add about 2½ cupfuls of flour, and beat vigorously to a smooth batter. Add 1 beaten egg, and mix. Then add ⅔ cupful of raisins or currants (or a combination of citron, nut meats and raisins). Add 2 ½ cupfuls of flour to make a soft dough. Knead on floured surface until smooth. Place in a greased bowl; cover and store in a warm place (about 80 degrees) until more than double in bulk. Pinch off pieces of dough the size of large walnuts, and shape into rounds with buttered hands. Place side by side, at least 1 inch apart, in oiled baking pans, and let rise until light. Bake in hot oven (375 to 400 degrees) for 20 minutes. Remove from the pans and cool slightly. Mark with a cross made by mixing to a paste confectioner's sugar with hot water. Flavor with vanilla. This recipe makes 30 buns.
–*Mrs. Mabel B. Miller,* 1205 Rhode Island St., Apr. 14, 1933.

Mrs. *C*arter's Blueberry Muffins

One cup blueberries, 2 cups flour, 3 teaspoons baking powder, 4 tablespoons sugar, ½ teaspoon salt, 2 eggs, 1 cup milk, 4 tablespoons shortening. Wash and drain blueberries well; sprinkle with three tablespoons of the measured sugar and a little sifted flour. Sift together remaining dry ingredients; add eggs, milk, and melted and cooled shortening to make a stiff batter. Mix in the blueberries. Half fill greased muffin tins and bake in moderate oven at 375 degrees F. for thirty minutes. Canned blueberries, carefully drained, can be used if fresh blueberries are not obtainable. Bake in small greased muffin rings for nice variety. Makes 24 small muffins.
–*Mrs. G. H. Carter,* 2229 West Drive,
July 14, 1933.

Mrs. *F*ey's Cheese Biscuits

One and a half cups flour; 2½ teaspoons baking powder; ¼ teaspoon salt; 1 teaspoon butter; 6 tablespoons American cheese, grated; ¾ cup milk. Sift flour, salt and baking powder together; add shortening and cheese, rubbing in very lightly. Add milk slowly, just enough to hold the dough together. Turn out on floured board, and roll about ½-inch thick. Cut with small biscuit cutter. Bake in a hot oven about 15 minutes. Serve hot.
–*Mrs. A. P. Fey,* 21 Winona St.,
Oct. 20, 1933.

LJW, 12-11-25

Mrs. *J*ennings's Boston Brown Bread

One cup fine cornmeal, 1 cup graham flour, 2 cups sour milk, ½ cup raisins, 1 teaspoon salt, ¾ tablespoon soda, ¾ cup molasses. Sift the dry ingredients together. Then mix the raisins into the dry mixture. Then pour in the sour milk and molasses and mix well. Grease well baking powder cans or mold. Fill half full of batter and put on lids. Steam three hours for baking powder cans. If larger molds are used, it will be necessary to steam longer. Keep kettle covered during steaming, and keep water boiling all the time. If a dry crust is preferred, the cans may be taken from the steamer and baked in a hot oven for the last fifteen minutes.

–*Mrs. George Jennings,* 1305 New York St., Jan. 26, 1934.

Mrs. *L*inscheid's Hot Cross Buns

One and one-half cakes yeast, ½ cup sugar, ½ teaspoon salt, 1 cup lukewarm milk, ½ cup butter, 3 eggs, 4 to 5 cups flour, 1 teaspoon cinnamon, ½ teaspoon nutmeg, ½ teaspoon cloves, ¾ cup raisins. Sprinkle a little sugar over the yeast and let stand a few minutes. Add butter, sugar and salt to warm milk; then yeast. To this mixture, add beaten eggs; then flour sifted with spices, and raisins dredged with flour. Knead lightly. Let stand until double in bulk. Roll out. Cut rounds ½-inch thick and 2 to 3 inches in diameter. With a sharp knife, mark a cross on top. Let rise until double or more in bulk. Bake in a hot oven, 450 degrees, about 20 minutes. While warm, trace the cross on top with powdered sugar icing. These buns may be partially baked the day before and reheated the next morning, or they could be cut out the night before, put in the refrigerator covered with waxed paper, and baked the first thing in the morning, after letting them have their second rising.

–*Mrs. J. E. Linscheid,* 900 Alabama St., Mar. 30, 1934.

Mrs. *N*icholas's Real Scotch Scones

Two and three-fourths cups flour, 4 teaspoons baking powder, one teaspoon salt, 4 level tablespoons shortening (butter preferred), ½ cup currants, 1 egg, ⅔ cup milk. Sift dry ingredients; cut in shortening, and add currants. Beat egg and milk together thoroughly. Reserve 3 tablespoons of this for brushing tops of scones. Moisten dry materials with the rest. Turn on mixing board with some flour as for biscuits, dividing into four parts. Work each round and smooth. Pat out about ¾-inch thick, and cut each one crosswise into four sections. Brush with the milk and egg kept back. Sprinkle lightly with cinnamon. Place on baking sheet; bake about 20 minutes in hot oven.

–*Mrs. C. D. Nicholas,* 1016 Alabama St., Sept. 28, 1934.

Mrs. *R*eed's Cheese Straws

One cup of flour, 3 tablespoons butter, 2 tablespoons grated Parmesan cheese, a pinch of salt, a few grains of cayenne pepper. Mix into a paste with the yolk of an egg. Roll out to the thickness of a silver quarter, about 4 or 5 inches long. Cut into strips about a third of an inch wide. Twist them as you would a paper spill, and lay them on a baking sheet, slightly floured. Bake in a moderate oven until crisp, but they must not be the least brown. If put away in a tin, these cheese straws will keep a long time. Serve cold, piled tastefully on a glass dish.

–Mrs. W. F. Reed, Route 5, Dec. 7, 1934.

Mrs. *R*idgeway's Hot Cross Buns

Two cakes compressed yeast; ⅔ cup sugar; 2 cups milk, scalded and cooled; 2 tablespoons sugar; ½ teaspoon salt; 7½ cups sifted flour; ½ cup raisins or currants; ½ cup butter; 2 eggs. Dissolve yeast and 2 tablespoons sugar in lukewarm milk. Add 3 ¼ cups flour to make sponge. Beat until smooth; cover and let rise until light in warm place free from draft–about one hour. Add butter and sugar (creamed), eggs well-beaten, raisins or currants, which have been floured, and rest of flour or enough to make a moderately soft dough. Turn onto board. Knead lightly and place in greased bowl. Cover and set aside in warm place until double in bulk, which should be in about 2 hours. Shape with hand into medium-sized round buns. Place in well-greased shallow pans about 2 inches apart. Cover; let rise again about 1 hour or until light. Glaze with egg diluted with water. With sharp knife, cut a cross on top of each. Bake 20 minutes. While hot, fill cross with plain frosting or jelly.

–Mrs. Guilford C. Ridgeway, Route 1, McLouth, Apr. 12, 1935.

Mrs. *A*llen's Southern Corn Bread

Two level cups of corn meal, 1 teaspoon soda, 1 teaspoon salt, 1½ cups sour milk mixed with ½ cup water, 2 eggs, ⅓ cup shortening (very hot). Mix meal, salt and soda. Add liquid, making a very thin batter. Add beaten eggs, and lastly the melted shortening. Have muffin rings or pan very, very hot, and put at once into a hot oven, about 500 degrees.

–Mrs. E. B. Allen, 911 Missouri St., Feb. 28, 1936.

Miss *T*owne's Southern Spoon Bread

One-half cup white corn meal scalded with 1½ pints boiling water, ½ cup cold boiled rice, 3 well-beaten eggs, 3 teaspoons baking powder, 2½ cups sweet milk, 1 teaspoon salt, 1 tablespoon sugar. Bake in a moderate oven until well-brown. When done, the bread should be of the consistency of very thick cream. Serve with a spoon and eat with butter.

–Miss Louise Towne, 1147 Ohio St., Nov. 6, 1936.

Mrs. *G*arvin's Ice Box Rolls

One cake compressed yeast, 1½ cups water (lukewarm), ⅔ cup sugar, ⅔ cup shortening, 1 cup mashed potatoes, 1½ teaspoons salt, 2 eggs, 7½ cups flour. Method: Dissolve yeast in ½ cup water. Cream shortening, sugar, ½ teaspoon salt; then add mashed potatoes, well-beaten eggs, and yeast mixture; mix well. Sift flour once and measure. Add the remaining 1 cup water and one-half of flour, and beat well several minutes. Mix in the rest of flour; knead in a bowl till smooth. Let rise in greased bowl till double in bulk; work down, then cover tightly and place in ice box. When wanted, form into rolls. Let rise in warm place until double in bulk. Bake in moderate oven, 400 degrees, 15 or 18 minutes. Care should be taken not to have the mixture too warm when rising.

–Mrs. A. W. Garvin, 2129 New Hampshire St., Feb. 5, 1937.

Mrs. *H*usted's Hot Cross Buns

Two cakes of compressed yeast; 2 cups milk, scalded and cooled; 2 tablespoonfuls of sugar; 7½ cups of sifted flour; ½ cup butter; ⅔ cup sugar; 2 eggs; ½ cup raisins; ½ teaspoon salt. Dissolve yeast and two tablespoonfuls sugar in lukewarm milk. Add 3¼ cups of flour to make a sponge. Beat until smooth. Cover and let rise until light, in warm place, free from draft, about one hour. Add butter and sugar, creamed, egg well-beaten, raisins which have been floured, rest of flour or enough to make a moderately soft dough, and salt. Turn on board; knead lightly. Place in greased bowl. Cover, and put in a warm place until double in bulk—usually two hours. Shape with hand into medium-sized round buns. Place in well-greased shallow pans about two inches apart. Cover and let rise again, one hour or until light. Glaze with egg diluted with water, and with sharp knife, cut a cross on each one. Bake twenty minutes. Just before removing from the oven, brush with sugar moistened with water. While hot, fill cross with plain frosting.

–Mrs. Charles Husted, Route 3, Mar. 19, 1937.

Miss *S*eiwald's Loganberry Muffins

One-fourth cup of shortening, 2 ⅔ cups flour, ⅓ cup of sugar, 3 teaspoons baking powder, 1 egg, 1 cup milk, ½ teaspoon salt, 1 cup fresh loganberries. Cream shortening and sugar; add egg, and beat smooth. Add milk alternately with flour, which has been sifted with baking powder and salt. A third cup may be used to dredge berries, but if the batter is stiff enough, the berries will not sink. Stir batter until smooth, then pour into muffin tins and bake.

–Miss Evelyn Seiwald, 712 Lincoln St., June 11, 1937.

Mrs. *S*timpson's Real Southern Cornbread

One and seven-eighths cups yellow corn meal, 2 tablespoons flour, 1 cup sour milk, 1 teaspoon baking powder, ½ teaspoon soda, ¼ teaspoon salt, 2 tablespoons sugar, 1 egg, 2 tablespoons melted fat (bacon drippings). Measure and mix all dry ingredients together in bowl. Add beaten egg and sour milk; beat batter thoroughly. Place melted fat in bottom of 9" x 12" pan. Pour in batter, and cut through with spoon to allow melted fat to mix with batter at the edge. Bake in hot oven 20 to 30 minutes or until slightly browned over the top. Serve while hot.

–Mrs. E. C. Stimpson, Route 1, Oct. 22, 1937.

Miss *O*wen's Cornmeal Muffins

Mix and sift 1 cup flour, 1 cup yellow cornmeal, 3 teaspoons baking powder, 2 tablespoons sugar, and ½ teaspoon salt. Beat one egg and combine with 1 cup of milk and 4 tablespoons melted shortening. With a spoon make a hollow in the dry ingredients, and pour in the milk and egg mixture. Stir just enough to moisten dry ingredients (this takes about 20 seconds). The batter should look lumpy. Pour into well-greased muffin pans or corn stick pans, filling two-thirds full. Bake in a hot oven (400 degrees F.) 30 minutes. Makes 12.

–Miss Marie Owen,
912 Indiana St., Jan. 7, 1938.

Saturday Specials

Cinnamon Rolls	15c per dozen
Pecan Rolls	40c per dozen
Parker House Rolls	12c per dozen
Sandwich Buns	12c per dozen
Vienna Rolls	12c per dozen
Health Muffins	15c per dozen
Puff Muffins	15c per dozen
Cloverleaf Rolls	20c per dozen

All these goods can be purchased at Brinkman's Bakery or at your grocer. Also include Jayhawk Bread, Whole Wheat Bread, Rye Bread, Cracked Wheat Bread.

BRINKMAN'S

LJW, 11-23-34

Mrs. *K*ennedy's Baked Boston Brown Bread

"I have found this especially convenient to make because it is baked, thus eliminating the long process of the steamer."

Three cups sour rich milk or buttermilk, ½ cup sugar, 1 teaspoon salt, 2 teaspoons soda, 4 tablespoons hot water, 5 cups whole wheat flour, 1 cup raisins, 2 teaspoons baking powder, molasses. Put the milk into mixing bowl and add sugar and salt. Put soda into measuring cup and add hot water. Stir until dissolved, then fill up cup with molasses. Mix thoroughly and add to milk. Stir in the flour with which the baking powder has been mixed, and add raisins last. Bake 1 hour in a slow oven. A little orange peel, which has been put through the food grinder, will make a pleasing addition.

–Mrs. L. W. Kennedy, Route 2, Jan. 14, 1938.

Mrs. *P*atterson's Refrigerator Rolls

One quart scalding milk, 1 cup mashed and sieved potatoes, 1 cup sugar, 1 cup shortening, 1 cake compressed yeast, ½ cup lukewarm water, 2 teaspoons salt, 14 to 15 cups sifted all-purpose flour, 2 tablespoons baking powder, 1 teaspoon soda. Combine milk, potatoes, shortening and sugar in a mixing bowl. Cool to lukewarm, then add yeast dissolved in lukewarm water. Add part of flour sifted with baking powder, soda and salt. Beat to a smooth batter, and continue adding flour until a stiff batter is formed. Turn onto a well-floured surface and knead lightly. Place in a greased bowl. Cover and place in a refrigerator. Remove portions as needed, and set in a warm place to rise. Allow plenty of time to rise. A variety of fancy rolls may be made from this basic recipe. This may be kept for over 2 weeks and is good to the last.

–Mrs. S. F. Patterson, 808 Mississippi St., Feb. 4, 1938.

Mrs. *D*rennon's Date-Nut Bread
"This is a moist, well-flavored bread suitable for sandwiches or to serve cut in thin slices with salads."

One cup dates, 1 cup nuts, 2 cups flour (white), 1 cup whole wheat flour, ½ teaspoon salt, 4 teaspoons baking powder, 3 tablespoons butter, ½ cup sugar, 1 well-beaten egg, 1 ¼ cups milk. Stone dates and cut fine. Chop nuts. (Never grind nuts for date-nut bread.) Sift white flour, then measure. To measure whole wheat flour, lift it with a spoon from the container into the cup. Combine flours; add salt and baking powder, and resift. Return any bran in the sifter to the sifted mixture, and stir until well-blended. Cream the butter until soft and plastic. Add the sugar gradually, and when all is in, add the egg and beat until the batter is a thick, creamy mass. Add the dry ingredients and the milk alternately. Add nuts and dates and stir only enough to distribute. Turn into well-buttered loaf bread pan. Bake in hot oven (400 degrees F.) for at least 50 minutes. Makes loaf 8x3x3 inches.

–Mrs. Harold Drennon, Route 2, Feb. 18, 1938.

Mrs. *R*eber's Honeymoon Ice Box Rolls

Two eggs, beaten separately until light; 1 cup mashed potatoes (no crumbs); 1 cake compressed yeast dissolved in ½ cup lukewarm water; ½ cup lard; ½ cup sugar; ½ cup sweet milk, scalded and cooled; 1 teaspoon salt; 3¼ cups flour, sifted. To the beaten eggs, add sugar, potatoes, sweet milk. Add 1 cup of flour, or make dough stiff enough to drop from spoon. Set to rise at 11:30; at 2:30 it should be ready to mix with 2 cups of flour. Add salt and shortening; make dough stiff as bread; knead until smooth; grease bowl and set to rise double in bulk. Set in warm place; let rise until 4 p.m. Knead lightly, using as little flour as possible on board. Roll thin like biscuits; spread with melted butter and make pocketbook rolls. Let rise until 6 p.m., then bake for 20 minutes at 350 to 400 degrees. Grease tops of rolls with melted butter.

–Mrs. L. Reber,
1536 New Hampshire St.,
Jan. 13, 1939.

Mrs. *B*arnhill's Hub-of-the-Universe Bread

One egg, 1 tablespoon butter, 1 cup sour milk, ½ cup molasses, ½ cup sugar, 2½ cups graham flour, ½ cup corn meal, 1 tablespoon soda, 1 teaspoon salt, ½ cup chopped raisins. Beat egg slightly; add melted butter and sugar, and mix well. Add molasses. Mix dry ingredients in sifter; sift in one-third of contents, and mix. Add milk and remainder of dry ingredients; add raisins, and beat. Grease four 1-pound baking powder cans and fill three-fourths full. Steam 2½ hours. Bake in oven 20 minutes. Remove from cans; slice into half-inch rounds, and serve hot.

–Mrs. Ellis B. Barnhill, 935 Maine St., Jan. 20, 1939.

Mrs. *M*iller's Boston Brown Bread

One-half cup sugar, 1 cup flour, 1 cup all-bran, 1 cup sour milk, 1 teaspoon soda, ¼ teaspoon salt, 1 tablespoon molasses, ½ cup raisins. Mix together the sour milk, all-bran, and raisins; then add the molasses, sugar, and flour–which has been sifted with the soda and salt. Put the mixture into a greased can; cover tightly and steam for three hours. Serve hot with baked beans. This bread is also good sliced when cold and spread with cream cheese, or made into sandwiches, using a filling of parsley butter or cheese, olives and nuts.

–Mrs. Ed Miller, 1809 Kentucky St., Feb. 23, 1940.

Mrs. *S*temmerman's Simple Ice Box Rolls

One cake yeast, ⅔ cup shortening, 1 cup mashed potato, 2 eggs (well-beaten), ½ cup lukewarm water, ⅔ cup sugar, 1 cup scalded milk, 1 teaspoon salt, flour to make a stiff dough. Dissolve yeast in lukewarm water; add shortening, sugar, salt, and mashed potato to scalded milk. When cool, add yeast. Mix thoroughly and add eggs. Stir in enough flour to make a stiff dough. Turn out onto slightly floured board, and knead thoroughly. Put into bowl large enough to allow for slight rising. Rub over with melted shortening. Cover tightly and place in refrigerator. About an hour before meal time, pinch off dough; shape, and let rise till light or double in size. Bake in 425 degree oven 15 to 20 minutes. This dough may be kept in refrigerator indefinitely and baked as needed.

–Mrs. A. W. Stemmerman, 422 Mississippi St., Oct. 18, 1940.

Mrs. *R*othwell's Cinnamon Rolls
"The Famous Dutch Sticky Rolls."

One cup scalded milk, ½ cup chopped raisins, 2 tablespoons currants, ½ teaspoon cinnamon, brown sugar, 2 tablespoons finely chopped citron, ½ yeast cake (dissolved in ¼ cup warm water), 3 cups flour; ½ teaspoon salt; 3 tablespoons butter. Dissolve yeast in warm water and add to milk, which has been allowed to become lukewarm. Add sugar (about 3 tablespoons), salt and flour. Knead thoroughly until it becomes a soft dough. Place the dough in a buttered bowl and butter the top of the dough. Cover bowl and put in a warm place. Permit it to stand until the dough becomes three times its original size. Roll until it is one-fourth of an inch in thickness. Brush with butter and spread with the raisins, currants, citron, brown sugar and cinnamon. Roll as a jelly roll and cut into slices three-fourths of an inch thick. Place slices in buttered pans. Spread well with brown sugar, and bake in a hot oven (400 degrees F.) for 20 minutes.

–Mrs. Glenn Rothwell, 913 Rhode Island St., Feb. 14, 1941.

Mrs. *L*owman's Hot Cross Buns

One teaspoon granulated sugar; 1 cake compressed yeast, crumbled; 1 cup milk, lukewarm; ¼ cup shortening, melted; 1 teaspoon salt; ⅓ cup brown sugar; ½ cup currants; ½ cup raisins; ½ teaspoon cloves; 1 teaspoon cinnamon; 1 egg, beaten; 4 cups flour, sifted. Mix the granulated sugar and yeast for 5 minutes. Add milk, shortening, salt, sugar, currants, raisins, spices and egg. Beat for 2 minutes. Fold in the flour. Cover and let rise until the dough has doubled in size (about 4 hours). Knead 2 minutes. Break off small pieces of dough and shape into 2-inch balls. Brush the top of each ball with slightly beaten egg whites. Place on a greased pan and let rise until double in size (about 3 hours). With scissors cut a cross on top of each bun, and then bake 15 minutes in a moderate oven. Frost by filling the "cuts" with a butter icing.

–Mrs. W. K. Lowman, 1100 W. 23rd St., Mar. 21, 1941.

Mrs. *L*efferd's Cornbread

One and one-half cups yellow corn meal; ¾ cup flour, measured after sifting; 1 ½ teaspoons baking powder; ¾ teaspoon baking soda; 1 teaspoon salt; 1 teaspoon sugar; 2 eggs, well-beaten; 1¼ cups buttermilk or sour milk; ¼ cup shortening, melted. Mix and sift dry ingredients. Combine beaten eggs and milk, and add to dry mixture, stirring until all is well-mixed. Stir in melted shortening. Bake in well-greased pan or corn stick pan in hot oven (400 degrees) for about 30 minutes.

–Mrs. W. S. Lefferd, 809 New York St., Nov. 21, 1941.

Mrs. *A*uchard's Refrigerator Rolls

One or two potatoes and 1 pint water, 1 pint milk (scalded), ¾ cup sugar, 1½ teaspoons salt, ½ cup shortening, 2 eggs, 1 cake compressed yeast. Method: In 1 pint water, boil one large or two small potatoes till soft. Drain off (and reserve) the water, and mash potato fine; then replace the 1 pint water in which it has been cooked. Scald 1 pint milk, and when cooled to lukewarm, dissolve 1 cake yeast in it. Cream sugar, lard or other shortening, salt and eggs, and add to it the potato water and milk and yeast. Sift in 8 or 9 cups flour to make a stiff dough. Place on a well-floured board and knead, adding more flour and kneading it in until the dough is smooth and not sticky. Rub the roll of dough with lard or butter, and place in a large greased pan and let rise till double in bulk. Then knead lightly and rub over with shortening. Place in a bowl, covering tightly, and put in refrigerator. About 2 hours before baking time, pinch off dough, shape into rolls, put in a warm place, and let rise till light. Then bake 30 or 40 minutes in a slow to moderate oven. Remove from pan, and while hot, rub butter over top, sides and bottom crusts to make them soft and moist.

–Mrs. V. M. Auchard, 1405 New York St., Jan. 9, 1942.

Mrs. *R*ockhold's Cinnamon Rolls for the Lunch Box

Four cups flour, sifted; 1 cake compressed yeast; 1½ cups milk, scalded and cooled; ½ cup shortening; ⅓ cup sugar; 2 eggs; 1¼ teaspoons salt. Method: Dissolve the yeast in lukewarm milk, and stir well. Add sugar, beaten eggs, salt, and half the flour. Mix well and add the melted shortening. Beat thoroughly; add balance of flour or enough to make a soft dough. Turn out onto floured board; knead into smooth dough. Place in well-greased bowl. Let rise; knead down and let rise 45 minutes. Shake dough. Let stand 5 minutes. Roll to half-inch thickness. Spread with melted butter and sprinkle with sugar and cinnamon that have been mixed together in the proportion of ½ teaspoon cinnamon and 2 tablespoons of sugar. Currants or raisins may be added. Roll as for jelly-roll. Press edges firmly together, and cut into pieces ½ to ¾ inches thick. Place in a well-greased pan. Let rise until very light. Bake in a moderate oven (400 degrees F.) 25 to 30 minutes.

–Mrs. John A. Rockhold, Route 3, Baldwin, Apr. 17, 1942.

Mrs. *B*lack's Strawberry Tea Rolls

Two cups flour, 1 teaspoon salt, 2 teaspoons baking powder, ¼ cup butter or shortening, 1 egg, 3 tablespoons milk, 2 tablespoons softened butter, 1½ cups strawberries, ½ cup sugar, 1 egg, 1 tablespoon milk, 1 tablespoon sugar. Sift together 2 cups flour, 1 teaspoon salt and baking powder. Cut in ¼ cup butter. Beat together 1 egg and 3 tablespoons milk, and add flour mixture to form a soft dough. Roll out on floured board into ¼ inch thickness, about 12 inches square. Spread with 2 tablespoons butter. Wash and stem strawberries; if large, cut into halves. Spread berries over dough. Sprinkle with sugar. Roll like jelly roll and cut into slices 1-inch thick. Beat together 1 egg and 1 tablespoon milk and pour over rolls. Sprinkle tops of rolls with 1 tablespoon sugar. Place on greased pan and bake in moderate oven, 375 degrees, for 30 minutes. Remove from pan and, when slightly cool, serve with sweetened whipped cream or thickened strawberry juice.

–Mrs. M. F. Black, Tonganoxie, May 15, 1942.

Mrs. *P*ardee's Boston Brown Bread

One cup white flour, 2 cups graham flour, 1 teaspoon salt, 2 teaspoons soda, ½ cup brown sugar, 1 egg, ¼ cup molasses, 2 cups sour milk or buttermilk, ½ cup seedless raisins, ½ cup chopped nut meats. Sift white flour; measure and sift with salt and soda. Add graham flour, brown sugar, nuts and raisins. Mix well. Add molasses and milk to well-beaten egg. Combine wet and dry ingredients. Pour into 4 well-greased and floured baking powder cans. Steam 1½ hours, or if preferred, bake in a moderate oven, about 325 degrees, for one hour.

–Mrs. Alice Pardee, 734 Arkansas St., Jan. 29, 1943.

Mrs. *G*allagher's Corn Meal Muffins

One tablespoon sugar, 1 cup sifted flour, 1½ cups corn meal, 1 teaspoon soda, 1 teaspoon baking powder, 2 teaspoons salt, ¼ cup shortening, 2 beaten eggs, 2 cups sour cream or milk. Sift flour, corn meal, soda, baking powder and salt. Cut in shortening until mixture is like meal. Combine eggs and milk, and stir into the dry mixture. Bake in greased muffin pans, 450 degrees F., 15 to 20 minutes or until brown.

–Mrs. Gene Gallagher, 634 Massachusetts St., Feb. 26, 1943.

Mrs. *J*ennings's Refrigerator Rolls

Two packages compressed yeast, 3 teaspoons salt, 1 cup lukewarm water, ¾ cup sugar, 1 pint milk, ⅔ cup shortening, 2 eggs, about 11 cups or more sifted flour–as needed. Pour the cup of water over yeast. Add 1 teaspoon sugar; stir, and let stand about 10 minutes. Scald the milk and dissolve in it the salt and sugar. Let cool. When milk is lukewarm, add to it the softened yeast. Blend yeast mixture with about half the flour, and beat until smooth. Add beaten eggs and the shortening (softened, but not hot). Add enough more flour to make dough softer than for bread. Knead smooth. Let dough rise in a moderately warm place until doubled. Knead down. Then store in refrigerator after placing it in a well-greased vessel, covered with a tight-fitting lid or with a double thickness of waxed paper tied down securely. About 2 hours before rolls are wanted, take out amount of dough required. Shape and

place in greased pans. Let rise in warm place until doubled. Bake about 15 minutes in a fairly-hot oven. This dough should keep for a week in a good refrigerator–if kept below 45 degrees F. All measurements are level.
  –*Mrs. George Jennings,*
  1528 New Hampshire St.,
      Apr. 9, 1943.

Mrs. Cross's Cornmeal Muffins

One cup cornmeal, 1 cup boiling water, ½ teaspooon salt, 1 egg, 2 level teaspoons baking powder, ½ cup sweet milk, 1 tablespoon melted butter. Grease generously 6 or 8 glass custard cups. Sift cornmeal and salt into mixing bowl. Pour boiling water over same and beat smooth; add cold milk at once to keep from lumping, then egg, and beat well. Sprinkle baking powder over batter; mix well, but lightly. Add melted butter and pour into cups. Bake in very hot oven, 475 to 500 degrees. This recipe should be put together quickly, so have everything ready before starting to mix batter. Bake to golden brown, remove from oven, split, put in a pat of butter, and serve at once.

–*Mrs. Anna R. Cross*, 921 Illinois St., Feb. 4, 1944.

Mrs. Puckett's Graham Muffins

"This will serve a small family."

One egg, 1 cup sour milk, ½ teaspoon soda, ½ teaspoon salt, 2 tablespoonsful lard, 1 cup graham flour. Beat the egg well, then add sour milk and soda, salt, then sugar and lard; beat again and then add flour. Grease pans and bake in moderate oven.

–*Mrs. Leroy Puckett*, Route 6, Apr. 28, 1944.

Mrs. Hunzicker's Ice Box Rolls

One yeast cake, ½ cup lukewarm water, ⅔ cup shortening, ½ cup sugar, 1 teaspoon salt, 1 cup mashed potatoes, 1 cup scalded milk, 2 eggs, 6 to 8 cups flour. Mash potatoes; add shortening, sugar, salt and eggs; cream well. Dissolve yeast in lukewarm water; add to lukewarm milk, then add to potato mixture. Add sifted flour to make a stiff dough. Toss onto floured board and knead well. Put into a large bowl and let rise double in bulk. Knead slightly. Rub over top with melted butter.

Place in casserole, cover tightly, and place in refrigerator cabinet until ready to bake. About 2 hours before baking time, pinch off dough, shape into rolls as desired; cover and let rise until light. Bake 400 degrees F. 15 to 20 minutes. These rolls can be kept in the refrigerator for a week.

–Mrs. Otto Hunzicker, 2045 Vermont St., July 14, 1944.

Mrs. *I*ngalls's Molasses Nut Bread

One-half cup molasses, 1 cup milk, 2 cups whole wheat flour, ¼ cup bread flour, ½ cup sugar, 1 teaspoon soda, ½ teaspoon salt, 1 cup chopped nut meats. Mix molasses and milk together in a bowl. Mix the whole wheat flour, bread flour, sugar, soda, salt and nut meats. Stir quickly into the liquid. Mix until just blended, then pour into a greased and floured loaf pan. Bake in moderate oven (350 degrees F.) 50 to 60 minutes. Cool in pan before slicing. Makes 1 loaf.

–Mrs. Maurine Ingalls, 921 Missouri St., Jan. 25, 1946.

Mrs. *R*alston's Hot Cross Buns

Dissolve 2 envelopes of dry granular yeast, or 2 cakes of compressed yeast, in a little lukewarm milk with 2 tablespoons of sugar added. When yeast is perfectly dissolved, add 2 cups of milk, scalded but cooled, and 3¼ cups flour to make a sponge. Beat until smooth. Put in a warm place, and let rise an hour, or until light. Add ¼ cup butter or margarine and ⅔ cup sugar, well-creamed; 2 eggs, well beaten; ½ cup raisins, after flouring them; ½ teaspoon salt; and enough flour to make a moderately soft dough. Knead lightly, either in a large pan or on a board. Place in a well-greased bowl; cover closely, and keep in a warm place, until double in bulk, or about 2 hours. Shape buns with hands to a medium size, and place in well-greased shallow pans about 2 inches apart. Cover and let rise, about one hour, or until light. Glaze the top of the buns with yolk of egg, diluted with water; then, with a sharp knife, cut a cross on each one. Bake 20 minutes. Before removing from the oven, brush with sugar moistened with water. While hot, fill the crosses with white frosting.

–Mrs. C. E. Ralston,
Route 2,
Mar. 29, 1946.

Miss **D**yche's Bread or Rolls

One cup sugar, 1 cup lard, 1 cup mashed potatoes (strained), 1 tablespoon salt, 1 cake compressed yeast. Dissolve sugar, fat, and salt in water (about 1 quart) from the water in which the potatoes cooked. When lukewarm, add soaked yeast. Sift in enough flour for a sponge batter, and beat well. Then add more flour (8 to 12 cups in all) to make a dough. Knead well. Let rise till double in bulk. Mold to loaves or rolls; let rise again and bake. Or put the dough, after mixing and kneading, into ice box, and use when needed. The dough will rise for baking in 3 hours after chilling in the ice box. Note: Less sugar and fat can be used. Two beaten eggs may be added to the sponge, but use less liquid unless additional volume is desired. Makes 4 loaves or 50 rolls.

–*Miss Ruth Dyche,* 1617 Massachusetts St., June 14, 1946.

Mrs. **B**arnard's Ice Box Rolls
"This is also good for making cinnamon rolls or coffee cake."

One cake compressed yeast, ½ cup lukewarm water, 1 teaspoon salt, ½ cup sugar, ⅓ cup fat (melted), 2 eggs, 1 cup mashed potatoes, 1 cup potato water, 5 cups flour. Crumble yeast, add to warm water, and let stand five minutes. Add salt, sugar, fat, eggs, potatoes, potato water, and 3 cups flour. Beat 3 minutes; add rest of flour, and knead until soft and elastic. Let rise until double in bulk. Knead down and store in ice box. When rolls are desired, let rise until double in size, and bake. This dough will last 3 to 4 days in ice box.

–*Mrs. Harry Barnard,* 1740 Massachusetts St., Mar. 7, 1947.

Heard In Lawrence

It will be Merry Christmas at the Douglas county jail tomorrow for the fifteen prisoners now wards of Sheriff Jack Dunkley, for Mrs. Dunkley has prepared an attractive menu. In their "stockings" tomorrow morning the prisoners will find, in addition to several special breakfast items, such delicacies as oranges, apples, nuts and candy. The big moment will arrive at noon when the prisoners will be served with chicken, fried southern style, mashed potatoes and gravy, baked spiced apples, celery, and home made mince pie. [LJW, 12-24-32]

Mrs. $\mathcal{P}$earson's Muffins

One and one-half cups flour, 3 tablespoons sugar, 3 teaspoons baking powder, ½ teaspoon salt, 3 tablespoons shortening, 2 eggs, ¾ cup milk. Grease and flour muffin tins. Sift dry ingredients together. Mix shortening in with fork. Add eggs and milk. Beat just enough to mix. Put into tins. Bake in 450 degree oven. Makes twelve large muffins.

–Mrs. Thomas Pearson, 1336 Massachusetts St., Mar. 14, 1947.

Mrs. $\mathcal{S}$mith's Cornbread

Two cups cornmeal, 1 teaspoon salt, 1 teaspoon soda, 2 cups sour milk or buttermilk, 2 well-beaten eggs, 3 tablespoons melted fat. Sift dry ingredients. Add milk to eggs and fat. Combine, stirring only enough to mix ingredients slightly. Pour into shallow, oiled pan. Bake in hot oven (425 degrees F.) about 25 minutes. Use half flour (in place of half the cornmeal) if preferred. If a sweet product is desired, add ¼ cup sugar. Makes ten servings 3 inches by 3 inches by 1 inch.

–Mrs. Albert C. Smith, 901 ½ E. 23ʳᵈ St., Jan. 30, 1948.

Mrs. $\mathcal{B}$eguelin's Ice Box Rolls

One cup boiling water, ¾ cup shortening, ½ cup sugar, ¾ teaspoon salt, 1 cake compressed yeast, ½ cup lukewarm water, 1 cup flour, 1 cup mashed potatoes, 2 beaten eggs, 5½ cups flour. Combine boiling water, shortening, sugar and salt. Cool to lukewarm and add yeast, softened in lukewarm water. Mix to smooth batter with one cup flour. Stir in potatoes and eggs; let rise two hours or until light and bubbly. Add remaining flour to make soft dough. Knead lightly on floured surface. Let rise again in greased bowl about two hours. Punch down. Cover and place in refrigerator until ready to use. About 1½ to 2 hours before serving, remove portion of dough, and form in rolls of desired shape. Arrange in greased pan and let rise until double in bulk. Bake in moderately hot oven (400 to 425 degrees) 20 to 25 minutes. Makes three to four dozen rolls.

–Mrs. Clifford Beguelin, 1511 Barker Ave., Feb. 20, 1948.

Mrs. *H*all's Ice Box Rolls

One cup boiling water, 1 cake compressed yeast, ½ cup sugar, ½ cup shortening, 1 teaspoon salt, 1 cup mashed potatoes, ½ cup warm water, 1 cup flour, 2 eggs, 5½ cups flour. Combine boiling water, sugar, salt and shortening. Cool to lukewarm and add yeast. Mix to smooth batter with one cup flour. Stir in potatoes and beaten eggs. Let rise two hours or until light and bubbly. Add remaining flour to make soft dough. Knead lightly on floured surface. Let rise again in greased bowl two hours. Punch down. Cover and place in refrigerator until ready to use. About 1 ½ to 2 hours before serving, remove portion of dough and form into rolls of desired shape. Arrange in greased pan and let rise until double in bulk. Bake in moderate oven (400 to 425 degrees) 20 to 25 minutes. Makes three to four dozen rolls.

–Mrs. Ray H. Hall, Route 1, McLouth, Apr. 30, 1948.

Mrs. *T*owne's Boston Brown Bread

Sift together: 1 cup yellow cornmeal, 1 cup flour, 1 cup whole wheat flour, ½ cup sugar, 1 teaspoon soda, 1½ teaspoons salt. Add ½ cup molasses and 1½ cups sour milk or buttermilk. Mix well. Then add 2 tablespoons of melted shortening. Stir until well-blended. Pour into greased baking powder tins two-thirds full. Cover tightly. Place on rack in a kettle of boiling water. Cover and steam 3 hours. Keep water boiling slowly and add as necessary. Serve hot. For variation, chopped dates or raisins may be added.

–Mrs. Roy Towne, 1209 Oread Ave., Jan. 21, 1949.

Mrs. *B*rown's Baked Boston Brown Bread

One and one-half cups sifted flour, 2½ teaspoons soda, 1½ teaspoons salt, ¼ cup sugar, 2 cups whole wheat flour, ½ cup shortening, 1 cup raisins, 1 well-beaten egg, 2 cups sour milk, ¾ cup molasses. Sift flour, soda, salt and sugar. Add whole wheat flour. Mix well. Cut in shortening until mixture resembles coarse meal. Add raisins; mix well. Add combined egg, milk and molasses to dry ingredients. Mix only until all flour is dampened. Turn into two greased loaf pans and bake 45 to 50 minutes at 350 degrees F. Makes two 8- x 4- x 3-inch loaves. Serve warm or cold.

–Mrs. Howard Brown, 1726 Kentucky St., Nov. 4, 1949.

Pancakes,
Waffles,

and
Doughnuts

"Table Talk" Butter It Is!

Mrs. Chas. Starkweather won the $25 in gold prize for submitting the best name for the new butter being made by the Lawrence Sanitary Milk and Ice Cream Co. The name chosen was "Table Talk." More than 2,000 names were sent in ranging from "Billy Goat Better Butter" and "Billy Goat Best Butter" on up through 2000 degrees to the name selected. Although the butter was marketed only locally, names were submitted from Chicago and California and a dozen different states. As indicated by the results of the contest, this new butter is meeting with a good reception. The demand is good because the quality is kept at the very highest. In a test conducted by a chemist recently, Table Talk scored five points higher than any other butter marketed locally. [DCR, 3-7-29]

Hallie *H*olmes's Griddle Cakes

One egg, 1½ cups sweet milk or water, 1½ cups sour milk, 2 cups flour, 1 scant teaspoon soda, 2 teaspoons baking powder, 1 teaspoon salt, 1 tablespoon melted fat. Sift dry ingredients together two or three times. Beat egg and sweet milk or water. Then add the sour milk, then the flour and lastly the melted fat. If sour milk is mild, use two cups and leave out the other liquid; but if quite acid, it is better to use the half cup of sweet milk or water.

–Hallie V. Holmes, 945 Kentucky St., Feb. 17, 1922.

Mrs. *M*cGee's Buckwheat Cakes

One cake compressed yeast, 2 cups lukewarm water, 1 cup milk (scalded and cooled), 2 level tablespoons brown sugar, 2 cups buckwheat flour, 1 cup sifted white flour, 1½ teaspoons salt. Dissolve the yeast and sugar in the lukewarm liquid; gradually add buckwheat, white flour, and salt. Beat until smooth, cover and set aside in a warm place, free from draft, to rise–about one hour. When light, stir well and bake on a hot griddle. If wanted for over night, use only one fourth cake of yeast and an extra half teaspoon of salt. Cover and keep in a cool place.

–Mrs. George McGee, 914 Kentucky St., Jan. 11, 1924.

Mrs. *H*arris's Waffles

Four level teaspoons of baking powder, 2 level cups of flour, ½ level tablespoon salt, 2 eggs–separated, 1½ cups of milk, 4 level tablespoons melted butter. Mix flour with baking powder and salt, and sift into bowl. Beat yolks of eggs; add butter and milk. Add this mixture gradually to dry ingredients, beating thoroughly. When well-mixed, fold in stiffly beaten whites of eggs. Pour from a pitcher into center of a hot, well-greased waffle iron. Serve with melted butter and maple syrup, or with cinnamon and powdered sugar.

–Mrs. Wallace C. Harris, 1113 New Jersey St., Jan. 18, 1924.

Mrs. *K*ieffer's Waffles

Two cups flour, 4 teaspoons baking powder, ¾ teaspoon salt, 1¾ cups milk, 2 eggs, 1 tablespoon melted shortening. Sift the flour, baking powder and salt together. Add the milk and egg yolks (which have been beaten together) to the dry ingredients. Add the melted shortening, then mix in the beaten egg whites. Bake in a greased hot waffle iron until brown; turn only once. Serve hot with butter and maple syrup.

–Mrs. F. H. Kieffer, 915½ Massachusetts St., Apr. 17, 1925.

Mrs. *B*ryant's Quick Waffles

Sift 1 pint of flour 3 times and add 1 teaspoonful of salt. Beat the yolks of 2 eggs until very light; add to them 1 cup of rich milk. Add this to the flour, with 1 tablespoon of butter, melted, and beat until light and smooth. Beat the whites of the eggs to a stiff, dry froth; add to the batter and beat again. When ready to bake, add 1 teaspoon of baking powder. Put the batter in a pitcher, and have the waffle iron very hot and thoroughly greased. Pour in the batter carefully, and as soon as the edges are set, turn the iron and bake the second side. In making waffles, as much depends upon the even and quick baking as upon the recipe used.

–Mrs. Ike Bryant, 740 Rhode Island St., Oct. 26, 1928.

Mrs. *B*artley's Love Knots or Fried Cakes Modernistic

"This is my favorite recipe for tea doughnuts or winter refreshments. Made with potato, any fried cakes keep fresh much longer."

One cup sugar, creamed with 4 tablespoons shortening; 3 eggs, well beaten; 1 cup freshly mashed potato, put through a sieve to be entirely free from lumps; 2½ cups flour, sifted with 1 teaspoon each of mace, nutmeg and salt; 4 tablespoons of sweet milk. More flour may be added if necessary, but the less used, the lighter and more tender will be the fried cakes. These may be rolled and cut as usual, but are far nicer if cut with a 2-inch cutter, or cut in small rectangles and triangles of about 1½ inches, or squares cut 4 or 5 times part way in towards the center. When fried, these cuts open up and give surprising shapes. These pleasurable surprises for her guests are counted as essential by a good hostess as are the palatable flavors of the refreshments she has to offer. Especially nice for bridal showers and Valentine parties are the Love Knots, made by tying a single knot in a strip of dough, cut about 4 inches long and 1 inch wide, before frying. No matter what shape you prefer, the usual or fantastic, shake a few pieces at a time very carefully in a paper sack with a little sifted confectioner's sugar and they become doubly delightful.

–Mrs. S. Howard Bartley, 1240 Ohio St., Oct. 31, 1930.

Mrs. *W*ood's Sour Cream Doughnuts

One cup of sour cream, 1 cup of sugar, 1 egg, ¼ teaspoon soda, 1 teaspoon baking powder, ¼ teaspoon salt, flavoring, flour. Mix in the usual way and flavor with nutmeg or rose extract and add

enough all-purpose flour for a soft dough–usually about four cups. Roll in a thick sheet and cut with a ring cutter, or break off small pieces, roll under the fingers and form into figure eights. Fry in deep fat heated to 360 degrees F. Drain on absorbent paper. Put a small quantity of powdered sugar in a box or bag, and put four or five of the cooled doughnuts at a time into the bag. Shake until well-coated with sugar. If chocolate doughnuts are desired, add 3 ounces of melted chocolate to the dough as you mix it, or sift ⅓ cup of cocoa with the dry ingredients. Flavor with 1 teaspoon of cinnamon and ½ teaspoon vanilla.

> –*Mrs. Naomi D. Wood,*
> 1133 Pennsylvania St.,
> Oct. 23, 1931.

Mrs. *B*rubaker's Angel Food Doughnuts

Four egg whites, beaten; 1 cup sugar; butter the size of an egg; 2 teaspoons baking powder; 1 cup sweet milk; 1 teaspoon vanilla; flour to make a soft dough (about 3 cups). Mix together as listed, roll thin, cut, and fry brown in deep fat.

> –*Mrs. Lanty Brubaker,* Route 2, Richland, May 27, 1932.

Mrs. *M*essmore's Pancakes

One cup cornmeal, 1 cup flour, ¼ cup sugar, 1 teaspoon salt, 1 teaspoon soda, 1 teaspoon baking powder, 1 egg, ¼ cup melted shortening, 2 cups sour milk. Mix dry ingredients. Beat egg; add milk, and stir into other mixture. Add shortening; let stand five minutes, and bake on hot griddle on both sides. If sweet milk is used, substitute four teaspoons of baking powder for the soda. Serve with creamed ham or dried beef or with honey.

> –*Mrs. Marie Messmore,* 1530 New Hampshire St., Nov. 18, 1932.

Mrs. *W*arner's Old-Fashioned Buckwheat Cakes

Two cups buckwheat flour, 1 cup white flour, 2¼ cups liquid (water or milk), 1 cake yeast, 1 teaspoon soda, 1 teaspoon salt, 2 tablespoons sorghum. Put into mixing bowl (not metal) the white flour and buckwheat flour; mix. Add liquid and mix. Dissolve yeast in ½ cup warm water and then add this to other mixture. Cover mixing bowl and set in warm place to raise. This must set at least 12 hours. When ready to bake, add salt, soda and sorghum. Mix well, and bake on hot greased griddle. These cakes have a much better flavor when part of the batter, one cup or more, is kept for a starter for mixing cakes for the next day. At night, make first mixture of the two flours and liquid, and use the cup of leftover batter instead of the yeast cake. Keep in warm place. In the morning, before baking, add the salt, soda and sorghum as before. These cakes acquire a desirable sour flavor after the second morning. Batter must always be kept in warm place.

–*Mrs. Warren Varner,* 1824 Barker Ave., Jan. 5, 1934.

Mrs. *L*eary's Doughnuts

One cup mashed potatoes, warm; 1 cup sugar; 3 eggs, beaten; pinch of salt; 1 teaspoon nutmeg; 3 tablespoons melted butter; 1 cup flour with 3 teaspoons baking powder added; enough flour to handle–about 2½ cups. Add sugar and salt to the warm potatoes. This helps to dissolve it. Add the melted butter and then the beaten eggs. Add the cup of flour with the baking powder, and enough more flour to make the dough handle easily. Fry in a deep fat, and roll in sugar. Makes about 2 ½ dozen doughnuts, which are nice because they do not become solid after standing.

–*Mrs. Eugene Leary,* Route 2, Feb. 8, 1935.

Mrs. *G*abriel's Buckwheat Cakes

Two cups buckwheat flour, 2 cups wheat flour, ½ cup yellow corn meal, 1 tablespoon salt, 2 tablespoons sugar, 1 yeast cake, ½ cup warm water. Mix dry ingredients together, and add the yeast cake that has been dissolved in ½ cup warm water. Add more lukewarm water gradually, and keep stirring until mixture runs freely from spoon. This is put in a warm place overnight, and again stirred well in the morning before adding 1 teaspoon baking soda dissolved in a little warm water with 2 tablespoons molasses. Bake on a hot griddle.

–*Mrs. Gus Gabriel,* Route 1, Eudora, Mar. 15, 1935.

Local Grocery Prices 1938

1 pkg. grapenut flakes	.10
5 lbs. pancake flour	.21
1 (2 lb.) jar jelly	.25
6 lbs. bananas	.25
1 pkg. Bisquick	.25
10 grapefruit	.25
1 dozen oranges	.27
2 lbs. coffee	.48
Total	$ 2.06

Mrs. *H*arding's Old-Fashioned Buckwheat Cakes

At night: ½ cup corn meal and ½ teaspoon salt mixed with 1 pint boiling water. Beat well, and when cooled, add ½ cup white flour and 1 cup buckwheat with ¼ oz. dissolved yeast. In morning: Pour off the discolored water that lies on top of the batter and dilute with ½ cup of milk in which is dissolved ¼ teaspoon soda. Butter the griddle lightly and bake in small cakes quickly. The batter is so

thin that they do not need much time, and should be thin, crisp, and full of bubbles. Beat the batter and add more milk and soda, if needed. Save a cup of batter and use as yeast for the next time. They improve with repeated use. Griddle or waffle iron for these cakes must be well greased.

–Mrs. W. R. Harding, Route 1, McLouth, Nov. 19, 1937.

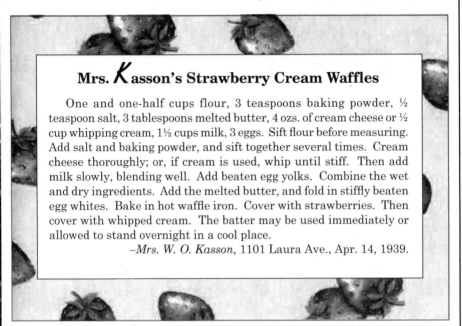

Mrs. *K*asson's Strawberry Cream Waffles

One and one-half cups flour, 3 teaspoons baking powder, ½ teaspoon salt, 3 tablespoons melted butter, 4 ozs. of cream cheese or ½ cup whipping cream, 1½ cups milk, 3 eggs. Sift flour before measuring. Add salt and baking powder, and sift together several times. Cream cheese thoroughly; or, if cream is used, whip until stiff. Then add milk slowly, blending well. Add beaten egg yolks. Combine the wet and dry ingredients. Add the melted butter, and fold in stiffly beaten egg whites. Bake in hot waffle iron. Cover with strawberries. Then cover with whipped cream. The batter may be used immediately or allowed to stand overnight in a cool place.

–Mrs. W. O. Kasson, 1101 Laura Ave., Apr. 14, 1939.

Mrs. *G*ettings's Favorite Griddle Cakes

Two beaten eggs, 2 cups milk, 2 tablespoons melted shortening, 3 cups flour, 1 teaspoon salt, 4 teaspoons baking powder, 2 to 4 tablespoons sugar. Combine beaten eggs, milk and shortening. Add flour sifted with salt, baking powder and sugar; beat smooth. Bake on ungreased griddle. Finer textured cakes are obtained if the melted shortening is cooled somewhat before adding to the batter, and if the egg whites are beaten separately and folded in last. Cakes should be turned carefully, only once, to avoid loss of lightness.

–Mrs. J. P. Gettings, Route 2, Feb. 2, 1940.

Mrs. *M*cKnight's Sour Milk Pancakes
*"When this recipe is properly made and baked, the pancakes
are very light and delicious and easily digested."*

Two cups sifted flour, 2 cups sour milk or buttermilk, 2 eggs, 2 tablespoons butter or shortening, 3 teaspoons baking powder, ½ teaspoon soda, 1 teaspoon salt; 1 tablespoon sugar. Beat yolks and whites of eggs separately. Add the milk to beaten yolks, then add dry ingredients. Beat well, and lastly fold in egg whites.

–Mrs. E. F. McKnight, 2203 Vermont St., Apr. 19, 1940.

Mrs. *N*eustifter's Sour Milk Waffles

Two cups flour, 1 teaspoon salt, ¼ teaspoon soda, 1 teaspoon baking powder, 1½ cups sour milk, 2 eggs, 3 tablespoons melted shortening. Sift flour, salt, soda and baking powder. Combine egg yolks, melted shortening and sour milk. Stir the liquid into the dry ingredients until smooth. Fold in the stiffly beaten whites of eggs. Bake on hot irons. Makes 6 waffles.

–Mrs. Edward C. Neustifter,
1101 ½ Massachusetts St.,
Apr. 2, 1943.

Mrs. *R*ichards's Crisp Waffles

Two cups flour, ¼ cup sugar, 3 teaspoons baking powder, ½ teaspoon salt, 2 egg yolks, 1¼ cups milk, ½ cup shortening, 2 egg whites. Mix and sift flour, sugar, baking powder and salt. Beat egg yolks until thick and lemon-colored. Add milk to yolks; add to dry ingredients. Melt shortening; add. Beat egg whites stiff, but not dry; fold in. Bake in hot waffle iron. Makes 8 waffles.

–Mrs. E. M. Richards, 606 Maine St., Mar. 31, 1944.

Mrs. *D*odds's Pancakes

Two cups sifted flour, 2 cups sour milk, 2 eggs, 2 tablespoons shortening (melted), 3 teaspoons baking powder, ½ teaspoon soda, 1 teaspoon salt, 1 tablespoon sugar. Separate eggs, and beat whites till stiff. Add milk to beaten egg yolks, then add dry ingredients. Beat well and fold in egg whites. Cook on hot griddle. Note: Sweet milk may be used. If so, use 4 level teaspoons of baking powder and no soda.

–Mrs. F. B. Dodds, 903 Alabama St., Mar. 9. 1945.

Mrs. *K*eefe's Griddle Cakes

One cup flour, ½ teaspoon salt, 2 teaspoons sugar, ¼ cup butter or other shortening, 2 teaspoons baking powder, 1 egg, 1 cup milk. Sift flour. Measure, resift twice with dry ingredients into mixing bowl. Beat egg until light and fluffy; add milk and melted shortening. Stir into dry ingredients and beat until smooth. For

each cake, pour about two tablespoons of batter onto a medium hot griddle. When full of bubbles and golden brown on under side, turn cake to finish baking. Serve with butter and honey or maple syrup. Yields about 17 cakes.

–Mrs. E. F. Keefe, 710 New Hampshire St., Feb. 22, 1946.

Mrs. *K*emp's Plain Waffles

Two cups sifted flour, 3 teaspoons baking powder, ½ teaspoon salt, 2 tablespoons sugar, 3 eggs (separated), 2 ¼ cups milk, ¼ cup melted margarine (or other shortening). Sift flour, baking powder, salt and sugar together. Combine beaten egg yolks, milk and melted butter, and stir into dry ingredients. Fold in stiffly beaten egg whites, and bake on hot waffle iron. Makes 6 waffles.

–Mrs. Sarah Kemp, 841 Ohio St., Jan. 17, 1947.

Mrs. *C*amp's Honey Bran Waffles

Two eggs (separated), 1½ cups milk, 1 tablespoon honey, ¾ cup bran; 1½ cups sifted flour, 4 teaspoons baking powder, 1 teaspoon salt, ¼ cup melted shortening. Beat egg yolks well; add milk and honey, and mix thoroughly. Add bran; let soak until moisture is taken up. Sift flour with baking powder and salt; add to first mixture and stir until flour disappears. Add shortening. Fold into stiffly beaten egg whites. Bake in hot waffle iron until no steam is visible. Makes 7 waffles.

–Mrs. Russell R. Camp, Apt. 28, Sunnyside, Jan. 9, 1948.

Mrs. *W*right's Pancakes

Two cups white flour, 3 teaspoons baking powder, ⅛ teaspoon salt, 1½ cups sweet milk, 2 eggs, 1½ tablespoons melted shortening (either bacon or sausage fryings). Sift dry ingredients together; add milk and mix thoroughly. Add whole eggs and beat till batter is well-mixed. Add melted shortening and beat again until batter is very smooth. Have the griddle pre-heated until it smokes. Grease griddle lightly for the first hot cake only; do not use grease for additional cakes. Drop two tablespoons of batter on the sizzling griddle for each cake. Let cook until it bubbles all over; turn with a cake turner and allow to brown on the other side. Serve piping hot with butter and any syrup you wish.

–Mrs. Faye Wright,
913 New York St., Dec. 31, 1948.

"Tailspin Tommy," LJW, 7-4-32

Mrs. *P*uckett's Waffles

Two cups sifted all-purpose flour, 3 tablespoons sugar, 1 teaspoon salt, 3 teaspoons baking powder, 2 eggs (separated), 1¾ cups milk, 4 tablespoons melted butter. Sift dry ingredients together into mixing bowl. Add egg yolks and milk slowly, beating until batter is smooth. Then add melted butter, and fold in stiffly beaten egg whites. This recipe may be varied by adding: ½ cup diced, crisply fried bacon, or 1 cup drained, crushed pineapple, or ½ cup finely chopped apricots, or ½ cup chopped dates.

–*Mrs. William Puckett,* Route 5, Mar. 18, 1949.

Mrs. *J*ohnson's Doughnuts

Four cups all-purpose flour, ¼ teaspoon cinnamon, ⅓ teaspoon nutmeg, ½ teaspoon mace, 1¼ teaspoons salt, 1 teaspoon soda, ½ teaspoon cream of tartar, 2 tablespoons shortening, ¾ cup sugar, 2 eggs plus 1 egg yolk, 1 cup thick sour milk.

Sift flour, spices, salt, soda, and cream of tartar together 3 times. Cream shortening and sugar until well-blended. Add eggs and mix well. Add sour milk and mix thoroughly. Add sifted dry ingredients and mix until smooth. With as little handling as possible, roll dough on floured board to three-eighths-inch thickness. Let dough stand 20 minutes. Cut with 2½-inch doughnut cutter. Fry in deep hot shortening (375 degrees) until brown. Turn when first crack appears. Drain on absorbent paper. Makes about 3 dozen.

–*Mrs. R. E. Johnson,* 21 Winona St., Oct. 21, 1949.

Sandwiches,
Fillings
and
Spreads

Chorus To Close Year With Picnic

The formal closing of the season for the Lawrence Choral Union will come Friday afternoon with the annual picnic of the organization which will be held at 4:30 o'clock in the west half of South Park. Between 4:00 and 5:00 persons are expected to be present.

Each year this choral union celebrates the close of its season with this huge picnic, and if present indications prove true, the party this year will be bigger than ever.

Plans for the picnic are fast being completed under the chairmanship of Mrs. C. M. Sterling. All picnickers are asked to bring coffee, cups and spoons. Ladies attending are asked to bring sandwiches for their own party and for five other people, and enough salad, baked beans (hot), deviled eggs, or cake, for five other persons.

Picknickers living away from home, and not having access to kitchens, are asked to bring any two of the following articles sufficient for five persons: Saratoga chips, olives, pickles or bananas. All men are expected to pay twenty-five cents.

The annual outdoor soft ball game between the basses and tenors, which find the two sections meeting in heartless combat, is being arranged for. Eli Wamego will captain the tenors, and Henry Werner will lead the basses. Robert Myers will umpire the conflict. [LJW, 5-14-29]

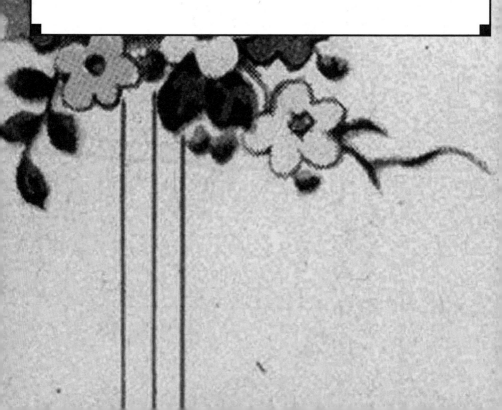

SANDWICHES THAT YOU WILL LIKE!

Mrs. *M*itchell's Mock Chicken Sandwich

Take a piece of fresh good ham or shoulder, cook in sufficient water to cover. When done, grind thoroughly in a food chopper. Mix in enough of the stock the pork was cooked in to make moist. Add pepper, a little chopped pickle, or chopped olives. The seasoning may be varied with good results; some like a little sage or onion. Chopped celery is also nice. Spread the above mixture between slices of buttered bread, and you have a delicious sandwich that can hardly be told from chicken.

–*Mrs. Frances Mitchell,* 1312 Vermont St., Oct. 14, 1921.

Miss *M*yers's Savory Sandwiches

Three tablespoons butter, 1 teaspoon capers, 6 olives, 1 tablespoon chopped mustard pickle, 2 teaspoons chopped parsley, a few drops of onion juice, slices of buttered white or graham bread. Beat the butter to a cream; add the capers and olives chopped finely. Mix these well with butter and stir in the pickle, parsley and onion juice, with salt if necessary. Spread between either white or graham bread.

–*Miss Gladys Myers,* Route 5, June 2, 1922.

Miss *J*ones's Delicious Sandwiches

Boil one and one-half cups light brown sugar, teaspoon butter, three- fourths cup water, until quite thick. Remove from the fire and add one- half pound grated cocoanut, one-half pound chopped figs, one-half cup chopped nuts. Stir until creamy, and spread on thin buttered slices of whole wheat bread.

–*Miss Marie Jones,* 1324 New Hampshire St., July 7, 1922.

Mrs. *R*ohman's Potted Ham Sandwiches

Six tablespoons of potted ham; six small sweet pickles, diced real fine; 3 pimientos, also diced very fine; 3 tablespoons of mayonnaise. Mix well and spread on thin slices of fresh bread with lettuce between.

–*Mrs. W. C. Rohman,* 1704 Kentucky St., Mar. 24, 1923.

Mrs. *B*eck's Sweet Sandwich Filling

One package dates, 1 package figs, ½ box cocoanut. Grind, then add enough orange juice to spread.

–*Mrs. Paul V. Beck,* 1808 Vermont St., July 11, 1924.

Mrs. *P*almer's Sandwich Filling

One-half pound cream cheese, ¾ cup homemade chile sauce or ketchup, ⅓ cup chopped pickles (preferably sweet mixed peppers). Grind cheese, and mix in sauce and pickles (pickles may be omitted). Spread on one slice of bread, and butter the other slice. It is good to have one slice of sandwich graham bread and the other white bread.

–Mrs. H. C. Palmer, 920 Louisiana St., Aug. 21, 1925.

Mrs. *H*ouk's Rolled Chicken Sandwiches

The bread for these sandwiches must be firm, of even texture, and fresh. Wrap loaves first in napkins wrung out in cold water, then in dry napkins, and put in cool place several hours. Have butter softened. Put the chicken meat, which should be boiled until tender, through the food chopper. Mix with a little mayonnaise. Cut crust off the loaf–top, bottom and sides. Cut sandwiches lengthwise. Cut bread in slices so thin it curls as it is cut. Spread lightly with soft butter, then with thin layer of chicken paste. Sandwiches may be rolled closely with a little care and should be laid close together so as to hold their shape. Wrap all in dampened napkin until ready to use. Then slice in thin rounds.

–Mrs. H. A. Houk, 1103 New Hampshire St., Mar. 8, 1929.

Miss *S*mith's Mock Chicken Sandwiches

Boil until very tender a small piece of lean, fresh pork (about one pound); cool, then grind in food chopper. Cut 3 sweet pickles, 2 hard-boiled eggs, a little celery and ½ cup of pecans or English walnut meats, chopped into very small pieces. Mix with the ground meat. Add enough mayonnaise to hold all firmly together. Spread between bread slices and serve.

–Miss Marjorie Smith, 1524 Rhode Island St., July 5, 1929.

Mrs. *P*earson's Five O'clock Tea Sandwiches

Grind one pound raisins, one pound stoned dates, and one-half pound English walnuts. Mix with the juice and pulp of two lemons and two oranges. This filling will keep indefinitely if packed in a jar and kept in a cool place. The sandwiches are best if made of nut or brown bread. The filling can also be used between graham crackers or wafers which do not have too pronounced a flavor.

–Mrs. Jacob Pearson, Simpson, Kans., July 16, 1926.

Heard In Lawrence

The Missouri game here Saturday is a real business opportunity for the hot dog venders who sell to the crowd at the stadium. One of the local bakeries this week is filling an order for 1,500 dozen buns to be used in making hot dogs. It will take nearly a ton of wieners to make up this order of 18,000 sandwiches. And as an appetizer the head chef has ordered four gallons of mustard. Doughnuts are another favorite of football fans and there will be 125 dozen doughnuts for sale at the stadium Saturday. [DCR, 11-21-29]

Mrs. $\mathcal{S}$pear's Pimiento Cheese Sandwich Filling

Five cents worth fresh salted peanuts, ½ lb. cheese, ½ can pimientos, 12 sweet pickles. Put all through food chopper and mix with the following dressing: 2 eggs, 1 teaspoon mustard, 1 teaspoon flour, 1 cup vinegar, ½ cup milk. Cook, and let cool before mixing with first part.

–Mrs. Roy D. Spear, 1000 Missouri St., July 26, 1929.

Mrs. $\mathcal{M}$yers's Peanut Butter

Pass the shelled, roasted peanuts, divested of skins, through the smallest cutter of food-chopper. To each cupful, add 2 tablespoons boiling water, 2 tablespoons olive oil, ¼ teaspoon prepared mustard, and ⅛ teaspoon salt. For sandwiches, add any desired salad dressing.

–Mrs. N. Myers, 916 Kentucky St., Dec. 13, 1929.

Mrs. $\mathcal{R}$obinson's Sour Cream Sandwich Spread

"I find this method fine for using up surplus cream."

One pint green tomatoes measured after being ground and drained, and 4 sweet peppers (2 red and 2 green, ground). Mix ground tomato and peppers, and sprinkle with 1 teaspoon salt. Let stand 5 minutes and drain. Put into kettle with ½ cup of water, and cook until tender (about 30 minutes). More water may be added if necessary. Next, add 6 ground sweet pickles. Keep this boiling hot while making the following dressing: 1 cup sugar, 2 level tablespoons flour, 2 level tablespoons prepared mustard, 3 eggs (well-beaten), ½ cup vinegar, 1 cup sour cream added after the dressing is cooked. Combine and seal while hot. This is delicious and lends itself to many variations. Salad oil may be used in place of part of the cream, or nuts may be added. The tomatoes and peppers can be canned by adding the vinegar, and opened and made into spread as convenient.

–Mrs. E. E. Robinson, 127 E. 19th St., Nov. 9, 1934.

Mrs. *I*ce's Salad Sandwich Rolls

Two cups cold chopped cooked veal, chicken, pork, or flaked white tuna fish; 1 cup diced celery; ½ teaspoon salt; ½ teaspoon sugar; 2 hard-cooked eggs, chopped (save several slices for garnishing); ¼ cup stuffed olives, sliced. To the diced cold meat, add celery, salt, sugar, eggs and olives. Moisten with mayonnaise and chill thoroughly. Cut bread lengthwise of the loaf, having it about one-fourth inch thick. Trim the crusts and place the bread in a damp linen cloth for about an hour so it will roll easily. Spread the bread with soft butter, then with a generous layer of the salad, and roll firmly. Place each roll on a plate and garnish the top with slices of hard-cooked egg, sprigs of parsley and slices of olive, and at the side, place pickles.

–*Mrs. LaVern Ice,* 1308 Oak Hill, Mar. 1, 1935.

Mrs. *F*ey's Hot Oyster Sandwich with Sauce
"For Sunday night supper, there is no nicer dish than hot oyster sandwiches."

The oysters, of medium size, should be crisply fried and left in the wire basket to keep piping hot until the toast is made. Then they should be laid neatly crosswise on toast panels, and a second piece of buttered toast pressed firmly on top. The whole sandwich is then covered with a white celery sauce. This is made by cooking until tender one cup of finely chopped celery in two tablespoons of butter. When the celery is done, one cup of hot milk is added, and the whole is thickened with two tablespoons of flour mixed with water. Each dish may be garnished with cress, and a relish of finely chopped pickled beets should be served.

–*Mrs. A. P. Fey,* 21 Winona St., Nov. 8, 1935.

Mrs. *N*ichols's Green Tomato Sandwich Spread or Dressing

Part No. 1: Grind enough green tomatoes to make one pint after juice has been drained off; add two red peppers and two green peppers, ground with one teaspoon salt. Let stand a few minutes. Add ½ cup water and boil till tender, then set aside. Part No. 2: 3 eggs, well-beaten; 1 cup sugar; ½ cup vinegar; 2 tablespoons prepared mustard; 2 tablespoons flour; 1 cup sour cream. Mix together and stir while cooking to a boil. Cut sweet pickles into small pieces. Add pickles and part No. 1 to part No. 2 and mix lightly. Put into sterilized jars and seal. Makes 3 pints.

–*Mrs. A. C. Nichols,* Route 5, Oct. 30, 1936.

Mrs. *P*ardee's Rolled Chicken Sandwiches

"These sandwiches are especially dainty for parties."

Wrap a fresh loaf of bread in a damp cloth, then in a dry one, and place in the refrigerator for several hours or over night. Trim the crust off the loaf–top, bottom and sides. Have the butter softened so it will spread easily. Put chicken meat, which should be boiled until very tender, and seasoned with salt and pepper, through the food chopper, using a fine knife. Mix to a paste with mayonnaise. Lightly spread the bread lengthwise of the loaf with the soft butter, then with a layer of the chicken paste. Sprinkle with celery salt. Cut the bread in very thin slices, using a sharp knife. Roll carefully. Wrap in damp cloth until ready to use. The rolls may be held in shape with tooth picks. Any other favorite sandwich filling may be used such as walnut-cheese, peanut-date, tuna-celery, peanut butter, jam, or jelly.

–*Mrs. Frank Pardee,* 734 Arkansas St., Mar. 3, 1939.

Mrs. *J*ames's Green Tomato Sandwich Spread

"This is a delicious spread for the school lunch."

One-half pint green tomatoes, ground and drained; ½ pint carrots, ground; 2 green and 2 red peppers, ground. Mix all and sprinkle with salt. Let stand a few minutes; drain and put into kettle with ½ cup of water, and cook until tender. Keep hot until the following dressing has been prepared: ½ cup sugar, 2 tablespoons prepared or ground mustard, ½ cup vinegar, 1 cup sour cream, 3 well-beaten eggs. Let come to a boil, stirring all the time. Pour over tomato mixture, and stir enough to mix. Can while hot.

–*Mrs. J. F. James,* Perry, Oct. 30, 1942.

Mrs. *G*lenn's Valentine Frosted Sandwich Loaf

Remove crusts from a loaf of day-old bread. Cut four lengthwise slices. Place a slice on a platter, spread with mayonnaise, and cover with peeled sliced tomatoes. Spread another slice with mayonnaise, and place with dressing side on tomatoes. Spread the top of this slice with cream cheese, and cover with third slice of bread. Spread it with mayonnaise and cover with lettuce. Spread the fourth slice of bread with mayonnaise and place on the lettuce. Soften three packages of cream cheese with milk, and frost the outside of the loaf. Garnish with parsley. Place in refrigerator an hour before serving. Canned pink tuna fish, salmon or ground lunch ham may be substituted for the tomatoes.

–*Mrs. Viola Glenn,* Lecompton, Jan. 26, 1945.

Mrs. *A*vey's
Squash Butter
*"A delicious spread
with little sugar."*

Six cups squash pulp, 1 cup crushed
pineapple, 3 cups honey (or 3 cups white
syrup and ⅔ cup sugar), 1 teaspoon
salt, 1 teaspoon ground cinnamon, ¼
teaspoon ground cloves.

Cut squash in half, remove seeds,
place halves in oven, shell side up, and
bake at 350 or 400 degrees until you can
pierce the shell with a tooth pick. Scoop
from shell and press through a sieve.
Mix with dry ingredients. Add pineapple
and honey and cook over slow fire (or in oven) until it has a glassy sheen, 15 to 30
minutes over slow fire, or 30 to 40 minutes in oven at 350 degrees. Stir often. Pour
into sterilized jars and seal.

–Mrs. C. O. Avey, 1306 Oak Hill, Nov. 1, 1946.

Mrs. *R*alston's Green Tomato Sandwich Spread
"This is a nice and inexpensive spread."

One pint of green tomatoes when ground; 1 green pepper and one ripe red
pepper, ground. Sprinkle with salt, and let stand 10 minutes. Drain. Put into a
kettle and cook with ½ pint of water until tender. Add 6 chopped sweet pickles.
Keep hot for the following dressing.

Dressing: ½ cup sugar; 2 teaspoons flour or
part cornstarch; 3 teaspoons mustard flour or 2
tablespoons of prepared mustard; ¼ teaspoon
tumeric powder; ½ cup vinegar–diluted a little
if too strong; 2 large or 3 small eggs, beaten
well; ⅓ cup sour cream to be added when
mixture is done. Combine this dressing with
the tomatoes and peppers, and bring to a boil.
Stir often to prevent sticking. Seal in small
jars while hot, and keep in a cool place.

–Mrs. C. E. Ralston, Route 2,
Oct. 15, 1948.

Local Grocery Prices
1934

1 dozen sandwich buns	.12
1 lb. bacon	.15
1 (6 oz.) can tuna fish	.15
1 lb. Longhorn cheese	.17
1 lb. frankfurters	.18
1/2 lb. sliced ham	.25
1/2 lb. Swiss cheese	.38
1 lb. Canadian bacon	.60
Total	$ 2.00

Soups, Stews, and Chili

Farmers Asked To Double Tomato Acreage This Year

Good Profits Assured for Growers If All Conditions Are Favorable

A shortage of canned tomatoes in the United States for the army and for shipment to England is of interest to local farmers. The Columbus Food Cooperation has been asked to double its pack this year. The factory wants 300 acres of tomatoes planted in this community. This will be necessary if the government gets the 15,000,000 cases of tomatoes that it is asking for to be used by British and American soldiers. The normal pack in one year is approximately 20,000,000 cases. Unless production of tomatoes can be doubled in the United States, very few cans will be available for home consumption after the government requirements are filled.

Anyone who is interested in planting tomatoes should get in touch with Will Pendleton at the Columbus Food Corporation immediately for details. [DCR, 5-15-41]

Beef Supply Slim

Indications are that Lawrence housewives will have to serve meals with less beef and veal for the next seven or eight weeks, according to information received this morning by several local markets.

Since the invasion started, local markets report beef has been a scarce article and several stores are practically out of beef. Most markets have an ample supply of pork, fish and lamb. One market owner said this morning he had been in business here for 38 years and he had less meat for his weekend trade than he had had at any one time since he had been in business.

Demand orders from the government during the past few days have taken the better cuts of beef and pork. Another market manager said this morning he had more meat coming tomorrow but no beef was included in the order. [LJW, 6-9-44]

Mrs. *L*ackey's Philadelphia Pepper Pot Soup

To make the pepper pot, wash, scald, drain, and cut in half-inch pieces, one pound of boiled tripe, and place in deep sauce pan with four cups of meat stock, 2 cups of diced raw potatoes, 2 cups diced carrots, and one-half cup of finely chopped onion. Boil 30 minutes and add enough vegetable stock to 8 cups. Add one tablespoon of parsley or celery tops, one tablespoon of sweet marjoram (dried and powdered), and two cups of dumplings. Make dumplings with one cup of flour, one teaspoon baking powder, one quarter teaspoon salt, and enough sweet cold milk to make a smooth dough. Roll out in dumplings, one quarter-inch thick; cut in quarter-inch strips, then crosswise. Boil the soup ten minutes after adding the dumplings. Season with finely chopped green peppers and salt.

–Mrs. Roy B. Lackey, 433 Michigan St., Nov. 5, 1921.

Miss *H*umphrey's Vegetable Soup

Purchase a piece of beef shank weighing about two pounds. Cover the bone with boiling water and boil vigorously for one and one-half hours, adding more water as it evaporates. Then, after skimming off the scum that rises, remove the bone and cut up the meat in small pieces. Return the meat to the kettle, and add two carrots, two medium-sized onions, two small white turnips, one medium-sized parsnip, all washed, pared and cut very fine. Add also 2 tablespoons of minced parsley, one stalk of celery, leaves and all, and one cupful of green beans, cut fine, together with peas from a dozen pods, and one-half cupful of canned tomatoes. Let cook one-half hour. Then add four medium-sized potatoes, cut very fine, five teaspoons of salt, one-eighth teaspoon each of paprika, ground cloves and nutmeg, and one-fourth teaspoon of Worcestershire sauce. Let cook another half-hour. This will serve eight persons generously.

–Miss Cecile Humphrey, Richland, Jan. 26, 1923.

OLD-FASHIONED BEAN SOUP

Dorothy *H*anks's Vegetable Soup
Put your soup bone on to cook, covering it with water. Let cook for one hour, then add one large potato, one medium-sized onion, one medium-sized carrot and two small tomatoes, all chopped fine. Also add two tablespoons of rice, one tablespoon of navy beans, and a small handful of macaroni. Season to taste. Keep the kettle full of water, or just so it covers the meat. Cook till the meat is tender and the added ingredients are cooked. Serve with crisp crackers or toasted bread. A small red pepper may be added to the seasonings.
–Dorothy L. Hanks, 1234 Tennessee St., Mar. 16, 1923.

Mrs. *M*ikesell's Vegetable Soup
One quart or more rich beef stock, 1 small Irish potato, 1 small onion, 1 carrot. Cut into cubes and add ¼ cup finely cut celery, one tablespoon of rice, ½ cup tomato pulp. Add vegetables to the beef stock and cook until about half done, turn fire low and simmer for one hour. Serve with crisp wafers. Season with salt and pepper.
–Mrs. Charles F. Mikesell, Denzer Station, Jan. 25, 1924.

Mrs. *H*arwood's Chili
One pound good fresh hamburger, 2 lbs. brown chili or pinto beans (pintos preferred), 1 medium-sized onion, 1 lb. chili loaf. Carefully pick over beans and remove all pebbles and hulls; wash several times. Put on to cook in plenty of lukewarm water. Warm water gives the beans a chance to swell and expand without scalding the outer hull. When the beans begin to soften, put in a separate cooker the meat and chopped onion in about 1½ quarts of water, and cook until tender. When the beans are well done, add the cooked meat and onion, all salted to taste, then cut up the chili loaf and add to the other ingredients. Plenty of water must be kept on the beans and meat while cooking so that when the two mixtures are poured together there will be plenty of liquor to add to each serving. After the chili loaf has been added, the mixture should not be allowed to boil again, but kept very hot. This amount should make about 1 ½ gallons, and will keep for several days, and warmed over each time. The last serving is as good as the first. The amount may be made smaller by using half the ingredients.
–Mrs. W. T. Harwood, 925 Mississippi St., Dec. 12, 1924.

Mrs. *L*ackey's Vegetable Soup
Two pounds beef with bone, and ½ gallon water. Cook slowly for four hours, then strain stock. Add ½ cup beans; 2 tablespoons finely cut onion; 3 medium-sized potatoes and 2 carrots, cut fine; 1 cup tomatoes; 1 cup finely chopped cabbage. A few minutes before removing from the fire, add a handful of celery leaves.
–Mrs. F. B. Lackey, 1611 Massachusetts St., Feb. 6, 1925.

Mrs. *S*choewe's Potato Soup with Dumplings

Pare and dice finely two medium-sized potatoes and put to cook in a quart of boiling water. Brown one sliced onion in a small pan containing one large tablespoonful of butter. When the potatoes are soft, add this to the soup, then drop in the dumplings and cover tightly and cook until they are well done. Salt and pepper to taste. Dumplings: One whole egg, well-beaten; to this add one tablespoonful of milk or water. If the egg is small, it will take two tablespoons of milk or water. Sift together one level teaspoon baking powder, ¼ teaspoon salt, and ¾ cup of flour. Mix the flour and egg together and stir well. This should not be stiff, but should drop well from the spoon.

–Mrs. W. H. Schoewe, 1631 Illinois St., Feb. 27, 1925.

Miss *T*hompson's Irish Stew

One pound of beef, 1 large carrot, 1 onion, and six potatoes. Cut the beef up fine and cover with cold water. Keep water over the beef, adding more as it boils away. Boil for two hours, then add the carrot, onion and potatoes, cut fine. Season with salt and pepper. Boil until the vegetables are cooked, then thicken with flour and butter. Serves six persons.

–Miss Marion Thompson, Williamstown, Jan. 29, 1926.

Miss *B*rown's Potato Soup

Four potatoes, 1 quart milk, 1 small onion, 1 teaspoon salt, ½ teaspoon celery salt, 2 tablespoons butter, pepper to taste. Wash, pare and cook the potatoes, without salt, until soft. Cook the milk and onion in a double boiler. When the potatoes are cooked and drained, mash them with a wire masher. Add to hot milk and rub the mixture through a sieve. Return the soup to the double boiler and add salt and pepper. Add the butter and cook five minutes. If desired, add one tablespoon of finely chopped parsley. Serve with croutons.

Foods Cooked Electrically Retain All the Health-Giving Vitamins and Minerals—and Taste So Much Better!

–Miss Margaret Brown, West 21ˢᵗ St., Mar. 11, 1927.

LJW, 3-18-39

Heard In Lawrence

Chief of Police Jude Anderson said today that numerous complaints have been coming into the police station concerning chickens running loose in the city. Anderson said that with the coming of spring and the planting of vegetable and flower gardens the police will enforce an ordinance prohibiting the practice. [LJW, 3-12-37]

Mrs. *M*iller's Cream of Potato Soup

Three medium potatoes; ½ onion, sliced; ½ teaspoon salt added to water in which potatoes are cooked; 1 cup potato water; 3 cups milk; 3 tablespoons butter; ⅓ cup flour; 2 teaspoons salt added to soup; ½ teaspoon pepper; ⅛ teaspoon celery salt, if desired; 1 tablespoon chopped parsley, if desired. Cut the washed, peeled potatoes in slices. Put these and the onion to boil, in a tightly covered kettle, in 1¼ cups of boiling, salted water. Cook until very tender. Rub through a sieve, using the potato liquor (this should be now reduced to about one cup) as well as the pulp. Melt the butter. Remove from the fire and stir in the flour and seasonings. Gradually stir in one-half of the milk. Stir and cook until the mixture thickens. Add the potatoes and the remaining milk. Heat over a protected low flame for at least fifteen minutes. This being a starch mixture, it is best to cook very well.

–Mrs. H. H. Miller, 1205 Rhode Island St., Jan. 27, 1928.

Mrs. *C*oker's Chili

Two tablespoons fat, 1 pound round steak (ground), 1 tablespoon flour, 1 can tomatoes, 1 can red kidney beans, 1 teaspoon chili powder, 1 quart of boiling water. Melt the shortening, add meat and cook until well-browned. Add remaining ingredients and boil one and one-half hours. Serves eight.

–Mrs. Paul A. Coker, 1634 Alabama St., Feb. 1, 1929.

Mrs. *P*ower's Chili
"This is splendid."

One pound ground beef, one-third pound of ground suet, two cups of chili beans, one cup tomatoes (cooked or raw), one small onion, chili powder to suit taste, salt. Soak beans overnight and cook until tender. Put suet in frying pan, and when melted, add ground beef, and fry until brown. Run onion and tomatoes through a food chopper, and add all to the beans, with enough chili powder and salt to suit the taste, and boil forty-five minutes. Keep plenty of water in beans, and add sufficient for the soup.

–Mrs. N. P. Power, 1016 Connecticut St., Nov. 22, 1929.

Mrs. *E*berhart's Noodle Soup

One egg, one-half cup flour, and one tablespoon water. Beat the egg well for three minutes, then add the water and beat for two minutes. Mix in the flour, making a very stiff dough. Put dough on bread board and work with a rolling motion until the dough, when cut, shows pores and is very elastic. This takes about thirty minutes.

Roll out into a large thin sheet, then stretch with hands until it is so thin one can almost see through it. Place on the bread board and let dry. When almost dry, fold the sheet of dough several times until the roll is about two inches wide. Then with a sharp knife slice in thin shreds. Drop the noodles into a kettle of meat stock (either beef, chicken or mutton) about 1½ quarts, seasoned to taste, and boiling. Boil for about one-half hour or until the noodles are tender. Sprinkle chopped chives, or parsley, and grated nutmeg on top of each bowl of soup before serving. This amount makes 4 large servings. Noodles, when thoroughly dried, may be kept for a long time in an air-tight container, and are ready for use anytime.

–*Mrs. I. F. Eberhart,* 945 Tennessee St., Jan 3, 1930.

Mrs. *L*efferd's Cream of Potato Soup

Three potatoes, 1 quart milk, 2 slices of onion, 3 tablespoons flour, 1½ teaspoons salt, ¼ teaspoon celery salt, ⅛ teaspoon pepper, 2 tablespoons butter. Cook the potatoes in boiling, salted water. When soft, rub through a sieve. Scald the milk with the onion in a double boiler, remove the onion, unless the family likes it left in; add the salt, celery salt and pepper. Melt the butter in a small sauce pan, stir the flour into it, and then add this mixture to the hot milk, stirring briskly. Cook for ten minutes over boiling water in the double boiler.

–*Mrs. Nannie Lefferd,* 809 New York St., Mar. 7, 1930.

Mrs. *C*allahan's Chili

"I lived in San Antonio, Tex., and learned to make this chili there. It is real Mexican Chili Con Carne."

Take two pounds of beef, cut in small pieces, and put in a frying pan where half a cup of lard has been heated, or fry out suet for this purpose. Sear well on all sides. Have ready two buttons of chopped garlic, salt and pepper to taste, a medium-sized onion chopped fine, and a half can of tomatoes. Add onion and garlic to brown with the meat; then add seasonings, tomatoes, and a small amount of water. Sift about two tablespoons of flour over the meat. Cover and steam over a low fire for about one hour and a half. Watch to keep from sticking, and add water a little at a time when needed. The flour added will thicken the gravy. Leave quite a little gravy to serve with the chili. About the last half hour of cooking, add 2 tablespoons of chili powder. This amount will serve eight people, and half the amount can easily be made. Never grind the meat for real chili. The lower round of beef steak is a very good, and not too expensive, cut.

–*Mrs. Albert B. Callahan,* 1621 Kentucky St., Nov. 21, 1930.

Mrs. *H*ill's Noodle Soup

Sift 2 cups flour, add 1 teaspoon salt. Break 2 eggs into flour and salt. Mix well with a fork. Add enough cream or whole milk to make a stiff dough. Knead, adding a little more flour if necessary. Turn out on a floured board and roll to a very thin sheet. Let dry (but not too dry), turning over often. Cut in strips 5 or 6 inches wide. Place strips on top of each other and roll crosswise. Slice very thin, shaking noodles apart. Spread on board and let dry a few minutes. Add to boiling beef or chicken broth, and boil until tender, about 15 or 20 minutes.

–Mrs. Ray Hill,
1405 New Jersey St., Jan. 30, 1931.

TODAY

Stop at George's Lunch for a piece of that good, home-made pie or a bowl of the best chili you ever ate. We use only the very highest quality of meats in our chili.

George's Lunch
1011 ½ Mass St.

DCR, 3-17-27

Mrs. *M*artin's Chili

One pound hamburger; ¼ lb. suet (ground fine), 1 medium-sized chopped onion, 2 cups chili beans, 1 can tomato soup, about 2 tablespoons chili powder, salt to taste. Cook beans until tender. Fry suet, hamburger and onions until hamburger turns white. Add tomato soup and chili powder. Simmer 30 minutes, adding a little water if necessary. Mix with beans and serve hot with crackers.

–Mrs. Frank O. Martin, Route 6, Jan. 8, 1932.

Mrs. *K*irchhoff's Vegetable Soup

"This has been used in the family for years, and many people have said it made the finest soup they had ever eaten."

Use a large soup bone or a piece of soup meat, one to two pounds. Put in a large kettle and cover with cold water. Add a tablespoon of salt, and allow this to cook slowly. After it has come to a boil, skim well. Add ½ cup of rice, ½ cup of barley, and 2 or 3 bay leaves. Grind through the coarse grinder 4 or 5 medium-sized carrots, and about the same amount of potatoes, 3 medium-sized onions, ¼ head of cabbage, the outside and top of a stalk of celery, a handful of parsley. As this boils down, add more water to make soup the right consistency. About one-half hour before serving, add one quart can of tomatoes, and a fourth of a package of noodles. Add more salt and pepper to taste. This recipe, served with crackers and celery, makes two complete delicious meals for a family of six.

–Mrs. George Kirchhoff, Jr., [address unavailable], Mar. 4, 1932.

Mrs. *J*ngham's Chili

Two cupfuls chili beans, 1 lb. beef hamburger, 2 tablespoonfuls salt, 3 cupfuls cooked tomatoes, 3 small onions, 1 tablespoon chili powder, 4 cupfuls hot water. Soak beans over night in cold water. In the morning, drain and cover with fresh water. Cook slowly for one-half hour and then drain and cover with freshly boiling water. Cook slowly until tender. Fry hamburger and onion, sprinkled with chili powder, for five minutes. Turn into a kettle, add tomatoes, salt and hot water. Cook this mixture about two hours, and then add beans with the liquid in which they were cooked. Cook this combined mixture very slowly for about an hour. This recipe will serve eight.

–Mrs. H. G. Ingham, 1714 Illinois St., Feb. 17, 1933.

Mrs. *D*ollnig's Potato Soup

Pare and slice thinly six medium-sized potatoes. Chop finely one medium-sized onion and four stalks of celery. Keep vegetables just covered with water, and cook slowly until tender. Add one quart whole milk (skim milk may be used), and two tablespoonfuls of butter. Season with salt and pepper, and serve with crackers. Serve cheese with the crackers if you desire, and have a more complete meal.

–Mrs. W. W. Dollnig, Route 1, Eudora, Jan. 18, 1935.

Mrs. *L*a Mont's Cream of Corn Soup St. Germain

Chop canned corn as fine as possible and press that to be used for the timbales through a sieve. Cook what is left in the sieve with the rest of the corn for the liquid part of the soup. To ⅓ cup of the corn puree, add 1 egg and the yolk of another, beaten without separating the white and yolks; ¼ teaspoon each of salt and black pepper; and ½ cup of thin cream or rich milk. Mix thoroughly and turn into four buttered timbale molds. Set to cook on several folds of paper in a dish of boiling water. Cook in the oven and do not allow the water to boil. When firm, and the soup is ready, serve an unmolded timbale in each plate of soup. To make the soup, cook half of an onion, sliced fine, and two branches of parsley, in 2 tablespoons of vegetable oil or butter until softened and yellowed. Add the rest of a pint of corn and a pint of boiling water or broth, and let simmer 20 minutes. Press through a fine sieve. Melt 2 tablespoons of butter; in it cook 2 tablespoons of flour and ½ tablespoon salt. Add 2 cups of milk and stir until boiling; add the corn and broth with ¼ cup cream, and serve hot.

–Mrs. Ethel La Mont,
1321 Tennessee St.,
May 10, 1935.

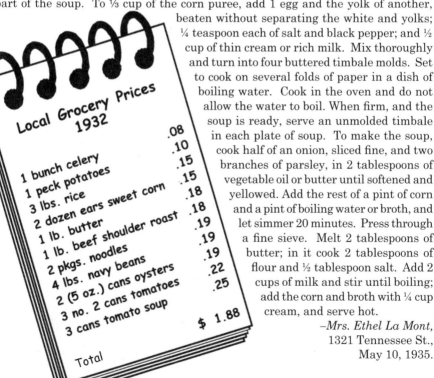

Local Grocery Prices
1932

1 bunch celery	.08
1 peck potatoes	.10
3 lbs. rice	.15
2 dozen ears sweet corn	.15
1 lb. butter	.18
1 lb. beef shoulder roast	.18
2 pkgs. noodles	.19
4 lbs. navy beans	.19
2 (5 oz.) cans oysters	.19
3 no. 2 cans tomatoes	.22
3 cans tomato soup	.25
Total	$ 1.88

Heard In Lawrence

Three local lads picked the wrong car yesterday evening to use as a target for throwing potatoes and as a result the trio appeared in County Attorney John Riling's office this morning for a lecture.

Sheriff Rody Skinner had a complaint three lads in the vicinity of Indian Village, north of Lawrence, were throwing potatoes at passing motorists. He at once drove to the scene and when he arrived one of the lads cut loose with a potato striking the side of the sheriff's car. The officer jumped out of the car. The boys ran, but Skinner soon had three boys in custody and told the lads to appear at Riling's office this morning at 9 o'clock. [LJW, 7-28-45]

Mrs. *T*eich's Lentil Soup
"This soup is very nourishing and good for a cold day."

Soak ½ package lentils over night. Next morning, add 2 good-sized onions and 2 potatoes, cut up in cubes; paprika, salt and pepper to taste. Then add ½ lb. smoked sausage or smoked ham, and enough water to cover all. Simmer 2 hours. Smoked sausage gives the soup the best flavor.

–*Mrs. Pauline Teich,* 505 Ohio St., Feb. 21, 1936.

Mrs. *V*iets's Vegetable Chowder

One teaspoon granulated sugar; ¼ cup butter; 1 cup thinly sliced carrots; 1 large onion, chopped fine; ¼ cup diced celery; ¼ cup spaghetti, inch lengths; 1 small bay leaf; 1 quart boiling water; 6 cups soup stock; 1 cup canned tomatoes; 1½ cups cooked (or canned) kidney beans; salt and pepper to taste; croutons. Melt the sugar in a soup kettle, and when golden brown, add the butter. Put in the carrots, onion, celery, spaghetti and bay leaf. Pour in the boiling water; cover and simmer until the celery is tender–about forty minutes. Then remove the bay leaf, and add the soup stock and tomato. Stir in the beans and boil fifteen minutes to blend the flavors. Season to taste with salt and pepper, and serve in bowls with a garnish of croutons.

–*Mrs. I. D. Viets,* 716 Arkansas St., Apr. 17, 1936.

Mrs. *D*enny's Vegetable Soup

One soup bone, 1 cup diced celery, 1 cup shredded carrots, 1 cup green peas, ½ teaspoon pepper, 1 cup tomatoes, ½ cup shredded pimiento or pepper, 6 cups water, 1 tablespoon salt, macaroni rings. Prepare vegetables. Place in thrift cooker, kettle or steam cooker kettle with soup bone. Add seasonings and water. Cover. Cook over low heat 8 to 10 hours. The last hour remove soup bone, add macaroni, and cook 20 minutes.

–*Mrs. Ed Denny,* 709 Mississippi St., Feb. 10, 1939.

Mrs. *G*regory's Beef Stew

Two and one-half lbs. beef plate or brisket; 3 quarts cold water; 1 tablespoon salt; ¼ teaspoon pepper; a few dried onion peels; ¼ cup each onion, carrot and celery, diced; ½ cup tomatoes, raw or stewed; 1 teaspoon chopped parsley; 1 tablespoon of chopped green or red pepper. Wipe and salt meat; place in soup kettle and let stand one hour. Add the cold water and let stand ½ hour longer. Place on stove and let come to boiling point. If clear soup is desired, skim now. This scum contains the chief nutritive value of the soup. If allowed to remain, a large part of it will pass through the strainer. Let soup simmer 3 hours or longer, then add the vegetables. Cook one hour longer, adding more hot water if too much has evaporated. Strain, cool, skim off the fat, add seasonings, reheat, and just before serving, add the parsley. If the meat is to be served at the table, remove from soup as soon as tender, and serve with any well-seasoned sauce. Horseradish sauce, made by mixing ¼ cup prepared horseradish with 1 cup mayonnaise, is excellent.

–Mrs. Howard Gregory, Route 1, Jan. 5, 1940.

Mrs. *P*rice's Potato Soup

Three large potatoes, diced; 1 large onion, minced fine; 3 cups milk, or more, as desired; salt, pepper, and celery salt to taste; 1 egg white, beaten stiff; 1 tablespoon butter. Boil potatoes and onions in small amount of water. When potatoes are soft, mash fine and add seasonings, butter and milk. Heat to desired temperature, and just before serving, fold in the beaten egg white. If desired, the egg white may be omitted, and diced green pepper may be added to each bowl of the soup.

–Mrs. William Price,
1305 Kentucky St., Jan. 17, 1941.

Mrs. *H*unsinger's Irish Stew

Two and one-half lbs. good beef with some fat. Dice, cover with water, salt and pepper to suit taste. Boil 1½ hours, then add 4 carrots, diced; 4 potatoes, diced; 2 onions, diced; 1 cup tomatoes; ½ teaspoon celery seed; 2 cups shredded cabbage; 1 turnip, diced. Simmer until vegetables are tender. Add water so there will be broth to cover vegetables. When done, just before serving, add 1 cup canned corn. Serve with crackers. Serves 6 or 8.

–Mrs. Lucy Hunsinger,
1132 New York St.,
Jan. 31, 1941.

Miss $\mathcal{S}$tocks's Grandmother's Soup
"This soup is really a meal in one."

Use one shank bone, and have the butcher crack it so you will get the full flavor of the marrow. Wash and dry the bone, and put it in the kettle of cold water, which will slightly more than cover it. Take onions, potatoes, carrots, and celery in equal proportions, and one parsnip. Wash and peel and chop them together; add one cup of shredded cabbage. After the bone has been simmering for about 1 hour, add the above vegetables, together with one cup of barley, a sprig of parsley, salt and pepper to taste. Simmer for one hour. Add water when necessary. The meat should fall from the bone when done. Serves 6.

–Miss Ruth Stocks, Atlanta, Ga., Jan. 2, 1942.

Mrs. $\mathcal{C}$omfort's Vegetable Soup

Three to four pound soup bone or shin of beef; 2 quarts of water; 1 small onion, quartered; 1 teaspoon salt; 2 cups tomatoes; 6 sprigs parsley; ¼ head young cabbage, chopped; ¼ cup rice or barley; 5 or 6 carrots, sliced; 2 cups green beans; 1 cup diced potatoes; ½ cup chopped celery. Cut half the meat from bone and brown in fat. Add remaining meat and bone to cold water, and allow to stand 30 minutes. Add browned meat, onion and salt. Bring to boiling and simmer 2 hours. Add vegetables and continue simmering 1 hour. If canned green beans are used, add last 15 minutes. Serves 8 to 10.

–Mrs. Winifred Comfort, 741 New York St., Jan. 8, 1943.

Mrs. $\mathcal{O}$'Brien's Limas and Lamb Stew
"This is a wholesome, satisfying one-dish meal.
Add a green salad and dessert and you have a complete dinner."

Two pounds lamb stew meat, cut up (breast of lamb is very good). Sift a little flour over meat, then brown well, preferably in bacon fat. Put meat, one slice onion, and one cup dried limas into a sauce pan with 1 cup canned tomatoes and water to cover well. Cook slowly three hours–or until beans are cooked, adding water as needed. Add 1 cup canned corn. Season to taste, and cook half an hour.

–Mrs. F. P. O'Brien,
612 Louisiana St.,
Jan. 22, 1943.

LJW, 3-12-26

Mrs. *F*rost's Potato Noodle Soup

"This may be used as a one-dish meal."

Cube six medium-sized potatoes, and mince one medium-sized onion. Cook in salted water until potatoes will mash easily with a fork or masher. Add water until there is about three pints of the potato liquid. Make noodles using one egg, and instead of cutting noodles in strips, pinch off small amounts of the dough and drop into the boiling potato liquid. Cook 15 minutes, and add one quart of milk and two tablespoons butter. Serve immediately with crackers.

–*Mrs. Robert M. Frost,* 313 N. 2nd St., Feb. 5, 1943.

Mrs. *G*ephart's Vegetable Soup

Have a hind quarter soup bone cut into three parts so marrow will cook out. Put the meat and bones into kettle covered with cold water. Bring to hard boil, then turn down heat and simmer about three hours. Remove meat and bones from broth. Add the vegetables, all chopped: 2 cups potatoes, 2 cups carrots, 2 cups cabbage, 1 cup tomatoes, 1 cup dry noodles, ½ cup onions, ½ cup celery. Put salt and pepper in with the meat–and taste and add more salt and pepper to taste. While the vegetables are cooking, cut off enough meat from the bone to make two cups, chopped, and add to vegetables. If some green beans, peas or corn are left over, add them to the soup. And then, what meat is left may be put into meat grinder and used in browned hash for another meal. This is just a suggestion.

–*Mrs. Louise H. Gephart,* Lawrence Memorial Hospital, Jan. 21, 1944.

Mrs. *R*oper's Potato Soup

Wash, pare and slice thin four medium-sized potatoes. Chop fine 2 small white onions and about four pieces (or a fourth) of a stalk of celery. Cook celery, while preparing potatoes and onions, in a small amount of water in heavy kettle. Add potatoes and onions, and cook slowly until tender and rather soft, in enough water to cover them well. Season with salt and pepper, and add about one quart whole milk when the potatoes are done. Add one large spoonful of butter or butter substitute or fresh bacon drippings, and allow to simmer for a minute or two. This will serve four people, and is delicious with crackers or toast and crisp bacon slices.

–*Mrs. Laura L. Roper,* 913 Vermont St., Feb. 18, 1944.

Mrs. *P*fleger's Navy Bean Soup
"Keep a supply on hand to use in an emergency when unexpected guests come in. It makes a delicious meal."

Soak 1 lb. navy beans overnight. The next morning, put beans on to boil with 3 quarts of water, ¼ lb. lean bacon, 1 small onion stuck with 2 cloves, 1 carrot (cut into thin strips), and 2 stalks of celery (cut fine). Cook slowly until the beans are tender. I usually cook my soups at a simmering temperature for 6 hours or longer. The soup may be served this way, or if preferred, it may be strained through a sieve, forcing through as much of the vegetables as possible. Thicken the soup with 2 tablespoons of flour and 2 tablespoons of butter, which have been mixed together. Season to taste with salt and pepper. This may be kept in a cool place for several days during the winter.

–Mrs. Hanna Pfleger, Linwood, Dec. 29, 1944.

Mrs. *A*vey's Quick Vegetable Soup

Put 1 lb. of hamburger into a large stew pan with 1 quart of cold water. Add salt to season, and cook until meat is done, about 30 minutes. Crumble the meat as it cooks by tearing apart with a fork. While meat cooks, place in another kettle 4 medium-sized potatoes, diced; 1 cup carrots, diced; and 1 medium-sized onion, chopped. Season with salt and pepper. Cook until tender. When meat is done, add the potatoes, onions, carrots, 1 pint cooked tomatoes (chopped, or tomato juice); 1 cup chopped celery, and any other small amounts of cooked vegetables you may have on hand–such as ½ cup peas, ½ cup corn or navy beans. Cook all together about 10 minutes and serve. Dried celery leaves may be substituted for the celery. Serve with crisp toasted crackers. Serves 4.

–Mrs. C. O. Avey,
1306 Oak Hill Ave.,
Jan. 12, 1945.

1929 Colonial Range

Mrs. *M*iller's Vegetable Soup

Cook 1 cup of beans until tender. Then add several potatoes, 2 large onions and a stalk of celery, all sliced very thin; ¼ cup of rice, previously cooked; and a couple of slices of salt pork, chopped fine. Season with salt and pepper. Cover and cook 1 hour. Have some bread in the oven browning while the soup is cooking. When the soup is ready to serve, butter the brown bread and pour the soup over, while hot.

–Mrs. G. E. Miller, Route 1, Mar. 2, 1945.

Mrs. *O*tt's Cream of Potato Soup

One medium onion, finely chopped; 2 tablespoons butter or other fat; ½ cup finely cut dry bread crumbs; 1 quart chicken or meat broth; dash of pepper; 1 teaspoon salt; 2 cups finely cut raw potatoes; 1 cup whole or evaporated milk. Cook chopped onion in the butter for five minutes, but do not brown. Add crumbs, broth, pepper, salt and potatoes. Simmer until potatoes are tender, about 20 minutes. Add milk and reheat before serving. If broth is not available, dissolve three bouillon cubes in 1 quart boiling water and use as directed.

–Mrs. Edwin Ott, Eudora, Nov. 30, 1945.

Mrs. *S*eiwald's Oyster Bisque

One-half pint oysters, 2 cups milk, 1 cup water, 1 slice onion, 1 stalk celery (diced), 3 sprigs parsley, ½ teaspoon mace, 2 tablespoons butter, 2 tablespoons flour, 1 teaspoon salt, ⅛ teaspoon pepper, small piece bay leaf. Chop oysters, add water, and simmer about 10 minutes. Scald milk with seasonings. Add oysters and strain, rubbing oysters through a sieve. Melt butter; add flour and blend. Add strained oysters; season and cook until smooth.

Tasty Crackers: Spread crackers generously with creamed cheese, to which minced parsley and Worcestershire sauce have been added. Brown lightly in the broiler. Serve hot with the oyster bisque.

–Mrs. E. E. Seiwald, 431 Perry St., Jan. 4, 1946.

Mrs. *L*eonard's Beef Stew

Aitchbone (beef hipbone), weighing 5 lbs.; 4 cups potatoes, cut in ¼-inch slices; turnips and carrots, ⅔ cup each, cut in ½-inch cubes; ½ small onion, cut in thin slices; ¼ cup flour; salt and pepper. Wipe meat, remove from bone, cut into 1½-inch cubes, sprinkle with salt and pepper, and dredge with flour. Cut some of the fat into small pieces and fry out in frying pan. Add meat and stir constantly; when well-browned, remove to kettle. Cover with boiling water and cook until meat is tender. Add vegetables so they can cook about ½ hour. Thicken with ¼ cup flour mixed with ¼ cup cold water. Cook 5 minutes.

–Mrs. Clem Leonard, 828 E. 14ᵗʰ St., Jan. 10, 1947.

Mrs. *L*onnecker's Stew

Place a three pound soup bone in a large kettle, cover with cold water and cook slowly until the meat on the bone is tender. You should have about two quarts of stock after the bone has been removed from the kettle. To this stock add 1 small can of tomato puree or the contents of one No. 2 can of tomatoes, which has been run through a sieve; 1 cup of cream style corn; 2 cups finely shredded cabbage; 2 cups of raw diced potatoes; 2 cups of finely cut carrots; 2 large onions, cut up fine; and 1 cup of finely cut raw turnips may be added for those who like them. Cook this mixture until the vegetables are tender. Add 2 tablespoons Worcestershire sauce, 1 tablespoon salt, 1 teaspoon pepper. Cut the meat from the bone in fine pieces and add to the stew. For variation, a cup of cooked rice may be added.

If one cannot find a soup bone, a good substitute is 2 pounds of stew meat and one half pound of suet. Cook this as you would the soup bone. This stew may be warmed up and used for several meals as slow cooking only adds to its tastiness. Will serve eight.

–Mrs. Alta Lonnecker, 1104 New Hampshire St., Mar. 21, 1947.

Mrs. *B*arnes's Potato Soup

Two cups cubed potatoes, 2 cups water, 1 small onion, 2 tablespoons butter, 1 teaspoon salt, 2 cups milk, 2 stalks celery, sprig of parsley. Wash vegetables. Pare potatoes, onions and celery. Cook in water with parsley until tender. Add milk, butter and salt. Heat over slow fire, until hot, 2 hours. Amount makes six servings.

–Mrs. Cora L. Barnes, 733 Walnut St., Nov. 28, 1947.

Mrs. *M*cConnell's Cream of Onion and Potato Soup

Three cups scalded milk, 1 cup potato water, 2 tablespoons flour, 2 tablespoons butter, 4 medium potatoes, 4 onions, 1 tablespoon chopped parsley, salt and pepper. Boil the potatoes and onions together until tender. Drain. Save the water, and rub the vegetables through a coarse strainer. Make a white sauce of the liquid, flour, and fat, and combine with the potatoes and onion pulp. Season with chopped parsley, salt and pepper.

–Mrs. Don McConnell, 744 New Hampshire St., Jan. 2, 1948.

Mrs. *G*orrill's Chili Con Carne

One pound hamburger, ½ cup ground suet, 2½ cups cooked kidney beans, 2 cups cooked tomatoes, 1 cup water, 1 clove garlic or ¼ teaspoon garlic salt, ¼ cup chopped onion, chili powder and salt. Brown meat in suet. Add onion. Cook until brown. Add beans, garlic, water and tomatoes. Season to taste with salt and chili powder. Simmer until the flavors are well-blended. This makes eight servings.

–Mrs. Galen Gorrill, 2109 Vermont St., Feb. 6, 1948.

LJW, 1930

Miss *S*chopper's Potato Soup

Four large potatoes, 2 medium onions, 1 quart of water, pepper and salt, ¼ teaspoon of celery seed, 1 tablespoon of butter, 1 tablespoon of flour, 1 quart of milk.

Peel the potatoes and onions and cut into small pieces. Add to the water and cook slowly until tender. Add seasonings and butter. Heat again and add the flour mixed to a paste with the milk. Serves six.

–Miss Frances Schopper, 1246 New Hampshire St., Jan. 14, 1949.

Mrs. *K*line's Vegetable Soup

The ideal vegetable soup must be made with a shank bone. One shank bone, cracked, and placed in a good- sized kettle of cold water–enough to cover it completely, and then some. Let it simmer. Now prepare your vegetables according to the size of your family. Have about 4 quarts of water, as this boils away. I add more hot water to keep the amount about the same. I take onions, potatoes, carrots, celery, in reasonable proportions, not stinting on onions, and one parsnip, about a quart of this mixture, and 1 cup of shredded cabbage. An hour and a half or two hours before dinner time, I put the vegetables into the kettle with a cup of washed barley. Season with salt and pepper, boil slowly until the vegetables are done, and the meat falls from the bone, adding water as necessary.

–Mrs. William V. Kline, Linwood, Jan. 28, 1949.

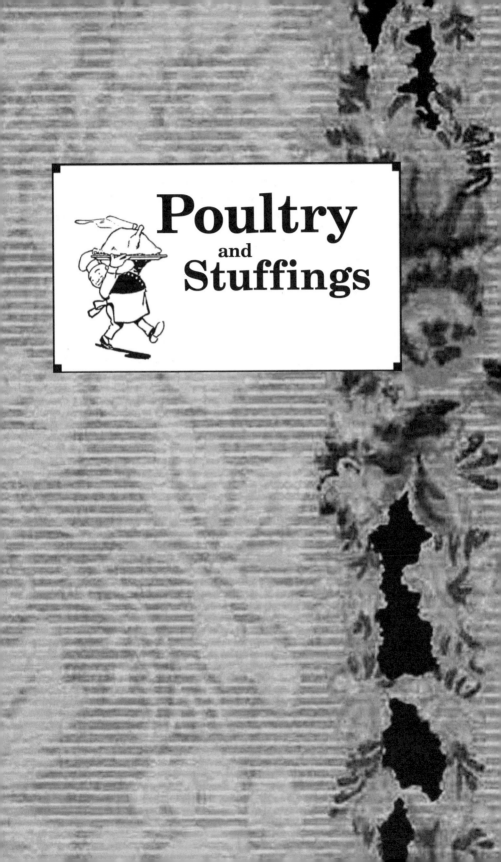

Poultry
and
Stuffings

Novel Scheme To Lure Ducks
To Tonganoxie

The continued dry weather has caused most of the sloughs and ponds in this section to go dry, but one group of enterprising duck hunters at Tonganoxie has evolved a novel scheme to insure water for the fall shooting.

A pond near Tonganoxie is used by this group, and although it has gone dry, water will be pumped into it in time for the duck season. The pond is some 1,000 yards from Big Stranger creek, and by means of a centrifugal pump and some water pipe, the pond will be flooded.

It is possible that because of the dry condition of the soil the water pumped from the creek will only slack the pond bottom, in which event the hunters believe it will hold rains if they are forthcoming.

Slouths in the vicinity of Lawrence are all dry, but the local nimrods hope that sufficient rain will fall before September 16 to insure shooting on the opening day. [LJW, 8-14-30]

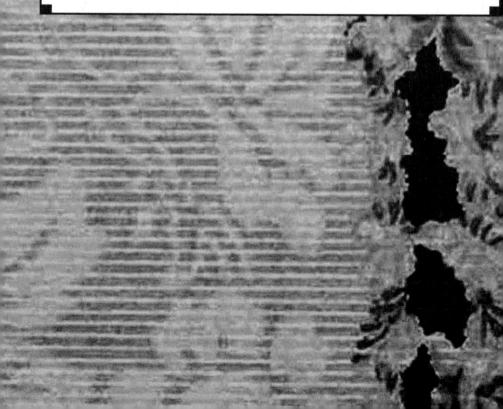

Ellen *L*ackey's Turkey Croquettes

Mix one and one-half cups (or desired amount) of minced turkey or chicken with one cup of very thick and highly-seasoned cream sauce. Use salt, pepper, celery salt, a scrap of onion, and a dash of cayenne. Spread on a shallow plate; let get cold and mold into croquettes. Dip each into crumbs, then into seasoned egg to which two tablespoons of cold water have been added, and fry in very deep, hot fat. Surround with little ducks molded from seasoned mashed potatoes to which an egg has been added. Brush the tops of the ducks with a little egg reserved for the purpose, and then brown slightly in a hot oven; or surround with a border of peas and diced carrots.

–Ellen Lackey, 838 Illinois St., Dec. 16, 1921.

Mrs. *S*haw's Roasted Capon

Dress and wash capon inside and out with cold water. Fill inside with dressing. Turn wings across back so that pinions touch. Tie firmly, leaving several inches twine. Press legs to body. Run needles through thigh, body, and second thigh. Return, going round bone in same way; tie. Run needle through ends of legs; return, passing needle through (if opening is large) and making one or two stitches to close. Rub all over with soft butter and sprinkle with salt and pepper. Place on rack in roaster and put into very hot oven. Make basting mixture with ½ cup each of butter and water; keep hot and baste every 10 or 15 minutes. Roast 3 hours for 8 pound capon. If bird is very large and heavy, cover breast and legs with several thicknesses of white paper to keep from burning. Dressing: 2 cups stale bread, 1 tablespoon fine cut onion, 1 tablespoon butter, 1 tablespoon finely cut parsley, ½ tablespoon salt, ⅛ teaspoon pepper, ¼ teaspoon paprika, sage if liked.

–Mrs. Ed Shaw, Route 1, Nov. 11, 1922.

Mrs. *K*rum's Oyster Stuffing

One pint oysters, 1 loaf stale bread (baker's bread is the best), 4 tablespoons melted butter (or fat from the fowl), 3 eggs, 1 tablespoon each of salt and pepper. Cut the loaf into small squares, and pour enough milk over the bread to moisten well. Add the eggs, beaten light, and the seasonings. A few celery leaves may be added if desired. Mix well together and put in a spoonful or two of stuffing, then 2 or 3 oysters, being careful not to break them. Continue adding stuffing and oysters till the fowl is filled. If more than enough, put balance in a small baking dish and bake in oven, adding a little grease from fowl, or butter, on top of dressing.

–Mrs. Jessie J. Krum, 432 Elm St., Dec. 9, 1922.

Mrs. *R*oper's Chestnut Dressing

Two cups chestnuts, 1 teaspoon salt, ¼ cup butter, pepper, 1 tablespoon minced onion, ½ cup milk, 2 cups stale bread crumbs, 2 tablespoons minced celery or lettuce leaves. Shell and blanch the chestnuts, then cook in boiling salted water until soft. Drain and mash them. Melt the butter and mix with the bread crumbs. Add the other ingredients and mix well.

–Mrs. E. W. Roper, [address unavailable], Nov. 16, 1923.

Miss *S*palsbury's Hot Tamales

Stew a chicken until very tender in just enough water to cover. Salt when half done. Remove meat from bones and chop fine. Remove and discard seeds from one dozen red chili peppers. Boil until tender, and scrape skin with a knife. Add chili to chicken. Moisten with chicken broth. Season with 1 teaspoon onion juice, and let simmer a few minutes. Stir enough hot chicken broth into three cups of corn meal to moisten. Let stand 15 minutes. Wash corn husks and dry with a towel. (Dry husks, steamed until pliable, may be used in place of fresh husks.) Use three husks for each tamale. Spread thin layer of cornmeal in center of each husk. On one of them place a tablespoon of chicken. Cover with other two husks arranged so the chicken is covered by corn meal and all by the husks. Fold back the ends of the husk and tie with strips of husks. Steam one hour and serve very hot. Beef or veal may be substituted for chicken.

–Miss Margaret Spalsbury, 721 Mississippi St., Nov. 14, 1924.

Mrs. Henry's Dressing for the Thanksgiving Fowl

One loaf of stale bread, sliced and dried, or toasted in the oven. Break in small pieces in shallow crock or pan. Add enough cold water to soften. After a few minutes, spread on this 1 ½ cups of finely broken crackers; next, 2 cups of finely cut and plentifully salted and peppered celery. (I use the small stems and some of the leaves culled from the table stalks.) Next, 1 pint of oysters, salted and peppered. Pour on top of all ¼ lb. of melted butter. Mix well with spoon. This is enough for 1 medium-sized turkey or two chickens. If fowl is lean, a little more butter can be used. If fowl is very fat, the butter can be omitted. For geese or ducks, use a small minced onion instead of the oysters.

–Mrs. J. M. Henry, 913 Tennessee St., Nov. 20, 1925.

Miss Brown's Heart Chicken Canapes

Cut bread a quarter of an inch thick, then form into hearts with a cooky cutter, and brown on both sides in butter. Cut cooked chicken into small dice and beat in a rich cream sauce, adding, if desired, a few canned mushrooms cut in pieces. Arrange the chicken on the hearts of fried bread, and place small hearts, cut from canned pimiento, in the center of each. As a final touch before serving, garnish the plates with parsley.

–Miss Ruth Brown, Route 10, Feb. 12, 1926.

Mrs. Keiffer's Stuffed Peppers

Six green peppers, 1 cup diced cold chicken, 1 medium-sized onion, 1 teaspoon of salt, ⅛ teaspoon pepper, ½ cup bread crumbs, 1 teaspoon melted butter, ½ cup milk. Halve the peppers lengthwise and remove seed and pith, and parboil about ten minutes. Drain and lay in a shallow buttered baking dish. Stuff with the filling, mixed in the order given above. Sprinkle each half with buttered bread crumbs. Bake twenty minutes, basting frequently with hot water. English walnuts, or any left over meats, can be substituted for the chicken.

–Mrs. F. H. Keiffer, 1300 ½ New York St., Sept. 3, 1926.

Mrs. Ulrich's Next-Day Christmas Turkey

Put carcass of turkey and all scraps, including left-over dressing, in roaster where turkey was baked. Add about one quart water, ¼ teaspoon salt. Cover closely and boil 20 minutes. Remove bones. If not much dressing is used, add ½ cup cream or rich milk in which 2 level tablespoons of flour has been blended. Put covered roaster in hot oven, and when mixture becomes very hot, drop the following dumplings, by small spoonfuls, on top without removing from oven. Bake 10 minutes uncovered, then 5 minutes covered so sauce will boil over the dumplings. Serve at once.

Dumplings: 1 cup flour, 2 level teaspoons baking powder, ⅛ teaspoon salt, 1 egg, 2 tablespoons milk. Sift flour, baking powder and salt together. Add to well-beaten egg and milk.

–Mrs. Robert Ulrich, Route 4, Dec. 24, 1926.

Mrs. Mueller's Chicken Pie

Cut up chicken–a year old is best–and place in enough hot water to cover. As water boils away, add more so as to have enough for the pie and for gravy to serve with it. Boil until tender. Line the sides of a pan with a rich baking powder or a soda biscuit dough. Put in part of the chicken, season with salt, pepper and butter. Lay in a few thin strips or squares of dough; add the rest of the chicken, and season as before. Some add a few new potatoes in their season. Season the liquid, in which the chicken was boiled, with butter, salt and pepper; add a part of it to the pie. Cover with crust with a hole in the center the size of a teacup. Keep adding the chicken liquid as needed, since the fault of some chicken pies is that they are too dry. There scarcely can be too much good, rich gravy. Bake one hour in moderate oven. Instead of baking chicken pie in crust, some prefer to roll and cut the dough into biscuits, then cover the top of the pie with biscuits–otherwise using the same process.

–Mrs. Lillie Mueller, 1140 New Jersey St., Dec. 31, 1926.

Mrs. Brown's Dressing for Thanksgiving Turkey

One loaf of stale bread, 1½ cups of fine broken crackers, 2 cups of finely cut celery, 1 pint of fresh oysters, ¼ lb. of butter. Have bread thoroughly dried, or better if toasted, and break into small pieces in pan or crock. Moisten until soft with cold water, and spread over this 1½ cups of finely broken crackers. To this add 2 cups of finely cut celery, 1 pint of fresh oysters, ¼ lb. of melted butter, and salt and pepper to suit taste. Mix thoroughly. For those not liking oysters, finely minced onion or sage may be used. This makes enough dressing for 1 turkey or 2 chickens.

–Mrs. Ella Brown, 1024 Pennsylvania St., Nov. 18, 1927.

Mrs. *H*arris's Turkey in Baskets

To 3 cups hot mashed potatoes add 3 tablespoons butter, one teaspoon salt, yolks of 3 eggs (slightly beaten), and enough milk to moisten. Shape in form of small baskets, using a pastry bag and tube. Brush over with white of egg, slightly beaten, and brown in oven. Fill with creamed turkey. Use parsley to form handles for baskets.

Creamed Turkey: 2 cups cold cooked turkey, cut in dice; 2 cups white sauce; ⅛ teaspoon celery salt. Heat turkey dice in sauce to which celery salt has been added.

White Sauce: 2 tablespoons butter, 3 tablespoons flour, 1 cup milk, ¼ teaspoon salt, few grains of pepper. Put butter in saucepan and stir until melted and bubbling. Add flour mixed with seasonings, and stir until blended; then pour on gradually, stirring constantly, the milk. Bring to a boiling point and boil 2 minutes. (If wire whisk is used, all milk may be added at once.)

–Mrs. J. F. Harris, 1108 Kentucky St., Dec. 23, 1927.

Mrs. *C*arter's Chicken Loaf

Four cups cold boiled chicken; 2 cups cracker crumbs; ½ cup celery; 2 eggs, well-beaten; lump of butter, size of walnut; salt and pepper to taste. Take enough of stock from cooked chicken to moisten the above mixture, and roll into loaf. Place in buttered loaf pan and bake three-quarters of an hour in moderate oven.

–Mrs. M. V. Carter, 841 Massachusetts St., Jan. 24, 1930.

Mrs. *W*atts's Chicken Pie

Cover chicken with cold water; simmer gently until two-thirds done, then salt to taste. Cook until it falls from bones. Then remove the large bones and lay the chicken in the bottom of a baking dish. Then prepare a sauce. Three tablespoons of butter, melted; three tablespoons flour; a little pepper. Mix well. To this add 5 cups of warm broth and one cup of cream or milk. Let this cook, and pour over chicken in baking dish. Reserve some for gravy. Keep this warm while you prepare crust.

For crust: 2 cups of flour, 2 scant teaspoons baking powder, ½ teaspoon salt, 2 tablespoons shortening (rubbed into the flour), 1 egg, 1 cup milk. Stir into a batter; lay over chicken and bake.

–Mrs. H. G. Watts, 1726 Kentucky St., Dec. 5, 1930.

Chicken Dinner
Complete 3-Course Dinner
Served Every Sunday.
Also Daily Meals.
TERRACE TEA ROOM
1316 Ohio
LJW, 9-3-37
Phone 547

Mrs. *W*illert's Procedure for Cooking Guinea Fowl

After guinea has been dressed, boil till partly tender, then place in roasting pan and fill with stuffing. Season with salt and pepper, dot with bits of butter, and place in moderate oven. Bake till tender and brown, about 1 hour, according to size.

Stuffing for guinea: 4 cups bread crumbs (using part corn bread or whole wheat bread), 1 teaspoon salt, ¼ teaspoon of pepper, 1 egg (slightly beaten), ½ teaspoon of poultry seasoning or onion, 2 tablespoons melted butter, 2 cups of the broth the guinea was boiled in, and a little sweet milk (saving the remainder of broth for the gravy). Serve with cranberry sauce. Young guinea is good fried in the same manner as chicken.

–Mrs. Mary D. Willert, 932 Mississippi St., Oct. 16, 1931.

Mrs. *S*uiter's Dressing for the Thanksgiving Fowl

Use three cups of grated white bread crumbs, one teaspoonful of grated onion, one-half cup of melted butter, one-half cup of finely chopped green pepper (sweet), one cup of chopped celery, one pint of well-washed and drained oysters, and salt and pepper to taste. Mix together in the order given. If desired, a beaten egg or two may be added to the dressing.

–Mrs. Maurice Suiter, Route 3, Nov. 20, 1931.

Mrs. *S*aunders's Procedure for Cooking a Wild Duck

Pick while dry, then scald and rub well with dry cloth. Wash well with soap and warm water. Rinse well and remove entrails, surplus fat, bloody spots, etc. Soak in salt water for at least twenty-four hours. Rinse again, put to boil in cold water to which a little salt, sage, and pieces of onion have been added. Cook until tender, remove from water, stuff with good dressing, well-seasoned with sage and onion. Spread the breasts with butter, dust with pepper, and brown nicely in hot oven. Remove the grease from the water the fowl was boiled in; add it to the water in roaster, and use for gravy.

–Mrs. J. C. Saunders, Route 2, Nov. 24, 1931.

SPECIAL THANKSGIVING DINNER
$1.50 PER PLATE

Menu

Roast Turkey
with Dressing
Mashed Potatoes
and Gravy
Candied Sweet Potatoes
Buttered Peas
Celery, Pickles, Olives
Hot Biscuits, Cranberry Sauce
Special Fruit Salad
Mince or Pumpkin Pie
Ice Cream and Cake, Mints
Coffee, Tea, Milk

MAKE YOUR RESERVATIONS EARLY
Dinner served from 12:00 to 2:30
No meals served
Thanksgiving evening.

Carolyn Tea Room

Phone 1450   801 Indiana.

LJW, 11-24-25

Mrs. *J*ohanning's Roasted Wild Duck

Clean a wild duck for roasting; soak in salt water one hour to draw out the blood and whiten the meat. Drain and wipe dry, rub slightly with salt inside. Have the following dressing ready. Dressing: 3 cups sliced apples; ½ cup buttered, toasted bread crumbs; 2 cups prunes that have been soaked in warm water one hour. Mix and put stuffing inside and sew up. Rub outside with salt, a little pepper, and ¼ teaspoon ground, sweet marjoram. Place fowl in roaster; add ½ cup water. Do not allow pan to get dry while roasting. Bake till it begins to get brown, basting occasionally with the juice that forms in the bottom of roaster. Reduce heat and cook slowly till done.

–Mrs. D. W. Johanning, Route 2, Baldwin, Nov. 4, 1932.

Miss *E*zell's Dressing for the Thanksgiving Fowl

Three cups of bread, broken in small pieces; ½ cup of cooked cream of wheat, corn meal mush or corn bread; four hard-boiled eggs, diced, or more if desired; butter the size of an egg; one onion, finely minced. Season well with salt, pepper, sage, if desired, and poultry seasoning may also be used. Cook giblets, chop fine, and add these and the broth to the mixture. Mix well and add more moisture if needed. Put in seasoned fowl; or partly cook fowl, and put the dressing around it and brown with fowl.

–Miss Lula Ezell, 1017 Kentucky St., Nov. 22, 1932.

Mrs. *G*abriel's Chicken Loaf

One egg, well-beaten; ½ teaspoon salt; ¼ cup scalded milk; 1½ cups mashed potatoes; 1½ cups cooked chicken, chopped; 1 teaspoon minced parsley; ¼ teaspoon paprika. Add well-beaten egg, salt, and scalded milk to mashed potatoes. Add chicken, parsley and paprika. Turn into greased baking dish and bake in moderately hot oven (350 degrees F.) until top is browned. Serves 6.

–Mrs. Gus Gabriel, Eudora, Nov. 25, 1932.

Mrs. *B*aker's Pressed Chicken

Four or five lbs. chicken, 1 small onion, 1 blade celery, 1 tablespoon salt, pepper to taste, 1 tablespoon granulated gelatine. Choose a year-old hen if possible. Wash and disjoint. Put chicken in kettle, cover with boiling water, add onion and celery, and simmer until tender. Remove from broth and take the meat from the skin and bones. Return skin and bones to broth and boil until the stock is reduced to 3 cups. Cut the meat in tiny neat dice. Cook broth after straining, and remove fat. Put broth and chicken in kettle and bring to the boiling point. Stir in gelatine softened in a tablespoon cold water. Season with salt and pepper, and turn into a deep brick-shaped mold. Let stand on ice to chill and become firm.

–Mrs. Susie Baker, 829 Ohio St., Aug. 4, 1933.

Mrs. *F*ranks's Roast Wild Duck

"If you care for game, and there's a hunter in your family, serve wild duck, preparing it this way."

Pick and singe, cut down the back, and draw bird; then soak in salt water over night. If there are pin feathers, they can be drawn with a pair of tweezers. Next morning, cover with boiling water, to which is added 1 teaspoon of soda. As soon as the scum has come to the top, pour it off and wash each bird in cold water. Place breast down in the roaster with 1 cup of boiling water, adding more water when necessary. Fifteen minutes before serving, pour over ducks one cup thick cream. Let cook until gravy is thick. There should be but very little gravy, however.

–Mrs. A. J. Franks, 1501 Rhode Island St., Nov. 24, 1933.

Mrs. *B*aker's Rice and Oyster Dressing
"This is especially good with roast chicken."

Two cups cooked rice, one and one-half cups oysters with liquor, two tablespoons chopped green pepper, two tablespoons pimiento, one tablespoon onion, one teaspoon salt, one-fourth teaspoon pepper. To the cooked rice, add oysters, liquor, finely chopped vegetables and seasonings. Mix well.

–Mrs. Harold Baker, 1601 W. 9th St., Nov. 28, 1933.

Mrs. *E*berhart's Chicken Loaf

Four cups of coarsely ground chicken, 1 cup of sweet milk, 1 cup of chicken stock, 1 ½ teaspoons salt, ¼ teaspoon pepper, 1 teaspoon of minced onion, 1 tablespoon of chopped parsley, 2 eggs, 2 cups of soft bread crumbs. Mix together all the ingredients. Pour into a buttered loaf pan. Set in a pan of hot water, and bake in a moderate oven (375 degrees) for 1 hour, until slightly brown. Serve either hot or cold on a platter garnished with parsley and candied red apple rings. Turkey may be substituted for chicken.

–Mrs. I. F. Eberhart, 945 Tennessee St., Dec. 29, 1933.

Mrs. *H*ines's Chop Suey Americanized

Two cups cold chicken, 1 cup cooked celery, ¼ cup fat, 1 tablespoon cornstarch, 2 cups chicken stock, 1 teaspoon salt, ⅛ teaspoon pepper, Worcestershire sauce, 1 onion, boiled rice. Cut chicken, celery and onion in strips. Fry onion in fat until a delicate brown. Mix cornstarch to a smooth paste, and add. Add chicken, celery, and stock, and stir until mixture thickens. Season with salt, pepper, and Worcestershire sauce. Serve on a mound of hot, boiled rice. To make Chinese chop suey, add 1 cup sauteed mushrooms, 1 can bean sprouts (drained), and 1 can bamboo to chicken mixture.

–Mrs. Blanche Hines, 786 Walnut St., Jan. 19, 1934.

Mrs. *O*tt's Chicken Souffle

Melt 2 tablespoons of butter, and cook 1 slice of onion in it without browning. Remove onion, add 2 level tablespoons flour, ½ teaspoon paprika, and stir until well-blended. Add 2 cups milk, and stir until thick. Add to this ⅔ cup soft bread crumbs or ½ cup dry crumbs, 2 cups chopped, cooked chicken, and the yolks of 3 eggs, well-beaten. Then fold in the whites, beaten until stiff. Turn into a casserole or baking dish. Bake in a slow oven (350 degrees F.) until firm in center. Serve at once with tomato sauce or catsup. Ham or other meat may be used in place of chicken. Or use a third pound good cheese, cut in cubes or grated.

–Mrs. William Ott, Eudora, Apr. 27, 1934.

Mrs. *H*ornberger's Roast Wild Duck

Clean a wild duck for roasting; soak in salt water one hour to draw out blood and whiten the meat. Drain and wipe dry; rub slightly with salt inside. Have the following dressing ready: 3 cups sliced apples; ½ cup buttered, toasted bread crumbs; and 2 cups of prunes that have been soaked in warm water one hour. Mix and put stuffing inside and sew up. Rub outside with salt, a little pepper, and ¼ teaspoon ground sweet marjoram. Place fowl in roaster, add ½ cup of water. Do not allow pan to get dry while roasting. Bake till it begins to get brown, basting occasionally with the juice that forms in the bottom of roaster. Reduce heat and cook slowly till done.

–Mrs. Henry Hornberger, Route 3, Nov. 27, 1934.

Mrs. *A*braham's Chicken Loaf with Mushroom Sauce

One four-pound chicken, cooked tender and diced; 2 cupfuls of fresh bread crumbs; 1 cupful of cooked rice (measured after cooking); 1½ teaspoonfuls of salt; ⅛ cupful of chopped pimiento; 3 cupfuls of milk or chicken broth, or half and half; 4 eggs well-beaten. Mix all together, adding eggs last. Bake 1 hour in a slow oven (325 degrees) in a baking pan or ring mold.

Mushroom Sauce: Melt ¼ cupful of butter in a sauce pan. Add ¼ pound of fresh mushrooms or ½ pound can of mushrooms cut rather coarsely. Cook gently for 5 minutes, stirring occasionally. Add ¼ cupful of flour and mix well; then add the chicken broth, about 1 pint. Cook, stirring constantly until thick and smooth. Add ¼ cupful of cream, ⅛ teaspoonful of paprika, ½ tablespoonful of chopped parsley, ½ teaspoonful of lemon juice, and salt to taste. Mix and let stand over hot water until ready to serve.

–Mrs. R. C. Abraham, 930 Missouri St., Nov. 30, 1934.

Mrs. *P*aasch's Roast Quail

Clean and wash birds well. The second water should have a teaspoon of baking soda dissolved in it. Wash well, then rinse in clear water. Wipe the inside of each bird with a soft cloth. Bind the legs and wings down with a cotton string, and put one oyster in the body of each bird. Have ready thin slices of salt pork, two slices to each bird. Cover the breast with these, and put into the roaster. Pour over a little boiling water and roast for thirty minutes or till tender. Five minutes before you take them up, remove the pork, add a little butter and dredge with flour. Remove to the oven to brown. Have ready slices of bread, toasted and buttered. Lay a bird upon each slice of toast; add a spoonful of gravy from the pan and serve. Seasoned bread crumbs and chopped oysters make a nice stuffing.

–Mrs. Ed Paasch, Route 2, Nov. 26, 1935.

Mrs. *M*artin's Canned Chicken

Let fowl fast 24 hours before killing. Kill, dress at once, washing carefully, and let cool 24 hours before canning. Cut in convenient pieces. Never wash after cutting up as it draws out delicious juices. It may be packed in jars raw, adding teaspoonful salt (but no water) and processed, but some good authorities do not advise it for canning in glass. Pre-cooking is better. For fried chicken, brown nicely in hot fat, and pack partly-cooked chicken in jars, adding two or three tablespoons of fat in which it was fried. Season before cooking. Old fowls may be used as above, but do not roll in flour as crust formed prevents processing. They may be roasted for 1½ to 2 hours; cut up, and packed in jars and processed. Season before cooking. Or they may be stewed and canned with the broth, processing in jars as for the others. Can only the better pieces. Steam, until tender, the bony pieces, such as neck, back and ribs. Pick meat from bones and pack in jars and process. They may be used for sandwiches or salads when opened, or used as creamed chicken on toast or croquettes. The bony pieces of chicken may be made into soup and canned. Gizzards and livers should be canned separately because they are dark and contribute a strong flavor to the rest of chicken. Processing time for all above: For pressure cooker, 60 minutes at 15 pounds pressure; 90 minutes at 10 pounds; for water bath, 180 minutes; for oven canning, 240 minutes at 250 degrees. For pressure cooker, seal before canning. For water bath, leave lid open one turn for metal lids, and tighten when removed from water. With jar caps that do not require rubbers, seal tight before canning. With glass tops with wire clamps, seal tight for pressure cooker, but do not clamp down with water bath until processed.

–Mrs. Jessie Martin, Route 4, Sept. 11, 1936.

Miss James's Turkey Loaf

Two cups of diced cooked turkey, 1½ cups of bread crumbs, 2 tablespoons of diced celery, 1 tablespoon of diced onion, ¼ teaspoon of sage, 1 beaten egg, 1 cupful of milk, 2 tablespoons of melted butter. Mix the above ingredients and pour into a buttered loaf pan. Bake in a moderate oven of 350 degrees for 30 minutes. Unmold and serve with Egg Sauce.

Egg Sauce: 3 tablespoons of butter, 4 tablespoons of flour, ¼ teaspoon of salt, ¼ teaspoon of celery salt, 2 cupfuls milk (part cream preferred), 1 beaten egg, pepper to taste. Melt butter; add the flour and salt, and smooth to a paste. Gradually add the milk and cook to a smooth sauce. Add the egg, beat thoroughly, and remove from the stove. Pour over the loaf and serve. A few oysters added to the sauce give a good flavor.

–*Miss Helen James,* Route 3, Nov. 24, 1936.

25¢ **SATURDAY LUNCH** 25¢
Country Fried Chicken and Cream Gravy
or
Roast Loin of Pork with Applesauce
Snowflaked Potatoes
Creamed Peas and Carrots
Cranberry Relish
Hot Rolls and butter
Choice of 5¢ Drink

H.W.Stowit's **Rexall**

LJW, 2-9-34

Miss Brown's Quail on Toast
"This makes a wonderful dish."

Cut the dressed quail in half and place in a baking dish with a close-fitting lid. Season with pepper, salt, a lump of butter, and sufficient water to steam-cook. Place in a slow oven, rather moderate fire, for one hour or until done. Remove the quail from broth, dip in egg which has been slightly beaten. Roll in flour or cracker crumbs; brown in deep fat. Serve on buttered toast, which has been slightly moistened with broth, and serve while hot.

–*Miss Fay Brown,* 1105 Connecticut St., Nov. 27, 1936.

Heard In Lawrence

Ice box bandits did a thriving business last evening as two Lawrence homes were visited. At both residences the bandits emptied the refrigerators of their contents. At the H. B. Lacy home, 716 Mississippi street, the robbers secured a turkey, a chicken, and all the fixings for a New Year's dinner. The thief laid in a good supply of rations at the Fred Shimmons home, 616 Kentucky street. At the latter place, the robber secured butter, bacon, half a pig and other food in good sized quantities. [LJW, 1-1-26]

Mrs. *A*lexander's Hot Chicken Loaf

Cut one and one-half pounds cooked chicken fine and add three-fourths cup cream and one-half cup chicken broth. Add one teaspoon salt, one-eighth teaspoon pepper, two beaten eggs, and one and one-half cups soft bread crumbs. Pour into a greased loaf pan and bake for forty-five minutes to one hour in 375 degree oven. Turn out on platter and garnish with water cress. Serves eight.

–*Mrs. E. E. Alexander,* 345 Mississippi St., Feb. 12, 1937.

Mrs. *N*oever's Canned Chicken

"No pantry shelf is complete without canned chicken, ready to serve at short notice, when unexpected company arrives, or when it becomes necessary to prepare a meal in a hurry."

To get the best results, poultry should be killed, and thoroughly cooled, 6 hours before canning. Soak liver and gizzard in weak salt water 3 hours–so they won't discolor rest of chicken when cooked. Pack chicken in well-sterilized jars, adding 2 level teaspoons salt to each quart jar. Place on jar ring and partly seal jar. Cold pack for 3 hours, or in a steam pressure cooker for 30 minutes at 10 pounds. Remove from canner and seal immediately. Meat juices (liquid contents) in canned meats should form into jelly.

–*Mrs. Albert Noever,* 1136 Connecticut St., Aug. 20, 1937.

Mrs. *M*cCanles's Dressing for the Thanksgiving Fowl

One loaf of stale bread, sliced and dried, or toasted in oven. Break into small pieces in shallow dish or pan. Add enough cold water to soften. After a few minutes, spread on this 1½ cups of finely broken crackers. Next, 2 cups of finely cut and plentifully salted and peppered celery (can use small stems and some of the leaves from the table stalks). Next, 1 pint of oysters, salted and peppered. Pour on top of all ¼ lb. of melted butter. Mix well with spoon. This is enough for one medium-sized turkey or two chickens. If the fowl is lean, more butter can be used. If fowl be very fat, the butter can be omitted. For geese or ducks, a small minced onion may be used instead of oysters.

–*Mrs. J. C. McCanles,* 207 E. 14th St., Nov. 23, 1937.

Mrs. $\mathcal{D}$oering's Turkey Ring

Pick all bits of meat off the bones and cut into small dice. The meat should measure three cups after being pressed into cups. If turkey meat is insufficient, add a bit of lean cooked pork or veal. Break up the carcass and all loose bones; put into kettle and cover with water. Let simmer over slow fire for an hour or more, then strain off liquor which should be one quart. Put back on fire; add to this a fourth cup butter, and season with salt. Thicken this with a smooth paste made from a heaping tablespoon of flour and sweet milk. Add the prepared meat to the thickened broth. Remove from fire, but keep hot. In the meantime, bake the ring by using your regular biscuit recipe. Form the dough into a long round roll, and arrange in a round ring on a large tin. (I use a lard can lid.) When done, place ring on chop plate or platter, and pour prepared turkey in center. Garnish with curled celery or watercress. This is a delicious dish and will serve from 8 to 10 plates.

–Mrs. Ella Doering, 1214 Tennessee St., Dec. 24, 1937.

Mrs. $\mathcal{H}$ertzler's Procedure for Cooking Wild Duck

To prepare: Pick ducks dry, then singe. Scrub well, using warm water and a mild soap. Rinse thoroughly several times. Remove the entrails; then place the fowls in a weak solution of salt water (¼ cup to 1 gallon of water). Let soak overnight. To cook: Boil until tender (1 to 1½ hours) in water salted to taste and a whole onion added. This water may be saved (part of the grease skimmed from it) and thickened for gravy. Stuff the ducks with a dressing made of chopped hard bread, moistened with hot water, a pinch of sage, a teaspoon of minced onion, salt and pepper to taste for each duck. Place in a roaster, no lid, with just enough water to avoid sticking, and brown in a moderate oven (350 to 400 degrees F.) for 1 hour.

–Mrs. H. B. Hertzler, 811 E. 11ᵗʰ St., Nov. 11, 1938.

Local Poultry Prices
1934

1/2 lb. pressed chicken loaf	.23
1 lb. goose liver sausage	.40
1 (3 lb.) fancy hen, dressed	.60
1 (2 lb.) frying chicken, dressed	.70
Total	$ 1.93

Mrs. $\mathcal{W}$estheffer's Picnic Dish

A plump, tender chicken; 4 tablespoons milk; salt and pepper; 2 eggs, slightly beaten; seasoned flour. Dress chicken just long enough before frying to chill thoroughly. Cut chicken, wipe dry, and dip in mixture of beaten egg, milk, salt and pepper. Then dip into flour seasoned with salt and pepper, and sprinkle liberally with paprika. Fry in deep hot fat until brown. Place in a casserole, covered dish, or pan, and let steam in oven at low temperature until tender.

–Mrs. Don Westheffer, Route 1, Eudora, July 7, 1939.

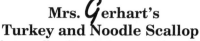
Mrs. *G*erhart's Turkey and Noodle Scallop

One pkg. noodles (6 oz.), 1 can condensed cream of mushroom soup, 4 ounces Velveeta cheese, ¼ teaspoon salt, pepper to taste, 4 tablespoons chopped green peppers (cooked), 2 tablespoons chopped pimiento, 2 cups cooked turkey (diced), 4 tablespoons rolled corn flakes. Cook the noodles in boiling salted water until tender, about 10 minutes. Put the mushroom soup in a saucepan and stir well; add the milk [probably what amounts to the volume of a soup can] and sliced cheese. Heat until the cheese melts. Remove from the fire and add the seasonings, chopped green pepper (which has been cooked 8 to 10 minutes in water), chopped pimiento, diced cold turkey, and noodles. Turn the mixture into a buttered casserole, and sprinkle with rolled buttered corn flakes. Bake in a moderate oven (350 degrees F.) for about 30 minutes. Serves 8. The same mixture can be used in making individual turkey and mushroom pies, or one large pie, using biscuit dough for the top. Bake the individual ones in shallow pottery bowls.

–Mrs. T. R. Gerhart, 2043 Tennessee St., Dec. 1, 1939.

Mrs. *S*tevens's Chicken Loaf

One 5 lb. chicken cooked tender and diced, 2 cups fresh bread crumbs, 2 cups cooked rice, 1½ teaspoons salt, ⅛ cup chopped pimiento, 3 cups chicken broth, 4 eggs (well beaten). Mix in order given, folding in eggs at the last. Bake in greased pan 1 hour in a slow oven (325 degrees F.). Serves 12. Serve with Mushroom Sauce: ¼ cup butter, ¼ lb. fresh mushrooms or ½ lb. can, ¼ cup flour, 2 cups chicken broth, ¼ cup cream, ⅛ teaspoon paprika, ½ tablespoon chopped parsley. Melt the butter, saute the mushrooms, add the flour, and stir well. Add the liquid, paprika and parsley. When well-blended, serve hot with the chicken loaf.

–Mrs. R. B. Stevens, 1123 Louisiana St., Mar. 15, 1940.

Mrs. *D*owney's Creamed Turkey in Mashed Potato Cups

One-fourth cup melted butter or margarine; 6 tablespoons flour; 2 cups milk, scalded; 1 cup hot turkey stock; 2 cups diced turkey; 1 cup sliced mushrooms; salt and pepper; 1 egg, slightly beaten; 3 cups hot mashed potatoes. Combine butter or margarine and flour. Add milk and turkey stock. Cook until smooth and thick, stirring constantly. Add turkey and mushrooms. Season to taste. Combine egg and potatoes; season to taste. Shape in 6 cups or nests. Place on baking sheet. Brush with melted butter or margarine. Fill with creamed mixture. Brown lightly under broiler. Serve.

–Mrs. H. P. Downey, 128 W. 13th St., Nov. 29, 1940.

Mrs. *I*ngalls's Roast Goose

Use a goose not over a year old, and have it dressed twenty-four hours before using. Make a dressing of three pints bread crumbs, two tablespoons butter, and two tablespoons salt pork (cut fine), a little chopped onion, one teaspoon sage, salt and pepper. Do not stuff very full, and fasten the opening firmly to keep flavor in. Place in a roaster and baste frequently with a little water (some use a little vinegar). Bake two hours or more. When done, take from the pan, pour off the fat, and to the brown gravy, add the chopped giblets, which have previously been cooked tender. Thicken with a little flour and butter rubbed together. Bring to a boil, and serve with currant jelly or apple sauce. If the wild flavor is disliked in wild fowls, soak overnight in salt water, or pare a fresh lemon without breaking the thin white inside skin, and put inside the fowl for a day. This will absorb unpleasant flavors from almost all game. The garnishes for prairie chicken, pheasants, and other wild fowl are sliced orange, currant jelly and apple sauce.

–Mrs. Maurine Ingalls, 921 Missouri St., Nov. 28, 1941.

Mrs. *A*dams's Scalloped Chicken

Use 4½ to 5 lb. chicken. Boil chicken until meat falls from the bones. Season to taste while boiling. Grind skin; chop meat into desired pieces. Place a layer of broken crackers on bottom of pan, place meat, then another layer of crackers. Thicken broth and pour over, boiling hot, and bake 15 or 20 minutes in a hot oven.

–Mrs. F. P. Adams, 1300 Oak Hill, Feb. 13, 1942.

Mrs. *O*lson's Aunt Susie's Chicken Pie
"Old fowls may be used in making this pie, making it more economical, and equally as good."

Cook a hen until very tender, and remove meat from bones. Sauce: 3 tablespoons chicken fat or butter, 3 tablespoons flour, melted and stirred together until the mixture bubbles; then add 3 cups chicken broth, season with salt, pepper and celery essence or celery salt. Cook until thick. Put the prepared chicken in the pan in which you will bake the pie, and pour over the sauce, leaving the pan on stove to keep hot while preparing the crust. Crust for pie: 2 cups flour, ½ teaspoon salt, 2 teaspoons baking powder, 1 egg, 3 tablespoons shortening, ¾ cup milk. Sift flour with baking powder and salt; work in shortening. Add beaten egg and milk, and beat well. Drop the mixture by tablespoons over the chicken, and bake quickly. Have extra sauce to serve with chicken pie.

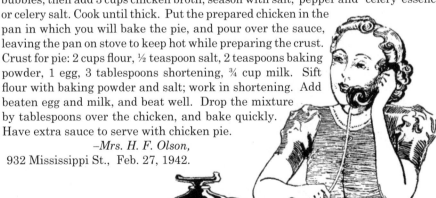

–Mrs. H. F. Olson,
932 Mississippi St., Feb. 27, 1942.

LJW, 3-19-42

UNCLE SAM SAYS:
Start Now To
Raise More Chickens
for National Defense

Mrs. $\mathcal{S}$mith's Arroz Con Pollo

"This recipe is one my father, Frank E. Jones, brought back from the Philippines. It is a traditional part of the menu for every special occasion in our family, and is delicious."

One plump hen, 1 pound rice, 1 cup diced ham, 2 tablespoons chopped onion, 1 cup diced celery, 2 tablespoons chopped green pepper, 20 pimiento-stuffed olives, salt and pepper to taste. Have hen cut into serving-size pieces. Simmer till tender in salted water. Meanwhile, boil rice in plenty of salted water, and drain so it is dry and fluffy. Brown diced ham in a little chicken fat, add onion and cook slowly till tender but not browned. Mix ham and onion, green pepper, olives, and celery with salt and pepper, and the cooked rice. Moisten well with chicken broth. Lay pieces of chicken in a large casserole and cover with rice mixture. Cover casserole, and bake in moderate oven 1½ hours. Uncover and brown, baking ½ hour longer. More broth may be added as needed, but should all be absorbed by the rice, so the finished dish is moist but not soupy. Several hard-boiled egg halves may be imbedded in the rice if desired. A few mushrooms, or a sprinkling of chopped parsley, are also nice additions to this recipe.

–Mrs. Marie J. Smith, 1129 Oregon St., Jan. 15, 1943.

Mrs. $\mathcal{H}$ouk's Emergency Chicken Pot Pie

Two tablespoons butter, 3 tablespoons flour, 1 medium-size can vegetable soup or mushroom soup, 1½ to 2 cups diced cooked chicken, pastry or rich biscuit dough. Melt butter, blend with flour, add soup and stir until thickened. Add the chicken and pour into a baking dish. Cover with a layer of pastry or biscuit dough and bake in a hot oven (450 degrees F.) until the pastry is well-browned.

–Mrs. Harry Houk, 1618 Rhode Island St., Feb. 12, 1943.

Mrs. $\mathcal{G}$lenn's Chicken in Patty Shells

Shells: 1 cup boiling water, ½ cup lard, ½ teaspoon salt, 1 cup flour, 4 eggs. Filling: 4 tablespoons flour, ½ cup water, 3 cups rich chicken broth, ¼ cup chopped onion, 1 cup chopped carrots, ¼ cup chopped green pepper, ½ cup chopped celery, 2 cups diced cooked chicken. Shells: Combine the boiling water, shortening and salt;

cook until the mixture is boiling briskly. Add the flour all at once, and cook until the dough forms a ball that clings to the spoon and is transparent. Remove from heat; cool to lukewarm. Add the eggs, one at a time, beating until smooth after each addition, and then continue beating until the spoon has a satiny appearance. Drop lightly by spoonfuls into muffin pans. Bake in hot oven (450 degrees) 10 minutes. Reduce heat to 325 degrees, and continue baking 45 minutes, or until firm to touch. Cool. Filling: Mix flour and water to a smooth paste and add to the chicken broth with other ingredients. Simmer 15 minutes, stirring frequently. Remove from heat. Slit the shells near the top, and fill with chicken mixture. Serves eight.

–*Mrs. Viola Glenn,* Lecompton, May 14, 1943.

Miss *C*hristenson's Chicken a la King
"An excellent way to use a small amount of chicken."

One-fourth cup butter, ½ cup mushrooms, ¼ cup flour, ½ teaspoon salt, 1 cup milk, ½ cup chicken gravy, 1 cup diced cooked chicken, 1 cup peas, 1 tablespoon chopped pimiento, ½ cup diced celery. Saute mushrooms in butter. Blend in flour and salt. Add milk and chicken gravy, and cook over hot water, stirring constantly until thick and smooth. Parboil celery for five minutes. Add to creamed mixture with chicken and remaining vegetables. Serve on toast points. Four servings.

–*Miss Emma Christenson,*
911 New Hampshire St., May 28, 1943.

V**ICTORY Poultry House**

★ More meat and eggs for victory! Produce them in your back yard in this 9-by-12 modern poultry plant. The house is easy to build with the complete plans, instructions and material.
—*A. Neely Hall Craft Patterns, c. 1943*

Mrs. *M*alone's Chicken and Ham Loaf

One cup chopped cooked chicken, 1 cup chopped cooked ham, 1 cup soft bread crumbs, 1 cup milk, 2 eggs, ¼ teaspoon salt, ¼ teaspoon celery salt, 1 teaspoon chopped parsley, 2 tablespoons pimientos, 2 tablespoons butter (melted), ¼ teaspoon paprika. Mix bread and milk; let stand 5 minutes. Add remaining ingredients, and pour into buttered meat pan. Bake 30 minutes. Take out loaf and let stand 5 minutes before unmolding. Cut in slices and serve.

–Mrs. James Malone, 1108 Kentucky St., July 9, 1943.

Mrs. *D*rennon's Baked Chicken and Dressing

One roasting chicken, stuffing (recipe follows), fat, salt and pepper. Wash, singe and draw the bird. Rub it with salt and pepper inside and out, and stuff with stuffing. Truss and tie the fowl. Brush skin with melted or softened fat. Turn breast side down, and cover bird with a cloth dipped in fat. Place in a moderate oven (325 to 350 degrees). Cook, uncovered, breast side down, about one half the total time. Turn breast side up. Over breast-bone, place strips of body fat–trimmings left from cleaning the bird–or bacon or salt pork strips may be used. Baste with extra fat. The cloth may be removed toward the end of the cooking if the bird is not well-browned. Allow 30 minutes per pound for small birds; 22 to 25 minutes per pound for larger birds.

Bread Stuffing: 2 to 3 tablespoons chopped onion, 1 cup dry bread-crumbs, 1 teaspoon salt, ¼ teaspoon pepper, 1 to 2 tablespoons milk or stock, ½ teaspoon each sage, chopped celery, parsley. Melt fat in frying pan; add onion, and saute until tender. Add bread crumbs and seasonings and mix well. Then add the milk or stock. This makes a loose, light stuffing, much preferred by many to the soft moist or compact type. It can be varied by leaving out the onion, or the sage, by adding chopped celery or by adding two tablespoons of seeded raisins. When the onion, milk and seasonings are omitted, and 1 cup canned oysters are added, a tasty stuffing is obtained.

–Mrs. H. C. Drennon,
23rd and Haskell Ave., Dec. 10, 1943.

Mrs. *S*tanwix's Chicken Pie

Take the left-over chicken, pick from the bones, cut into small pieces, and add one pint water. Put into kettle and bring to a boil. Add one heaping tablespoon butter, a little salt and pepper as needed. Pour into a casserole, and add one cup mushrooms cut in small pieces. Make a rich baking powder biscuit dough as follows: Sift one pint flour into a mixing bowl. Add a little salt, one heaping teaspoonful of baking powder. Mix well. Add one tablespoon lard, a cup of sweet cream, and milk enough to make a soft stiff dough. Roll out ½ inch thick, cut with a small biscuit cutter, and cover the top of chicken with the small biscuits. Dot the top with a little butter. Bake ½ hour, and serve in the pan in which it was baked.

–*Mrs. May Marie Stanwix,* Route 1, Apr. 14, 1944.

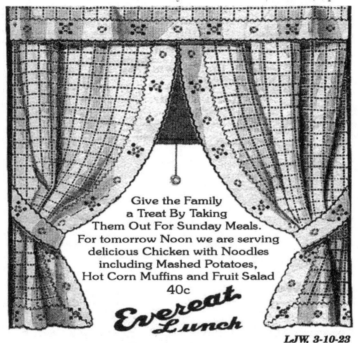

Give the Family
a Treat By Taking
Them Out For Sunday Meals.
For tomorrow Noon we are serving
delicious Chicken with Noodles
including Mashed Potatoes,
Hot Corn Muffins and Fruit Salad
40c
Evereat Lunch

LJW, 3-10-23

Mrs. Allen's Chicken Pie

"Very delicious. Pork or veal may be used instead of chicken."

Cook the chicken in plenty of water so there will be about four cups of broth when done. Take meat from bones in rather large pieces, and place in pan in which the pie is to be baked. Prepare a sauce from the broth by using 3 tablespoons of melted butter mixed with 3 tablespoons of flour and a little black pepper. Add 4 cups of the warm broth slowly and cook well; then add 1 cup of hot milk or cream. Pour this over the chicken in the pan, covering it till only small bits of chicken can be seen. Keep this where it will stay hot till crust is ready. Save the rest of sauce for gravy.

Crust: Mix together the four following ingredients: 2 cups of flour, ¼ teaspoon salt, 2 teaspoons baking powder, 2 tablespoons shortening. Beat one egg and add one cup of milk to it. Add this to the above dry mixture. Drop this from a teaspoon onto the hot bubbling chicken. Put at once into a very hot oven, 450 degrees. Bake 15 minutes.

–*Mrs. E. B. Allen,* 911 Missouri St., May 12, 1944.

Mrs. *C*arson's Roasted Wild Duck

Pull out all outside feathers, but do not bother with pin feathers or down. Cut off head and wings, then dip duck in hot, melted paraffin. Let stand on paper until cold; pull off paraffin and the result is a beautiful cleaned duck. Then draw and wash thoroughly. Make a dressing of dry bread crumbs, apples (cut in pieces), a large onion, celery, butter, salt and pepper. Rub entire surface of duck with onion and salt. Place in roasting pan, uncovered. Put into a hot oven at 450 degrees F. When well-browned, add a little water and cover roaster. Reduce heat to 300 degrees F., and roast for two and a half to three and a half hours, depending on size of duck.

–Mrs. Jesse Carson, Route 2, Nov. 24, 1944.

Miss *S*chopper's Pheasant with Cream Gravy

Singe, clean and cut a pheasant into pieces for frying. Dredge with flour, salt and pepper. Fry well-floured pieces in hot fat until browned on both sides. Place in a casserole and cover with milk or thin cream. Add one bay leaf and cover with thin sliced onions. Bake in medium oven until tender, about one hour. Remove to a hot platter. Add 3 tablespoons flour to the casserole, and blend well with the milk and juice from the pheasant, stirring until the mixture thickens. Serve in a gravy boat.

–Miss Frances Schopper, 1246 New Hampshire St., Nov. 2, 1945.

Mrs. *B*eurmann's Roast Wild Duck and Stuffing

For each duck: 1½ cups bread crumbs (stale is better), 1 apple, ½ onion, 1 egg, salt and pepper to taste. Break bread into small pieces, add enough water to make it soft, add egg, apple and onion, and stuff duck. Put duck into roaster and bake until done. Young ducks will roast in 1 ½ to 2 hours, while old ducks take 3 to 4 hours. Baste frequently and remove from the oven as soon as done as too long a baking makes the meat dry. Roast in hot oven (400 degrees) to sear, then reduce to 325 degrees. Reduce oven heat after ½ hour, and bake slowly until done. After duck has been picked and cleaned, it's best to leave in salt water for a few hours before baking.

–Mrs. L. A. Beurmann, Route 1, Nov. 23, 1945.

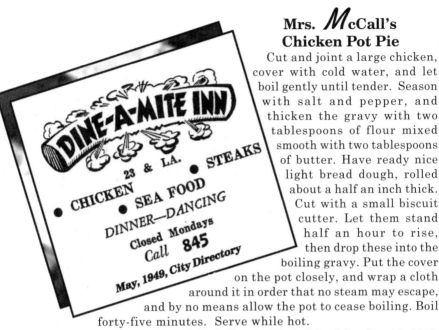

Mrs. *M*cCall's Chicken Pot Pie

Cut and joint a large chicken, cover with cold water, and let boil gently until tender. Season with salt and pepper, and thicken the gravy with two tablespoons of flour mixed smooth with two tablespoons of butter. Have ready nice light bread dough, rolled about a half an inch thick. Cut with a small biscuit cutter. Let them stand half an hour to rise, then drop these into the boiling gravy. Put the cover on the pot closely, and wrap a cloth around it in order that no steam may escape, and by no means allow the pot to cease boiling. Boil forty-five minutes. Serve while hot.

–Mrs. T. McCall, 1109 Rhode Island St., Jan. 18, 1946.

Mrs. *M*iller's Scalloped Chicken

Two cups chicken broth, ½ cup rich milk, ¼ cup butter, 6 tablespoons flour, dash nutmeg, ¼ teaspoon salt, dash celery salt, 2½ cups cooked chicken (finely cut), 1 cup bread crumbs. Heat milk and chicken broth together. Blend butter, flour and seasonings together, and blend into them the hot liquid. Cook until smooth and creamy (about 15 minutes), stirring constantly. Into greased 8-inch baking dish, 3 inches deep, place a layer of chicken, a layer of cream gravy, and a layer of bread crumbs. Repeat until ingredients are used. Dot with additional butter. Bake 30 minutes in a moderate oven (350 degrees). This recipe makes 6 servings.

–Mrs. Ed Miller, 1738 Massachusetts St., Feb. 8, 1946.

Miss *H*olcomb's Pressed Chicken

One chicken, salt and pepper, 1 tablespoon gelatine. Clean and cut up chicken. Put into a kettle with water to cover, and boil slowly until meat will fall from the bones, adding salt and pepper to taste about 30 minutes before taking up with a skimmer. Scrape all the meat from the bones, separating the white and dark meat. Soften gelatine in two tablespoons of cold water and add to boiling broth. Place the meat in the dish or crock it is to be pressed in, laying the white and dark in alternate layers, and adding broth enough to cover it. Lay a plate on top and a weight, and set away in a cool place.

–Miss Pauline Holcomb, 818½ Massachusetts St., June 28, 1946.

Mrs. *B*eecroft's Chicken Pie

Stew one chicken until tender; cool and pick from bones. Mix together 3 tablespoons butter, 3 tablespoons flour, 1 cup milk, 5 cups chicken broth. Cook until thick; add chicken. Place in baking dish and keep warm. Mix 3 cups flour, 2 teaspoons baking powder, ½ teaspoon salt. Add to 1 beaten egg, alternating with one cup milk. Pour over thickened chicken and bake in moderate oven 30 minutes or until golden brown.

–Mrs. C. S. Beecroft, 1237 Vermont St., Jan. 3, 1947.

Mrs. *P*reyer's Escalloped Chicken Loaf

One (5 lb.) chicken, cooked tender, and diced by hand (do not put through food chopper); 2 cups rice (measured after cooking); 1 large onion, minced fine; 5 eggs, beaten light; 2 cups fresh bread bits cut in small cubes; 1 can mushroom soup; 3 cups half milk and half chicken broth; 1 level teaspoon salt. Mix all ingredients together, adding mushroom soup and eggs last. Bake in slow oven for one hour. Serve, cut in squares, and covered with this sauce: 2 cans cream of mushroom soup, ¼ cup flour, 1 pint chicken broth, 1 cup cream, salt and pepper to taste. Bring chicken broth to boil. Thicken with flour dissolved in the cream. Add butter and mushroom soup. Bring to boil again and serve. Add more flour if sauce does not thicken enough. Loaf may be served with or without the sauce.

–Mrs. B. A. Preyer, 746 Alabama St., Feb. 21, 1947

Miss *H*elm's Scalloped Chicken

Four tablespoons butter or margarine, 3 tablespoons flour, 1 cup canned chicken broth, 1 cup rich milk, 1½ tablespoons salt, dash of pepper, 1 (6 oz.) package egg noodles, 1 can boned chicken, 1 package frozen carrots and peas, 1 finely minced onion (browned), ½ cup potato chip crumbs, ½ cup chopped almonds.

Melt butter or margarine in saucepan. Add flour, and stir until smooth paste is formed. Add broth and milk, and cook until thick, stirring constantly. Season with salt and pepper. Boil and drain noodles, and place half in baking dish. Add layer of chicken and vegetables, then another layer of noodles, topped with chicken and vegetables. Add thickened liquid. Cover with potato chip crumbs and almonds. Bake uncovered in a moderate oven (350 degrees F.) 20 minutes or until heated through and browned. Serves 6.

–Miss Lola Mae Helm, Route 5, Nov. 14, 1947.

Mrs. *R*othwell's Escalloped Chicken

Four cups cooked chicken (bones removed), 1 cup finely chopped celery, 1 cup soft bread crumbs, 2 tablespoons minced parsley, 2 teaspoons salt, 4 slightly beaten eggs, 2 cups chicken stock, 2 tablespoons butter.

Cut chicken in rather large pieces. Place in baking dish with alternate layers of celery, crumbs and parsley. Add salt and eggs to chicken stock. Mix thoroughly and pour over chicken; dot with butter. Cook in moderate oven (350 degrees) about 30 minutes, or until brown. Or cook in pressure cooker by placing rack with short pins in cooker, and adding two cups of water to bottom of cooker. Place baking dish on rack and cover with wax paper. Cook for 10 minutes at 15 pounds pressure. Serves 4 to 6.

–Mrs. Sylvester Rothwell, Route 1, Lecompton, Feb. 27, 1948.

Mrs. *B*anks's Escalloped Chicken

Cut up and boil one small or medium-sized chicken. In a small amount of water, cook chicken until tender, and season with salt to taste. Remove meat from the bones, and mix with 2 cups of dry bread cut in small pieces, or same amount of cracker crumbs, using any other seasonings one prefers, such as a little onion, sage or celery. Put into a baking dish, and pour over this 2 well-beaten eggs with 1 cup of the chicken broth and 1 ½ cups rich milk mixed together, and 2 tablespoons butter on top. Bake in a moderate oven around 35 to 40 minutes or until the egg mixture thickens or sets.

–Mrs. J. W. Banks, Route 6, Feb. 4, 1949.

Mrs. *W*ickey's Chicken Pie

One chicken, pie paste, flour, salt and pepper. Clean, singe and cut up chicken as for frying. Place in a kettle and add enough hot water to cover. Put the cover on the kettle, and simmer slowly until the chicken is tender, adding a little more water if needed. Make a gravy of the stock, using two tablespoons flour for each cup of stock. Use for the crust puff paste, or a good pie paste, rolled a little thicker than for fruit pies. Line the sides of a deep baking dish with crust. Invert in the middle of the dish a small cup or ramekin. Put in part of the chicken, and season with salt and pepper, then add the rest of the chicken, and season the same way.

Put in the dish two cups or more of the gravy, made from broth in which the chicken was cooked, and cover the top with crust. The cup or ramekin will hold the crust up, and will prevent evaporation. Most chicken pie is too dry; therefore, use a generous amount of the broth. Bake in a hot oven (450 degrees F.) until crust is done (one-half hour). When serving, after cutting the first slice, carefully slip the knife under the ramekin and release the gravy which is held there by suction. Additional gravy should be served in a gravy dish.

–*Mrs. Elmer Wickey,* Route 3, Tonganoxie, Feb. 11, 1949.

Beef, Pork, Veal, Lamb, Rabbit,

and

Variety Meats

Preparing The Buffalo Barbeque

Louis Bighorse, chairman of the Buffalo barbecue committee in connection with the stadium dedication celebration at Haskell Institute, October 27 to 30, was at the Indian school this morning making arrangements for the coming fete.

He requested that tables be built upon which the buffaloes will be cut up and prepared for cooking. He also asked that a shed be erected over the tables "for the squaws to work under" while preparing the meat and the squaw bread.

Bighorse is an Osage and has an enviable reputation among the people of his tribe for industry, enterprise and good sound judgment. For several years his children have been students at Haskell. He drove to Lawrence with members of his family in his Marmon sedan.

The Indian committeeman said he would arrive here two weeks before the celebration to have all plans perfected for the barbecue. He said he would superintend the building of a huge iron grate upon his return here. He intends to take a house in Lawrence during the celebration so as not to expose his infant grandchildren to tent life in camp.

Bighorse said the Indians prepared the buffaloes for barbecue without using saws or cleavers. When the meat is removed from the bones it is hung up in strips in the sun and cured a short time before being cooked. He explained that this old custom originated because it was found that the meat was better flavored and also cooked faster after being sun-dried.

When the Osage, who is a leader among his tribesmen, returns home to Pawhuska [Oklahoma] he will call together other Osage leaders, kill and barbecue a beef, and tell them the details of the big celebration here this fall. He predicts a huge crowd for the stadium dedication. Mr. Bighorse said it was probable that the noted chief, Bacon Rind, would be among those present. [LJW, 9-4-26]

Mrs. *W*atts's "Left Over" Meat and Potato Pie

One cup cold chopped meat, 2 tablespoons minced onion, 1 cup canned tomatoes, 2 cups mashed potatoes, salt and pepper. Put a layer of meat in the bottom of a baking dish, add a little onion, salt and pepper, and half of the tomatoes. Add another layer of meat, onion, salt and pepper, and the rest of the tomatoes. Cover with mashed potatoes, and bake in a hot oven about half an hour.

–*Mrs. William Watts,* 946 Connecticut St., Nov. 11, 1921.

Mrs. *M*yers's Casserole of Meat and Vegetables

Two cups macaroni (cooked), ½ cup grated cheese, 2 cups tomatoes, 2 tablespoons melted fat, ½ cup chopped green peppers, 1 teaspoon minced onion, 2 cups meat (chopped), salt, pepper, and bread crumbs. Mix in order given. Place in casserole, and cover with crumbs. Put lid on casserole and bake one hour in moderate oven.

–*Mrs. C. A. Myers,*
435 Michigan St., Feb. 3, 1922.

Mrs. *R*eed's Pressed Beef

Three lbs. boiling beef; 1 tablespoon gelatine dissolved in a little hot water; 1 teaspoon salt; 2 hard- boiled eggs; 1 tablespoon pimiento, chopped; 1 tablespoon green pepper, chopped; 1 tablespoon sweet pickle, chopped; ½ teaspoon celery salt. To the beef, which has been boiled till tender, then ground while hot, add the gelatine, then the other ingredients. Pack in a deep pan and press by putting a plate right on the meat. Set an iron on the plate; allow this to stand several hours. Chill and slice, and garnish with parsley.

–*Mrs. Dan Reed,*
1409 New York St.,
May 19, 1922.

Mrs. *W*ilcox's Directions for Cooking Steak
"The result is a dish fit for a king."

Take a piece of round steak, one-half inch thick. Have the butcher score deeply in both sides. Cut in pieces and work in as much flour as possible. Then fry in about as much fat as it would take to fry a chicken. Have the fat smoking hot, and fry brown as quickly as possible. Season liberally, cover with water, and let simmer at least half an hour, or until all the water has boiled out.

–Mrs. M. N. Wilcox, 726 Arkansas St., Sept. 1, 1922.

Mrs. *R*iggs's Meat Pie

Make a gravy by stirring flour into hot fat, and adding water and milk. Season to taste. Stir into this gravy small pieces of left-over meat, such as steak or roast. While still boiling hot, cover with small biscuits that have been dipped in melted fat. Bake and serve hot.

Biscuit: 3 cups flour, 1 teaspoon salt, 2 teaspoons baking powder, 2 tablespoons Crisco or lard. Mix well, then add sweet milk enough to make a soft dough.

–Mrs. H. C. Riggs, 907 Arkansas St., Oct. 20, 1922.

Miss *S*utton's Ham Loaf

One-half pound smoked ham, 1 pound fresh pork shoulder, 1 onion, 1 cup bread crumbs soaked in 1 cup of cold milk, ½ teaspoon pepper, no salt. Grind the meat and onion. Squeeze all the milk possible from the crumbs, and add to ground meat. Add pepper and mix well. Form in a loaf, and bake in moderate oven for three quarters of an hour. Serve cold with catsup.

–Miss Elizabeth Sutton, Colorado Springs, Colorado, Apr. 14, 1923.

LJW, 3-16-23

Mrs. *R*eed's Meat Pilaf

Grind two cups of any kind of left over meat. Add this to two cups of rice, one minced onion, one green mango pepper (chopped), and one can of tomatoes. Season with salt, pepper and celery salt. Pour in buttered baking dish, cover with water, and bake two hours. It is necessary to add a little water, at times, to prevent getting too dry. Serve hot.

–Mrs. Dan Reed, 730 Kentucky St., June 1, 1923.

Mrs. *R*iggs's Pressed Meat

Four lbs. veal shoulder, ½ can tomatoes (fresh or canned), 6 eggs, salt, pepper. Cover veal with water, add tomatoes, and boil until tender. When cold, grind, add stock, and season to taste. Put in molds and enclose hard-boiled eggs. Set in cold ice box, and it will be ready to slice in a few hours.

–Mrs. H. C. Riggs, 907 Arkansas St., Aug. 13, 1923.

Mrs. *L*owe's Baked Rabbit

Cut rabbit in pieces as for frying. Salt, pepper, and roll in flour. Put enough lard in a skillet to fry each piece quickly on both sides to a golden brown. Take from the skillet and put into a baking dish. Pour in half cup boiling water with small piece of onion. Cover and bake over a very slow fire for one hour or until tender. Remove cover of baking dish ten minutes before serving. Garnish with parsley, and serve with corn bread.

–Mrs. Charles B. Lowe, 216 4th St. North, Feb. 1, 1924.

Mrs. *B*rown's Method of Cooking Steak

"The toughest steak will be very tender when cooked this way."

One pound of round steak (one inch thick), ½ cup of flour, 3 tablespoons of fat, 2 teaspoons of salt, ½ teaspoon of paprika, ½ teaspoon of celery salt, 2 tablespoons of finely chopped onion, 2 cups of cooked tomatoes, 1 tablespoon of chili sauce, ½ cup of water.

Pound all of the flour into the steak. Place the fat in a frying pan, and when hot, add the steak and brown on both sides. Then add the onions and seasonings, and cook two minutes longer. Add the tomatoes, chili sauce and water; cover with tight lid, and cook slowly one hour. Tomatoes can be omitted by anyone not liking them, and more water added.

–Mrs. Ella Brown, 1105 New Hampshire St., Dec. 11, 1925.

Mrs. *E*ldridge's Veal Birds

One pound veal steak (sliced thin), 2 ozs. salt pork, 1 egg, 1 teaspoon of salt, ⅛ teaspoon pepper, ¾ teaspoon celery salt, ½ onion scraped (or 1 teaspoonful onion salt), 2 tablespoonfuls lemon juice, ¾ cupful bread crumbs, flour for dredging, butter for browning, 1½ cupfuls boiling water, ⅛ teaspoonful thyme. Wash the veal and trim the fat from it. Then cut the veal into five or six pieces, making each piece as nearly square as possible. Use the remainder of the ingredients, except the flour, butter and water, for stuffing. Prepare the stuffing as follows: Put the salt pork through a food chopper. Beat the egg and add it to the pork. Then add the remainder of the ingredients. Divide the stuffing into as many portions as there are pieces of veal. Place a portion of the stuffing on each piece of veal. Pin together the four corners of each piece of veal by means of a tooth pick. If necessary, thrust other tooth picks into the veal to hold the stuffing in place. Dredge the pieces of veal (or veal birds) with flour. Fry out the fat trimmed from the veal; add butter to it, and brown the meat in the fat. (Let the meat cook in the fat until it is dark brown.) While the veal is browning, add two tablespoonsful more of flour to the fat in the bottom of the frying pan so as to thicken the sauce around the meat when the latter is sufficiently cooked. After browning, sprinkle salt over the veal, and pour 1 ½ cupfuls of boiling water on it. Turn the meat and sauce into a casserole or pan. Cover and bake in the oven at 300 degrees for 1 ½ hours.

–Mrs. Seba Eldridge, 945 Rhode Island St., Dec. 25, 1925.

Mrs. *H*arris's Loin of Veal a' la Jardiniere

Wipe four pounds loin of veal, sprinkle with salt and pepper, and dredge with flour. Put one-fourth cup butter in deep stew pan. When melted, add veal and brown entire surface of meat, watching carefully, and turning often that it may not burn. Add one cup hot water; cover closely and cook slowly two hours, or until meat is tender, adding more water as needed, using in all about three cups. Remove meat. Thicken stock remaining in pan with flour diluted in enough cold water to pour easily. Surround the meat with two cups each boiled turnips and carrots, cut in half-inch cubes, and potatoes cut in balls. Serve gravy separately.

–Mrs. J. F. Harris, 200 W. 12th St., Feb. 25, 1927.

Mrs. *N*etzer's Liver Dumplings

Chop one-half pound liver and one-fourth pound bacon (both raw) as fine as possible, or grind through food chopper. Melt one-fourth cup butter to which is added one and one-half cup bread crumbs. Brown slightly and add to meat. Add also two well-beaten eggs, one tablespoon chopped parsley, salt and pepper to suit the taste. The mixture should be just stiff enough to make a paste which can be formed into balls. Add more crumbs if necessary. Divide into portions, roll smoothly in the hands, and poach in boiling water before boiling, cooking about fifteen minutes.

–Mrs. E. J. Netzer, 1533 Rhode Island St., June 3, 1927.

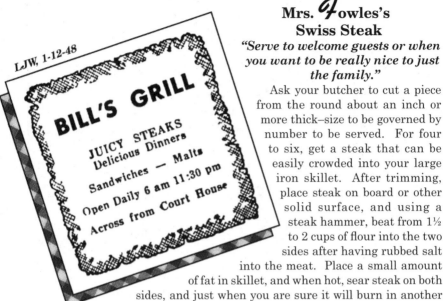

LJW, 1-12-48

BILL'S GRILL

JUICY STEAKS
Delicious Dinners
Sandwiches — Malts
Open Daily 6 am 11:30 pm
Across from Court House

Mrs. *Fowles's* Swiss Steak

"Serve to welcome guests or when you want to be really nice to just the family."

Ask your butcher to cut a piece from the round about an inch or more thick–size to be governed by number to be served. For four to six, get a steak that can be easily crowded into your large iron skillet. After trimming, place steak on board or other solid surface, and using a steak hammer, beat from 1½ to 2 cups of flour into the two sides after having rubbed salt into the meat. Place a small amount of fat in skillet, and when hot, sear steak on both sides, and just when you are sure it will burn in another minute, pour about ½ cup of boiling water down at the side of the steak, and cover quickly. Lower fire and allow to cook slowly two hours or more according to quality and thickness of steak. Add small amount of water as needed. It readily pierces when done, and should be well-browned. Remove carefully to hot platter, and add ½ tablespoon of flour and a sprinkle of salt to mixture in skillet. Mix smooth and add 1 pint or more of milk. Let boil up. Serve separate from meat, and you have a very tender meat and rich gravy.

–*Mrs. W. D. Fowles,* 624 5th St., North, Feb. 3, 1928.

Mrs. *Sterling's* Liver

"Try it–see if it is not delectable."

Cut liver the size for individual serving. Scald it or not, according to individual taste. Saute in skillet with butter, or part butter and bacon drippings, hot at first until it has been turned once, then turn down heat and cook slower until liver is tender but not dry or hard. Also have ready two cups of scraped, diced carrots. Cook in as little water as possible so that all the water will be used up in the cooking. Salt to taste, and butter with one tablespoon butter. Have bacon cooked brown and crisp, one small piece–one-half slice for each serving of liver. Also have apples (Jonathan apples are excellent) sliced about a half-inch thick, cored but not peeled. Cook in butter until tender and a pretty brown. Serve all piping hot, with a mound of buttered carrots in the center of platter surrounded with the liver. On each piece of liver, place a piece of bacon, and a slice of savory apple on top of each piece of bacon.

–*Mrs. C. M. Sterling,* 920 Louisiana St., Oct. 12, 1928.

Mrs. *C*lark's Meat Loaf

Dice two slices of bacon and fry to golden brown. Add bacon and fat to two pounds
ground round steak, ½ cup Minute Tapioca, 1 small chopped onion, 2 cups canned
tomato pulp, 2½ teaspoons salt, and ¼ teaspoon pepper. Mix well. Make into loaf
and bake in moderate oven about 45 minutes.

–*Mrs. John W. Clark,* 1929 Massachusetts St., June 7, 1929.

Miss *T*hompson's Bouchees of Meat

Two cups of cold mashed potatoes; one egg yolk, slightly beaten; one-fourth cup of
milk or cream, scalded; chopped meat added to thick white sauce. Pour the hot milk
over the egg yolk, stirring constantly. Add to the potatoes, beat well, and season to
taste. Line an oiled casserole with potato mixture. Fill with creamed meat. Bake
until slightly brown. Variations may be made by adding a bit of chopped onion or
a speck of sage. Individual casseroles may be used.

–*Miss Marion Thompson,* Williamstown, Jan. 17, 1930.

Mrs. *M*ettner's Ham Loaf

One pound of uncooked ham, 2 lbs. of lean pork, ¾ cup of milk, ½ cup cracker
crumbs, ½ green pepper (minced), 1 teaspoon parsley (minced), ½ onion (minced), 1
egg, 1 small can tomatoes. Grind meat; add all ingredients except tomatoes. Mix well
and pack in greased baking dish. Pour over the tomatoes, and bake in a moderate
oven 1 ½ hours. Garnish with shredded green pepper.

–*Mrs. C. W. Mettner,* 1637 New Hampshire St., Feb. 28, 1930.

Mrs. *C*ompton's Meat Loaf

One and one-half pounds ground beef, one half pound ground pork, 1 cup cracker
crumbs, 1 egg, 1 mango (sweet bell) pepper, 1 onion, milk, bacon, salt and pepper.
To cracker crumbs add enough milk to moisten well. Add one egg, well beaten, and
mango pepper, and onion, chopped finely. Add this mixture to the beef and pork, and
mix thoroughly. Add salt and black pepper to taste. Make into loaf; strip with bacon.
Add one half cup of boiling water, and bake one and one-half hours in medium oven. If
gravy is made, brown the flour before using. This makes a delicious brown gravy.

–*Mrs. J. H. Compton,* 1232 Louisiana St., May 31, 1930.

Mrs. *B*eery's
Braised Beef's Tongue with Mushroom Gravy

Wash a three pound tongue, and put it into a kettle. Cover with boiling water. Add seven cloves, one onion, size of a walnut, and a sprig of parsley. Simmer gently for two hours. At the end of the first hour, season well with salt and pepper. Take out the tongue, skin it, trim off the rough edges at the root, and remove any small bones. Now tie the tip of the tongue around to the thicker part, and fasten it. Put three tablespoons of butter in frying pan and brown it; then add two tablespoons of flour. Mix well. To the liquid drained from one can of mushrooms, add enough of the stock, in which the tongue was boiled, to make one and one-half pints. Mix this with the browned butter and flour; stir until it boils. Put the tongue in a covered roasting pan, and pour this gravy over and around it. Put in the oven for two hours, basting every fifteen minutes. Twenty minutes before the tongue is done, add two small carrots cut in rings. Just before serving, add one-half can of mushrooms cut in pieces. Remove the strings and serve the tongue on chop plates with the gravy poured over and around it. Garnish with parsley.

–*Mrs. B. B. Beery,* [address unavailable], Oct 10, 1930.

Mrs. *B*levins's Meat Loaf

One and a half pounds hamburger and ½ pound sausage, mixed; 1 large onion, cut fine; 3 eggs, beaten; 1 large teaspoon dry mustard; 1 teaspoon chili powder; ½ cup cracker crumbs. Work sausage and hamburger together with salt and pepper to taste. Add onion and other dry ingredients with the beaten eggs. Work all together; shape in a loaf. Put strips of thin bacon across the top, and bake slowly from 45 to 60 minutes.

–*Mrs. William H. Blevins,* 769 Maple St., Apr. 17, 1931.

Mrs. *W*atkins's
Jellied Meat Loaf

Soak one tablespoon gelatine in one-fourth cup of cold water for ten minutes. Dissolve in one pint of hot soup stock. Cool. Arrange in alternate layers in an oiled mold: one pound of cooked diced ham, one-half cup pimientos cut in small pieces, three tablespoons finely chopped pickles, a minced bay leaf, and a slice of onion (minced). Place several hard-boiled eggs in the center. Pour over all the gelatine, and chill. Turn out on lettuce leaves and serve. When sliced, the eggs show in the center of each slice.

–*Mrs. J. E. Watkins,* 728 New York St., June 19, 1931.

Miss *C*rim's Ham Loaf

One pound smoked ham, 1 pound fresh pork, 1 cup soft bread crumbs, 1 egg (beaten), ½ cup milk, salt. Grind the meat together, add the rest of the ingredients, mould into a loaf, and place in a shallow pan. Bake one hour at 350 degrees F., or in a moderate oven. Hard-cooked eggs, placed end to end through the center of the loaf, add flavor as well as color to the loaf. Vegetables such as potatoes, carrots, turnips and cabbage are also good cooked with the loaf. There should be enough liquid to make gravy.

–*Miss Adele Crim,*
746 Louisiana St., Oct. 30, 1931.

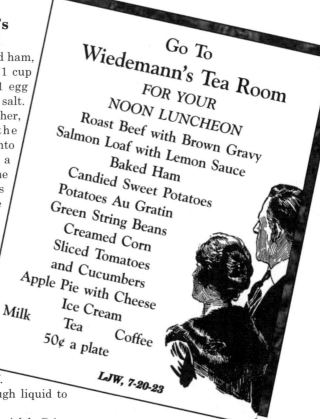

Go To
Wiedemann's Tea Room
FOR YOUR
NOON LUNCHEON
Roast Beef with Brown Gravy
Salmon Loaf with Lemon Sauce
Baked Ham
Candied Sweet Potatoes
Potatoes Au Gratin
Green String Beans
Creamed Corn
Sliced Tomatoes
and Cucumbers
Apple Pie with Cheese
Milk   Ice Cream
Tea   Coffee
50¢ a plate

LJW, 7-20-23

Mrs. *H*orr's Baked Meat Loaf

One pound round steak, ½ pound sausage, 3 slices moistened bread, 1 egg, 1 onion, ¼ pound salt pork, salt and pepper. Chop or grind the meat. Chop the onion and cook it in the fat, which has been tried out of a small portion of the pork. Add bread and cook a few minutes. When cool, mix with the other ingredients except the pork. Form into a long round roll, smoothing it by moistening the hands with cold water. Cut the salt pork in thin slices; lay them over the loaf and bake for forty minutes in a hot oven.

–*Mrs. W. H. Horr,* 1030 Maine St., Mar. 18, 1932.

Miss *S*tevenson's Pork Chops a la Creole
"This one dish makes a well-balanced meal
if followed by a fruit salad or dessert."

Six lean chops, thick, with bone; ½ cup rice, uncooked; 2 cans tomato soup; 1 large green pepper; onion. Cook rice, keeping it fairly dry. Pepper and salt chops on both sides. Put a spoonful of rice on each chop. Season rice with salt and paprika. Cut peppers in rings, putting one on each chop; fill the centers with chopped onion. Put in pan, pour soup around the chops, and bake two hours in a slow oven. Baste frequently, adding a little water if necessary.

–Miss Ruth Stevenson, Route 3, July 15, 1932.

Mrs. *S*moots's Sweetbread Cutlets

Two pairs sweetbreads, bread crumbs, 2 tablespoons water, toast points, 2 beaten eggs. Clean, trim and cook the sweetbreads in boiling salted water until tender. Drain, and cut in neat half-inch slices. Dip in fine, dried bread crumbs, then into the eggs beaten with the water, then in bread crumbs. Fry in deep fat to a golden brown. Lay on hot platter. Garnish with toast points and lemon, or serve with savory sauce. Serves six.

–Mrs. J. A. Smoots, Route 2, Eudora, May 5, 1933.

Mrs. *M*ueller's Ham Loaf
"I have used this many times, and find it makes a fine loaf."

Two pounds pork shoulder, ground; one pound smoked ham, ground; one cup cracker crumbs; one cup milk; 2 eggs, beaten; salt and pepper. Bake in moderate oven 1 ½ hours, or until done.

–Mrs. R. G. Mueller, 1140 New Jersey St., Nov. 17, 1933.

Mrs. *O*pperman's Jellied Veal Loaf

One knuckle veal (about 2 pounds), 2 quarts cold water, 1 onion (sliced), 1 tablespoon gelatine, 2 tablespoons cold water, ½ cup finely cut celery, salt and pepper, 2 tablespoons finely chopped parsley, 1 tablespoon lemon juice, 2 tablespoons finely chopped pimiento, ½ teaspoon celery seed, dash or two of tabasco sauce. Have the butcher crack the bones. Wash the knuckle well, and cover with the 2 quarts of cold water. Add the onion. Heat slowly to the boiling point, and then simmer, partly covered, until the meat is tender. Pour off and measure the liquid. There should be about a quart. Remove the meat from the bones, discarding all gristle and bone, and chop the meat very fine. Soften the gelatine in the 2 tablespoons of cold water and add to the hot stock. Chill, and when partly set, add the meat seasonings, and stir until well-mixed. Season to taste with salt, pepper and tabasco sauce. Rinse a large mold, pour in the mixture, and allow to stand several hours or overnight in a refrigerator.

–Mrs. J. C. Opperman, 1728 Kentucky St., Apr. 20, 1934.

Heard In Lawrence

The "got a dime for a cup of coffee?" boys are visiting Lawrence in increasing numbers and some are having more than ordinary success. The other day a Lawrence business man decided to spend twenty cents for lunch. On his way down the street he was accosted by a man who claimed to be very hungry. The business man gave the man a dime. Going on to a restaurant the business man was surprised to see the recipient of his help enter and order a large steak with all the trimmings. "The fellow seemed to be hungry, all right," the business man said. [LJW, 12-10-32]

Mrs. *H*ouser's Dried Beef Delight

Frizzle ½ cup dried beef in 1 tablespoon butter. Add 2 cups diced boiled potatoes or cooked rice. Beat 3 egg yolks till thick, add 3 tablespoons milk, and add to the above. Beat 3 egg whites stiff, and fold into the mixture. Season to taste, and cook as an omelet. Fold onto hot platter and serve.

–*Mrs. E. P. Houser,* 308 E. 19ᵗʰ St., May 18, 1934.

Miss *R*obinson's Spanish Meat Loaf

One and one-half pounds round steak, ground; ½ pound lean pork, ground; ¾ cup rolled crackers; 2 eggs; ¼ cup milk; 1 teaspoon salt; ¼ teaspoon pepper; 3 tablespoons chopped green pepper; 2 tablespoons chopped onions; 3 tablespoons melted fat; 4 tablespoons catsup (reserve for top). Mix ingredients, pack into loaf pan, spread catsup on top, and bake in moderate oven (325 degrees) one hour. Serves six.

–*Miss Eleanore Robinson,* 1545 Rhode Island St., Aug. 10, 1934.

Mrs. *O*tt's Meat Croquettes

One cup scalded milk, ½ cup Minute Tapioca, 1½ cups hot meat stock, 2 cups chopped cooked meat, 2 tablespoons chopped green pepper, 2 tablespoons chopped pimiento, ½ teaspoon salt, ⅛ teaspoon paprika, sifted bread or cracker crumbs, 1 slightly beaten egg, 2 tablespoons cold water. Cook tapioca in milk and stock in double boiler 15 minutes, or until tapioca is clear, stirring frequently. Add chopped meat, pepper, pimiento, salt and paprika. Cook 5 minutes longer. Cool. Shape into small cones. Roll in crumbs, dip in egg, to which water has been added, then roll again in crumbs. Fry in deep fat until golden brown. Serve with white sauce or creamed peas. Makes 12 croquettes. Chicken used in place of meats makes delicious croquettes.

–*Mrs. William F. Ott,* Route 1, Eudora, Aug. 31, 1934.

Mrs. *J*ohnson's New England Boiled Dinner

Select a 3 or 4 pound piece of corned beef, which is not too lean. Soak it over night in cold water. Early in the morning, drain and cover with boiling water in a large iron or porcelain kettle. Boil slowly and steadily. At 9 o'clock, add beets, taking care that

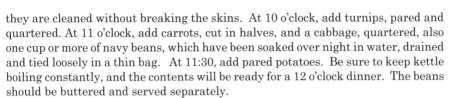

they are cleaned without breaking the skins. At 10 o'clock, add turnips, pared and quartered. At 11 o'clock, add carrots, cut in halves, and a cabbage, quartered, also one cup or more of navy beans, which have been soaked over night in water, drained and tied loosely in a thin bag. At 11:30, add pared potatoes. Be sure to keep kettle boiling constantly, and the contents will be ready for a 12 o'clock dinner. The beans should be buttered and served separately.

–Mrs. Vic Johnson, 846 Arkansas St., Dec. 28, 1934.

Mrs. *G*lenn's Baked Sweetbreads

Put a pair of sweetbreads on the fire in one quart of cold water, in which are mixed one tablespoonful of salt and one tablespoonful of vinegar. When the water boils, take them off, and throw them into cold water, leaving them until they get cold. Chop rather fine one-third of a medium-sized onion, four or five slices of carrot, half a stalk of celery, and one sprig of parsley. Put into the bottom of a baking dish trimmings of pork; on this place the sweetbreads, and sprinkle the chopped vegetables over the top. Bake them twenty minutes in a hot oven. Cut a slice of bread into an oval or any fancy shape, and fry it in a saute pan in a little hot butter, coloring it well. Put this crouton in the center of a hot platter, on which place the sweetbreads. Serve peas or tomato sauce around.

–Mrs. Viola Glenn, Route 1, Lecompton, Apr. 26, 1935.

Mrs. *B*ower's Stuffed Shoulder of Lamb

Bone a shoulder of lamb, leave the knuckle, and fill the cavity with rich bread stuffing. Tie neatly in shape and wrap in a buttered paper. Lay in a deep pan with 4 tablespoons butter, a sliced carrot and turnip, an onion stuck with cloves, and a bunch of sweet herbs. Pour on sufficient stock to cover the bottom of the pan. Set over a slow fire and simmer gently; baste every ten minutes. When nearly done, lift from the pan, remove the paper, and brush the meat with melted glaze. Set in oven to brown. Take up the shoulder on a heated dish. Strain the gravy and pour around it. Garnish with puree of green peas, and serve with mint sauce.

–Mrs. Donald K. Bower, Route 3, May 17, 1935.

Local Beef, Veal, and Rabbit Prices 1927

2 lbs. veal stew meat	.20
1 rabbit, dressed	.25
3 lbs. beef pot roast	.45
4 lbs. hamburger	.50
2 lbs. Porterhouse steak	.56
Total	$ 1.96

Mrs. *C*ummings's Jellied Meat Loaf
"This is fine for hot weather meals."

Get about 1½ pounds of pork pot roast and 1½ pounds of beef boil. Salt and pepper the meat as usual. Cook the meat together in a pot roaster or Dutch oven or a very heavy pan over a very slow fire for a long time. When it is well done, remove the meat from the broth. Take out all bones. Strain the broth to see that there are no small bones left in it. Take about a cup of broth and add to it 2 tablespoons of gelatine, which has first been dissolved in hot water. Taste the meat and add more salt and pepper if it seems to need it. Mix the meat all together and add a small amount of onion and some cucumber pickles cut into small pieces. Add the meat mixture to the broth and, when it is cool enough, put into the ice box and let stand several hours or until it is firm.

–Mrs. David Cummings, 1042 Ohio St., Aug. 2, 1935.

Mr. *B*roadwell's English Meat Pie
"This is a Melton Mowbray pie, named for the English town which first made them famous."

Two pounds lean pork (cut in small pieces), 1 small onion (minced) or 1 teaspoon onion juice, ½ teaspoon powdered sage, ½ teaspoon salt. Season with cayenne and black pepper as desired. Cover with water and simmer gently 2 hours. Add water as needed, but do not use too much, for you want the liquid to gelatinize when cold. Paste: 4 cups flour, 1 cup lard, ¼ teaspoon salt, ½ cup water. Boil water and lard, add to flour while hot, and knead till smooth. Set aside till wanted. When meat is done, re-knead the paste. Reserve one-fourth for lid to pie. Roll the balance, fit into a pan 4 inches deep, after lining pan with two thicknesses of paper. Put in the meat and 3 tablespoons of liquid. [Apply pastry lid.] Bake in slow oven 2 hours. When almost done, brush with beaten egg yolk. After taking from the oven, lift the lid and add the remainder of the meat stock. Serve cold.

–Mr. E. C. Broadwell, 832 Kentucky St., Dec. 20, 1935.

Mrs. *A*they's Meat Croquettes

One cup milk, scalded; ½ cup Minute Tapioca; 1½ cups hot meat stock; 2 cups cooked meat, chopped; 2 tablespoons pimiento, chopped; ½ teaspoon salt; 2 tablespoons green pepper, chopped; ⅛ teaspoon paprika; sifted crumbs, crackers or bread; 1 egg, slightly beaten; 2 tablespoons cold water. Cook tapioca in milk and stock in double boiler 15 minutes, or until tapioca is clear, stirring frequently. Add chopped meat, pepper, pimiento, salt and paprika. Cook 5 minutes longer. Cool, and shape into small cones. Roll in crumbs, dip in egg to which water has been added, then roll again in crumbs. Fry in deep fat until golden brown. Serve with white sauce or creamed peas. Makes 12 croquettes. Chicken used in place of meats makes delicious croquettes.

–Mrs. Elmer Athey, Route 3, Jan. 17, 1936.

Mrs. *K*eefe's Chop Suey
"This makes a good supper dish."

One pound of veal steak, cubed; 4 tablespoons butter or at least half butter; 1 cup of celery, cubed; 1 cup of onions, cubed; 2 teaspoons salt; 1 can of mixed Chinese vegetables or 1 can of bean sprouts; 3 tablespoons soy sauce; 1¼ tablespoons cornstarch; chicken and mushrooms, if desired; cooked rice. Fry veal in fat until brown; season, add celery and onions to meat. Cover closely and steam and cook until it is tender, 1 hour or more. Drain the Chinese vegetables or sprouts, add to first mixture, and stir. Heat thoroughly and add enough soy sauce to give the flavor you like. Thicken with the cornstarch. It will get dark and thick and very yummy as you cook it. Chopped sauteed mushrooms and the breast of chicken may be added to the mixture if you wish. Put molded rice in the center of a large platter, and the chop suey around the rice.

–Mrs. Ed Keefe, 710 New Hampshire St., Jan. 24, 1936.

Margaret *R*oper's Mock Chicken Loaf

Use 20 cents worth of veal hock and 15 cents worth of lean pork. Place in kettle with 5 cups of water, and boil two hours, or until two cups of liquid are left. Pick meat off bones and put through food chopper. Place in square pan. Pour liquid over meat and place in ice box. Leave over night or from four to five hours.

–Margaret Roper, 737 Arkansas St., July 31, 1936.

Mrs. *B*roadwell's Ham Loaf

Three-fourths pound smoked ham, ¾ pound fresh pork, ½ pound beef. Grind all together. Add 1 egg (slightly beaten), 1 cup rolled cornflakes, ½ cup tomato soup, ⅛ teaspoon pepper, no salt. Shape into loaf and roll in cornflakes. Bake 1 ½ hours in moderate oven. Baste with ½ cup tomato soup and ½ cup water. Raisins (½ cup) may be added to the pan and basted over the meat, or 1 cup of mushrooms may be used. Either one gives fine flavor.

–Mrs. Estelle Broadwell, 942 Mississippi St., Oct. 16, 1936.

Mrs. *G*reen's Sweetbreads a la King

Parboil 1 ½ lbs. sweetbreads. Melt 4 tablespoons butter, add 3 tablespoons flour. Blend well; add 1 teaspoon salt, and stir in 2 cups milk. Mix to a smooth white sauce. Add to this the diced sweetbreads, 2 tablespoons chopped pimiento, and one small can mushrooms, or 1 cup fresh, cooked mushrooms. When heated, stir in the yolk of one egg. Cook one minute. Nice served in patty shells or on toast points. Preparing sweetbreads: Plunge into cold water as soon as received, soak for one hour, then parboil in acidulated water (one teaspoon salt, 1 tablespoon vinegar, to one quart water) for twenty minutes. Drain and plunge into cold water to make them firm. The little strings and membranes, which are easily detached, should be removed.

–Mrs. A. A. Green, 829 Missouri St., Oct. 23, 1936.

Mrs. *S*haw's New England Boiled Dinner

Four pounds corned beef, 4 white turnips, 1 small head cabbage, 4 carrots, 6 or 8 potatoes, 6 beets, 6 small onions, ½ teaspoon pepper. Put the meat into the kettle with cold water to cover. Bring it rapidly to the boiling point; skim, and reduce the heat and simmer until meat is tender. About an hour before serving time, remove some of the liquid, in which the meat has been cooking, to another kettle and in it boil the vegetables, which have been prepared, with the exception of the beets, which should be cooked separately, as they will color the other vegetables. When vegetables are tender, arrange on a large platter around the meat.

–Mrs. Edward Shaw, Route 4, Jan. 15, 1937.

Miss *F*riend's Sausage

Three pounds tenderloin; 3 pounds of trimmings from hams, shoulders, and sides, with plenty of fat. Grind fine and add 1 tablespoon of pulverized leaves of sage, 1 teaspoon of red pepper (use pods of red pepper, chopped fine), ⅓ cup of salt. When seasoning is thoroughly distributed in finely ground meat, press the sausage into homemade cotton cloth sacks of about 3-inch diameter (cases may be used instead of sacks) and place in screened porch for cooling in open air. Smoking over hickory fire adds to flavor of the meat.

–Miss Susan Friend, 940 Kentucky St., Jan. 22, 1937.

Mrs. *K*ennedy's Vegetable Meat Loaf

Mix together one pound hamburger, one-half pound ground pork, and one-fourth cup minced onion. Peel and chop three ripe tomatoes and one red pepper. Add to meat mixture with two eggs. Season with salt and pepper. Into a well-greased ring pan, pour one-half cup of ketchup. Put in loaf mixture and bake in a moderate oven about one hour. Turn out of mold or pan, bottom side uppermost. Fill center with hot potato salad and garnish with parsley sprays.

–Mrs. A. R. Kennedy, 935½ Massachusetts St., Sept. 24, 1937.

Miss $\mathcal{S}$aunders's New England Boiled Dinner

One and one-half pounds veal for stewing, 4 cups water, 2 teaspoons salt, ¼ teaspoon pepper, 1 bay leaf, ¼ cup chopped onions, 4 tablespoons flour, 4 cups cubed carrots, 2 cups green peas. Dredge veal with 2 tablespoons flour, and brown in hot fat. Add water, salt, pepper, bay leaf, and onion, and stew until tender (about 1½ hours). Add carrots last 20 minutes of cooking. When tender, remove the bones from the stew. Thicken the gravy with 2 tablespoons flour, which has been mixed with a little cold water. Add peas. Place dumplings on top of meat. Cover tightly and cook until dumplings are done. Dumplings: 2 cups flour, 4 teaspoons baking powder, ½ teaspoon salt, 1 tablespoon shortening, ¾ cup milk. Sift flour once before measuring. Mix and sift flour, baking powder and salt. Cut in shortening. Add milk gradually to make a soft dough. Roll and cut with biscuit cutter or drop by spoonfuls on top of stew. (Dumplings should rest on meat and vegetables and not settle into the liquid.) Cover kettle closely and cook without lifting cover. Cook 12 minutes.

–*Miss Mildred Saunders,* Route 2, Jan. 21, 1938.

Miss $\mathcal{B}$artz's German-Style Kraut with Spareribs

Cut a side of spareribs into 5 or 6 pieces. Place in a shallow earthen dish, sprinkle 1½ tablespoons of salt over the ribs, and allow to stand for a day or so in a cold place. Wipe meat, put into a kettle, and add hot water to cover. Bring to the boiling point. Add 3 carrots and an onion with 2 cloves inserted. Cover and cook slowly until tender. Thirty minutes before serving time, add 3 potatoes, peeled and cut in cubes. Fifteen minutes before serving time, add 1 quart of kraut. When ready to serve, pile vegetables in center of hot platter and arrange the spareribs around them.

–*Miss Elizabeth Bartz,* Route 1, Mar. 18, 1938.

Mrs. $\mathcal{G}$ regory's Strawberry Ham Slice

One slice ham (1 inch thick), 1 cup crushed strawberries, ⅔ cup sugar, 8 cloves, 2 tablespoons lemon juice. Brown ham slice (in one piece or cut into 4 servings) in an iron skillet. Place in baking dish with pan drippings and 2 tablespoons each of water and strawberry juice. Cover and bake in moderate oven (375 degrees F.) for one hour to ninety minutes or until almost done. Combine berries, sugar and lemon juice, and bring to a boil. Remove ham from oven, stick fat with cloves, pour hot juice over it, and return to oven for 15 minutes longer. Garnish with fried pineapple slices with sugared strawberries in center of each. With the ham, serve these: Oven Hashed Potatoes: chop raw potatoes into very fine pieces, allow to stand in cold water a few minutes, drain and let cold water run through them. Drain. Butter a shallow glass baking dish. Place layer of potatoes in dish, season and dot with butter. Repeat; then add cream or whole milk until you can see it through the potatoes. Bake in a slow oven for 1 ½ hours. Cover during the first part of baking.

–Mrs. Howard Gregory, Route 1, Apr. 7, 1939.

Mrs. $\mathcal{D}$ unkley's Stuffed Peppers
"This is a delicious and inexpensive one-dish meal."

Six medium-sized green mango sweet peppers. Cut the tops off and scrape out seeds. Cover with water and boil with 1 teaspoon salt for 10 minutes. Cool. One tablespoon butter or drippings; 1 pound ground beef (beef should be quite lean, and lean shoulder meat can be ordered ground); 1 medium-sized onion, diced; 1 tablespoon flour; ½ cup sweet milk; ¼ to ½ cup crushed crackers or ground dry bread crumbs; 1 egg (may be omitted). Dice the usable parts of the tops of the peppers, and the onion, in the fat. Then add the meat, and stir and cook the meat into the hot fat until all of the meat has turned slightly brown. Season with salt and pepper. Scrape meat to one side of skillet, add the flour, brown slightly, then add milk. Mix all through the meat. Add cracker or bread crumbs, and stir in beaten egg. Stuff peppers with this mixture, being careful not to pack down too much.

Set peppers up carefully in a baking dish. Put about ¼ cup water in bottom of dish and place in 375 degree oven for 30 minutes to brown and blend the flavors. With a salad made of assorted vegetables or fruits, stuffed peppers make an entire meal.

–Mrs. George B. Dunkley, 628 Maine St., Sept. 29, 1939.

Mrs. *C*haffin's Ham Loaf

One pound ground smoked ham, ½ pound ground beef, ½ pound ground pork, ½ cup cracker crumbs, ½ teaspoon salt, pepper and paprika to taste, 1 onion (chopped), 1 green pepper (chopped), ½ cup celery (chopped), 1 small can pimientos (chopped), 1 egg, ½ cup milk. Mix all ingredients together thoroughly. Shape into loaf in pan and bake in a 375 degree oven, 1½ to 2 hours.

–Mrs. H. L. Chaffin, 1657 Indiana St., July 12, 1940.

Mrs. *H*icks's New England Boiled Dinner

Two pounds boiling beef, 6 medium-sized carrots, 6 small onions, 6 medium-sized potatoes, 1 small head cabbage (cut into one-sixths), 1 teaspoon salt, ¼ teaspoon pepper, ½ teaspoon celery salt. Wash meat and put into a large kettle. Cook 1 ½ hours. Add vegetables and cook until tender. Serves 6.

–Mrs. Eva Hicks, 210 W. 7th St., Jan. 24, 1941.

Mrs. *R*eed's Meat Loaf

One and one-half pounds raw beef, ground twice; 1 ½ lbs. raw pork, ground; ½ cup fine bread or cracker crumbs; ½ cup milk or tomato juice; 1 egg; 2 tablespoons grated onion; 2 tablespoons chopped parsley; 2 teaspoons salt; ¼ teaspoon poultry seasoning. Mix ingredients well. Pack into a greased loaf pan. Arrange strips of bacon over top. Bake uncovered in preheated oven, 375 degrees F., for one hour. Serve with tomato sauce. Tomato Sauce: 1 onion, chopped; ½ cup diced celery; 2 tablespoons butter; 1 tablespoon green pepper, chopped; ½ teaspoon salt; ⅛ teaspoon pepper; ¼ teaspoon nutmeg; ½ bay leaf; 2 cups strained tomatoes; 1 tablespoon chopped parsley. Fry onion and celery in butter over low heat. Add remaining ingredients, except parsley; cover and simmer for 20 minutes. Thicken if desired with a thin paste prepared with 1½ tablespoons flour and water, stirred to a smooth consistency. Add parsley.

–Mrs. D. A. Reed, 908 Massachusetts St., Sept. 5, 1941.

LJW, 1930

Mrs. *M*cKittrick's New England Boiled Dinner

Get an English pot roast cut or a piece of corned beef, 4 or 5 pounds. Put into a kettle with a tight cover, boil quickly in water almost covering the meat. Remove all scum. When no more scum rises, add the following vegetables, peeled and sliced into 1-inch pieces: 4 carrots, 4 beets, 4 turnips, 1 yellow turnip (cut in medium pieces), 6 medium onions, 6 or 8 small potatoes, stalk of celery. Place pot where contents can cook slowly until meat is tender and vegetables remain whole, 2½ to 3 hours. To serve, place meat on a large platter, and arrange vegetables around it. Serve gravy in a gravy boat. Beets can be cooked separately. Salt and pepper to suit taste. Put potatoes in to cook in time to be ready for serving so they will remain whole. The united flavor of the meat and vegetables characterizes the dish. Add vegetables to suit taste.

–Mrs. John McKittrick, 705 New Hampshire St., Jan. 23, 1942.

Mrs. *A*vey's Summer Meat Loaf

Mix thoroughly: 1 egg, 1 lb. twice-ground beef, ⅔ can canned milk or cream, 2 tablespoons finely cut onion, 1½ tablespoons finely cut parsley, 1½ teaspoons salt, ⅛ teaspoon black pepper, 1 cup finely ground cracker crumbs. Shape into loaf. Place in baking dish with about 2 inches of space on each side. Put liquid in spaces (either milk, water or tomato juice) and bake in moderate oven, 350 degrees, about 45 minutes. Lay slices of American cheese on loaf and bake 10 minutes longer or until cheese is melted. Serve at once. Dashes of tomato catsup may be used on baked loaf in place of cheese, if preferred.

–Mrs. C. O. Avey, 1306 Oak Hill Ave., June 19, 1942.

Mrs. *H*oley's Sausage Meat
"This is delicious and will keep indefinitely."

Fifteen pounds of pork, 2 ozs. of pepper, 4 ozs. of salt, 1 oz. of sage, ½ oz. of coriander (note: coriander may be omitted). Have the meat about ⅓ fat and ⅔ lean. Cut into small pieces, and sprinkle seasonings over meat. Grind fine. If you have no good sausage grinder, take seasoned meat to your local meat market. Your butcher will grind it for a small sum. Work this ground mass thoroughly so all seasoning is well mixed through. You may mold this into a 1-lb. butter mold, wrap in wax paper, and keep in cold place. When wanted, slice and fry. Or, from thin muslin, make casings not over 12 inches long and no more then 2½ to 3 inches in diameter. Stuff sausage into these, tie securely and hang over hickory smoke for at least 48 hours.

–Mrs. W. E. Holey, Sr.,
Route 3, Jan. 1, 1943.

Mrs. $\mathcal{S}$eiwald's
Brisket of Beef with Beans

Two cups navy beans, ½ teaspoon dry mustard, salt and pepper, ½ cup brown sugar, ½ cup maple syrup, 3 to 4 lbs. brisket of beef. Soak beans over night in cold water. Drain and place in large casserole or Dutch oven. Add seasonings, sugar and syrup. Trim excess fat from meat and put meat on top of beans. Cover with cold water. Bake in a moderate oven, 350 degrees F., until meat is tender–or about 3½ hours. Add water if necessary.

–*Mrs. W. J. Seiwald*, 909 Connecticut St., Jan. 28, 1944.

Heard In Lawrence

One local restaurant man serves "Jiggs" on Wednesdays. He says
"Jiggs" is his pet name for corned beef and cabbage.
[LJW, 3-31-34]

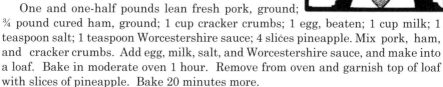

Mrs. *P*earson's Ham Loaf

One and one-half pounds lean fresh pork, ground; ¾ pound cured ham, ground; 1 cup cracker crumbs; 1 egg, beaten; 1 cup milk; 1 teaspoon salt; 1 teaspoon Worcestershire sauce; 4 slices pineapple. Mix pork, ham, and cracker crumbs. Add egg, milk, salt, and Worcestershire sauce, and make into a loaf. Bake in moderate oven 1 hour. Remove from oven and garnish top of loaf with slices of pineapple. Bake 20 minutes more.

–*Mrs. Gerald Pearson,* 708 Ohio St., Mar. 3, 1944.

Mrs. *A*llen's Meat Croquettes

One tablespoon fat, 3 tablespoons flour, 1 cup milk, 2 cups ground cooked meat, 1 tablespoon chopped onion, ½ teaspoon salt, ⅓ teaspoon pepper, 1 egg, fine dry bread crumbs. Melt fat, add flour, and blend. Add milk and cook until very thick, stirring constantly. Add meat, onion and seasonings. Chill thoroughly. Form into desired shape and dip into crumbs, then into beaten egg mixed with two tablespoons water, and into crumbs again. Fry in hot, deep fat until brown. Serves six.

–*Mrs. Nellie Allen,* 1407 Kentucky St., Jan. 24, 1947.

Local Lamb & Pork Prices
1924

1 lb. pork brains	.15
2 lbs. pork liver	.15
2 lbs. lamb breast	.30
1 lb. lamb chops	.45
2 lbs. pork chops	.50
1 (3 lb.) pork loin roast	.54
Total	$ 2.09

Mrs. *B*rubaker's Six Layer Dinner

"Six layers of six blended flavors and it serves six. Have hard rolls, tossed salad, and apple crisp."

Two cups sliced raw potatoes, 2 cups chopped celery, 2 cups ground beef, 1 cup sliced raw onions, 1 cup finely cut green peppers (or less if desired), 2 cups cooked tomatoes.

Season layers with 2 teaspoons salt, ¼ teaspoon pepper. Garnish with green pepper slices. Bake about 2 hours in 350 degree oven.

–*Mrs. Lanty Brubaker,* 1937 Learnard Ave., Jan. 23, 1948.

Mrs. *A*ltenbernd's Hamburger-Potato Pie

One medium-sized onion, chopped; 2 tablespoons fat; 1 pound ground beef; ½ teaspoon salt; ¼ teaspoon pepper; 1 cup cooked peas, frozen or canned; 1 cup canned tomatoes; ½ cup catsup; 3 cups hot, seasoned mashed potatoes; 1 beaten egg.

Cook onion in hot fat until golden. Add meat and seasonings. Cook until meat is lightly browned. Add peas, tomatoes, and catsup. Mix well. Pour into greased 2-quart casserole. Combine mashed potatoes and egg. Spoon to form mounds or spread over meat mixture. Bake in moderate oven (350 degrees) 20 to 30 minutes.

–Mrs. Homer C. Altenbernd, Route 2, Feb. 25, 1949.

Miss *M*ast's Ham Loaf

One and one-half pounds fresh ham (pork shoulder), ground; 1½ pounds smoked or cured ham, ground; 1 cup cracker crumbs; 1 egg; pepper (no salt). Combine the above ingredients in the order given, and form a loaf. Place in a baking dish. Bake in a moderate oven, 350 degrees, 1½ hours. Baste frequently with the following dressing: 1 cup brown sugar, ½ cup vinegar, ½ cup water, 1 scant tablespoon mustard. Combine and boil on top of stove until ingredients are well-mixed.

–Miss Mildred Mast, 1545 Rhode Island St., Apr. 8, 1949.

Fish
and
Seafood

Lone Star Lake Grand Opening
More Than 2,000 Permits Sold; Fishing Is Good

"What'll I do? What'll I do? I got one. Can I pull him in?" The cry of distress came from a woman in a boat on Lone Star Lake on the opening day. She had sent her husband on shore to buy a county permit. While he was buying the license she baited her hook and let it hang just at the edge of the water waiting for her husband to get back with the licenses. A hungry blue gill that did not understand about permits and such things grabbed the bait and the woman started yelling for help. Elmer Bahnmaier, who was selling licenses for the county, waved a dollar bill at the lady and told her to get her fish. She got that one and the rest of her limit within an hour.

Over 2,000 county permits have been sold. The opening crowd was estimated at 2,000; the next day, Sunday, was too windy for fishing but at least a thousand fishing enthusiasts turned out to try their luck.

The best part about the opening was the fact that almost everyone caught some fish. Only a few bass were caught. Blue gill, bull heads and channel cats made up the most of the catches. Some 12 pound channel cats were taken from the lake.

A large number of the fishermen on the first day had their limit by 7 o'clock. It was an interesting sight to see the many boats that dotted the lake at the sound of the bomb that started the fishing. By actual count there were 435 cars on the grounds at 3 o'clock Saturday morning. Cots and sleeping fishermen were everywhere.

The crowd was orderly and well behaved. Everyone had a good time and enough fish were caught to make them happy. The county commissioners, county clerk and sheriff had everything well organized so there was no serious trouble or accidents. [DCR, 8-1-40]

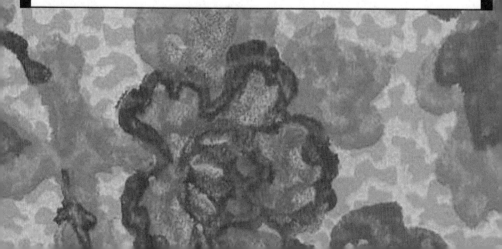

Mrs. *A*they's Fish and Corn Scallop

Two cups cooked fish, one cup white sauce, one can sweet corn, stale bread crumbs. Mix the thick white sauce into the corn, and season to taste. Place in the bottom of a bake dish a layer of bread crumbs, then a layer of fish; cover with a layer of the canned corn, and continue until the dish is full, placing a layer of crumbs on the top, and a little butter. Bake in a moderate oven about thirty minutes.

–Mrs. Martha Athey, Route 5, Sept. 16, 1921.

Mrs. *L*earned's Creamed Tuna Fish in Patty Shells

Two cups tuna fish (17 oz. can), 1 cup white sauce made from following recipe: 1 cup milk, 2 tablespoons flour (level), 2 tablespoons butter, ⅛ teaspoon of salt; cook until thickened.

Patty Shells: for these, a quick puff paste is made in the following manner: 1 cup bread flour, 1 tablespoon of lard, seven-eighths cup butter, ¼ cup ice water. Work lard into flour, then moisten with water. Roll into strip, place one half butter on top, sprinkle on a little flour, and double paste over three times (double one end over, then the other end over on that). Roll out again, and put remaining butter on in small lumps, and fold over again, and roll out in strip. Cut into shape for patty shells, chill a few minutes, and bake in an oven at temperature of 235 centigrade. [Ed. note: temperature converts to 455 degrees fahrenheit.]

–Mrs. Z. M. Learned, 739 Alabama St., Oct. 13, 1922.

Mrs. *P*ontius's Pot Roast of Halibut

Three or four pounds of halibut, one-half cup oil, two carrots, three large onions, two cups minced celery. Parboil the vegetables; pare and mince finely. Skin halibut by slipping a knife under skin and working away from you. Heat the oil in a frying pan and brown the fish lightly on each side. Lift the fish into a low casserole. Pour the oil from the pan over the top, rinsing out the pan with a little boiling water and adding that to the dish. Season the fish with salt and pepper. Add the parboiled vegetables and the water in which they were cooked (about a cup). Place a tight cover on the casserole and bake in the oven for about an hour. Serve the fish in the center of a hot platter with the vegetables around it.

–Mrs. Brooke Pontius, 709 Arkansas St., Mar. 12, 1926.

Mrs. Carter's Salmon and Macaroni Loaf with Lemon Sauce

One cup milk, 4 tablespoons cream, 2 cups dry bread crumbs, 2 eggs, 1 cup cooked macaroni cut in small pieces, 2 cups salmon, 4 tablespoons melted butter, 1 teaspoon salt, paprika.

Heat milk and crumbs together. Stir in egg yolks, macaroni, salmon, cream, butter and salt. Fold in stiffly beaten egg whites. Pour in buttered mould, sprinkle with paprika, and bake about 30 minutes in moderate oven, in pan of hot water.

Sauce: ¼ cup butter, 2 tablespoons flour, ¾ cup milk, ½ teaspoon salt, ⅛ teaspoon pepper, 2 egg yolks, grated rind of ½ lemon, 4 tablespoons lemon juice. Melt butter, add flour slowly, blending to smooth paste. Add milk; boil, stirring until it thickens. Add salt, pepper, rind, and egg yolks. Stir until smooth, without boiling; add lemon juice gradually. Serve on slices of loaf.

–Mrs. Ella Carter, 1335 Vermont St., Mar. 18, 1927.

Mrs. Cook's Creamed Tuna with Mushrooms

"This is a delicious party or luncheon dish."

One can tuna fish, 1 cupful of pecan meats, 2½ tablespoonfuls of flour, salt and pepper, 3 cupfuls of sweet milk, 1 can of mushrooms. Make a creamy sauce of the flour, butter and milk, seasoning to taste. Add the tuna, mushrooms and nuts. Serve in patty cases. Garnish with sprigs of parsley.

–Mrs. J. E. Cook, 936 Missouri St., Apr. 8, 1927.

Mrs. Pennington's Salmon Souffle

One cup of salmon, 2 tablespoons of butter, 2 tablespoons of flour, 1 teaspoon of salt, ¼ teaspoon of pepper, 1 cup of sweet milk, 3 egg yolks, 3 egg whites (stiffly beaten). Melt the butter, add the flour, salt and pepper. When well mixed, add the milk, and cook until creamy. Cool. Add the egg yolks and beat for two minutes. Then add the salmon, and cut and fold in the egg whites. Pour into a greased mold. Set in a pan of hot water, and bake in a moderate oven 35 minutes. This amount will serve 4 people.

–Mrs. May Pennington, 1024 Pennsylvania St., Jan. 13, 1928.

Heard In Lawrence

Justin Hill and Hovey Hanna did some research work on the behavior of fish during an eclipse. They went fishing last night at Lakeview and reported that fish do not bite any better during an eclipse than at other times. "In fact, I think, from our experience last night, that they are a little more reluctant to bite," said Hill this morning. Both the fishermen brought home fish, but fewer than they had expected to land.
[LJW, 4-13-49]

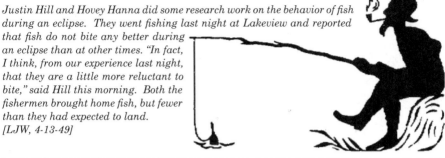

Mrs. *O*bley's Baked Halibut

Butter a baking dish, preferably one that may be sent to the table. Cut pieces of halibut for serving, and lay on bottom of dish. Mix one level cup of soft bread crumbs, one-fourth cup of melted butter, and one-fourth level teaspoon each of salt and paprika. Spread the mixture over the fish, add another layer of fish, and finish with two slices of salt pork. Cook six minutes in hot oven, then reduce the heat and cook half an hour longer, basting often with the fat in the pan. When the fish is done, remove the pork, sprinkle the top of the fish with three tablespoons of cracker crumbs mixed with one tablespoon of melted butter, and return to the oven to brown the crumbs.

Serve with the following sauce: Melt one-fourth cup of butter. In it cook one-fourth cup of flour and half a teaspoon each of salt and pepper. Add one cup of fish broth and one cup of cooked tomatoes, strained, and stir until boiling.

–Mrs. William Obley, 836 Mississippi St., Mar. 16, 1928.

Mrs. *B*urnett's Canned Oysters

One cup canned large oysters, 1 tablespoon butter, 2 tablespoons flour, 1 cup milk, ½ cup diced celery, ½ cup nut meats (pecans or walnuts), ½ teaspoon salt, 4 long French rolls or 4 slices toast. Scald oysters in skillet until edges curl; remove from liquor. Add butter and flour (creamed), and milk, then cook until thick. Add diced celery and nuts (broken in small pieces). Season to taste, add oysters, and heat thoroughly, but quickly. Remove tops from rolls, scoop out soft part and toast remainder slightly. Fill with oysters, cap with the toasted tops, and serve at once. Makes four servings.

–Mrs. W. W. Burnett, 909 Missouri St., Mar. 23, 1928.

Mrs. *S*uiter's Mushrooms with Oysters

One can mushrooms, one pint oysters, one large tablespoonful butter, one large tablespoonful flour, one cup cream, two yolks of eggs, one teaspoon salt, dash of paprika. Put the butter into the chafing dish when slightly melted, add the flour and stir until well blended. Pour in the cream and one half cup of the liquor from the mushrooms; stir until smooth, add the oysters and the small mushrooms, whole or sliced. Bring to the boiling point and add the well-beaten yolks slowly. Remove at once from the fire; season and serve on squares of toast.

–*Mrs. Maurice Suiter,* Route 3, May 4, 1928.

Mrs. *R*eed's Fried Haddock Fillets

Cut 2 pounds fillets in portions for serving. Roll in flour; shake off all loose flour. Beat 1 egg lightly with a fork. Add 1 tablespoon water, 1 tablespoon lemon juice, ½ teaspoon salt, ⅛ teaspoon pepper. Beat all together. Dip fish in egg, then roll in finely sifted dried bread crumbs (¾ cup). Fry in sizzling hot fat for 8 minutes, turning it once. Serve with tartar sauce, or lemon slices, and chopped parsley.

–*Mrs. Arthur Reed,* 1009 Maine St., Sept. 21, 1928.

Mrs. *B*artley's Salmon Puffs

"These Salmon Puffs are extremely convenient
when prepared in the morning if one is coming home late
with only a short time to prepare dinner."

These are glorified croquettes made much softer and creamier by a thick cream-sauce foundation. The following are the ingredients: 2½ tablespoons of butter or substitute, ⅓ cup of flour, ¼ teaspoon salt, a dash of pepper, 1 cup of scalded milk, bread crumbs, 1 egg, 1 can salmon, 1 cup mashed potato (may be varied according to what may be left over).

Melt the butter. When it bubbles, add the flour, salt and pepper, and stir until well blended. Pour the milk in slowly and beat with a fork until very smooth. Add to this the salmon, entirely freed of all bone and skin, picked into small bits with a fork, and mixed with the potato. Remove from the fire and spread on a platter to cool. Let it get thoroughly cold before using. The mixture should be as soft as can be handled, and will be found to be delicious and creamy. Cover a platter or board with finely rolled crumbs. Lift a large spoonful of the mixture, toss on the crumbs until a dry surface is formed, then lay in a dish that contains the beaten egg, in which one tablespoon of water has been mixed. Pour the egg over the croquette, lift on a large fork to drain off the egg. Then roll in the crumbs again and shape. Be careful about the crumbing and egging, for if the puff is not well covered, it will soak fat and crack open. Fry in deep fat until slightly browned. A wire basket is helpful though not necessary. If served for luncheon, "golf balls" made of hard-boiled egg cut

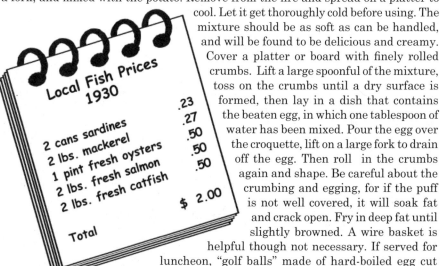

Local Fish Prices
1930

2 cans sardines	.23
2 lbs. mackerel	.27
1 pint fresh oysters	.50
2 lbs. fresh salmon	.50
2 lbs. fresh catfish	.50
Total	$ 2.00

lengthwise and stuffed with finely minced cabbage (mixed with the yolks and a snappy mayonnaise) are a relish to eat with these puffs. Potato rosettes and rings make a pretty garnish. A lemon pudding or pie is the best dessert to accompany such a luncheon.

–*Mrs. S. H. Bartley,* 1021 Maine St., Jan. 18, 1929.

Mrs. *I*nce's
Hot Oven Baked Haddock

Add one rounding teaspoon salt to one half cup top milk, and pour into shallow dish. In another dish have rolled and sifted dried bread crumbs. Cut fish into portions, dip in milk, then in crumbs, and place in well-buttered shallow pan. Pour melted butter over fish, and bake 15 minutes. Serve with any relish or sweet pickle.

–*Mrs. J. W. Ince,* 1729 Vermont St., Mar. 1, 1929.

Mrs. *H*oward's Scalloped Oysters

One quart oysters (fresh or cove), 1 cup bread crumbs, ½ cup melted butter, 1 cup cracker crumbs, and enough milk to moisten. Stir the bread and crackers crumbs into the melted butter. Sprinkle the bottom of an oiled baking dish with some of the crumbs. Place on these a layer of oysters, and season. Add crumbs and oysters, alternately, until dish is full, with a layer of crumbs on top. Add milk to moisten the crumbs until the milk shows at sides of dish. Bake in hot oven 15 to 20 minutes.

–*Mrs. Chester Howard,* Route 6, Dec. 27, 1929.

Mrs. *H*ammig's Scalloped Salmon

One can salmon, 1 can peas, 2 tablespoons fat, 4 tablespoons flour, 2 cups milk, ½ teaspoon salt, 2 tablespoons chopped chili peppers, ½ teaspoon pepper, half a lemon, ½ cup cracker crumbs. Break up salmon. Melt fat; add flour, salt, pepper and milk, and bring to boiling point, stirring constantly. Add salmon, chili peppers and peas, and pour into greased casserole. Squeeze juice of lemon over the top, cover with crumbs, and bake until brown.

–*Mrs. Erwin Hammig,* [address unavailable], Apr. 11, 1930.

Mrs. *V*iets's Oven Haddock

Cut haddock into individual portions. Dip each piece in milk, then roll in dry bread crumbs, finely ground and sifted. Afterward, place in large pan, which has been well-greased with cooking oil. Repeat with other portions; then sprinkle each piece slightly with the oil, and place pan, without cover, in very hot oven. The fish will be done in from ten to twelve minutes. If not sufficiently brown, place under gas broiler for one minute. Serve at once with sliced lemon for garnish.

–*Mrs. Ivan Viets,* 716 Arkansas St., Mar. 20, 1931.

ANDWICHES
HORT ORDERS
HRIMP ON FRIDAY

•

WE SERVE QUALITY
MEALS

•

L A R G E ' S
C A F E
PHONE 959

18 E. 9TH
Nov., 1938, Jayhawker

Miss Athey's Salmon Loaf

One level tablespoon gelatine, yolks of two eggs, 1½ teaspoonsful melted butter, 2 tablespoons mild vinegar or lemon juice, 1 teaspoon mustard, ¼ cupful cold water, 1 teaspoon salt, ¾ cupful milk, 1 can salmon, a few grains cayenne or paprika. Soak gelatine in cold water about five minutes. Mix egg yolks, slightly beaten, with salt, mustard and cayenne; then add butter, milk and vinegar. Cook in double boiler, stirring constantly, until mixture thickens. Add soaked gelatine and salmon, separated into flakes. Turn into wet mold, chill, and remove to bed of crisp lettuce leaves. Serve with mayonnaise.

–Miss Pearl Athey,
Route 3, Jan. 20, 1933.

Mrs. Robinson's Escalloped Salmon

Shred one can of salmon, removing all the skin and bones, but saving all the oil. Mix with cream sauce made of one tablespoon of butter, 1½ tablespoons of flour, and one cupful of milk. Put into a pan on the stove two cupfuls of cracker crumbs and two tablespoons of butter, stirring until butter is melted and mixed thoroughly with the cracker crumbs. Then take out one half of the crumbs, put in the salmon, and cover with the crumbs taken out. Bake in oven until slightly brown.

–Mrs. James E. Robinson, 1642 Tennessee St., June 30, 1933.

Mrs. Eberhart's Codfish Souffle

One-half cup of salt codfish, 1½ tablespoons butter, 2 eggs, 2 cups milk, ½ cup uncooked rice. Cook rice with the milk in double boiler until tender and dry. Add the well-beaten egg yolks. Add the butter and the codfish, which has been soaked in water several hours or even over night. Cool the mixture, fold in the egg whites (beaten stiff), and bake in a moderate oven (375 degrees) for 30 minutes. Serve with Maitre d'Hotel butter made thus: ¼ cup butter, ½ teaspoon salt, ⅛ teaspoon pepper, ½ teaspoon chopped parsley, 1½ tablespoons lemon juice. Cream butter, add salt, pepper and parsley, then lemon juice very slowly.

–Mrs. I. F. Eberhart, 945 Tennessee St., Feb. 9, 1934.

Miss $\mathcal{S}$cott's Baked Haddock a la Preston

Two haddock fillets, one and one-half tablespoons lemon juice, salt and pepper, two-thirds cup buttered bread crumbs, two-thirds cup cream or milk, mushroom stuffing. Brush fish with lemon juice and sprinkle with salt and pepper. Put one fillet in buttered pan or an oven-proof platter. Spread with stuffing, and cover with remaining fillet. Pour over cream or milk, and bake 25 minutes in moderately hot oven (375 degrees F.). Sprinkle with bread crumbs, and bake until crumbs are brown. Remove to hot serving dish, and strain liquid remaining in pan over it.

Mushroom Stuffing: Mix one-half cup bread crumbs with three tablespoons butter and one-third cup mushroom caps (cut in slices), one-half teaspoon salt, and a few grains of pepper.

–Miss Grace Scott, 808 Walnut St., Feb. 23, 1934.

Miss $\mathcal{C}$urtis's Salmon Loaf

Two and one-half cups flaked salmon, 1 cup bread crumbs, ½ pint milk, 4 eggs, 1 heaping tablespoon butter, 1 heaping tablespoon flour, 1 teaspoon salt. Flake salmon, sprinkle with lemon juice. Melt butter in sauce pan; blend in flour, and add milk. Stir until smooth. Add beaten egg yolks and salt; stir in salmon and bread crumbs; then fold in beaten egg whites. Pour into buttered baking dish, set in pan of hot water, and bake 40 minutes. Garnish with lemon and parsley.

–Miss Margaret Curtis, 846 Rhode Island St., Mar. 23, 1934.

Miss $\mathcal{C}$adwell's Scalloped Tuna and Noodles
"This makes a nice luncheon dish."

One package noodles, 1 can tuna, 1 package pimiento cheese, 1 small can mushrooms, 1 green pepper (chopped), 3 hard-cooked eggs, 12 ripe olives, 1½ cups milk, 3 tablespoons butter, 3 tablespoons flour, seasonings. Cook the noodles in boiling, salted water; drain. Make a white sauce of the butter, flour, milk and seasonings. Combine all ingredients and bake in a moderate oven at 350 degrees F. Serves 8 to 10 persons.

–Miss Ruth Cadwell, 1712 Learnard Ave., Nov. 2, 1934.

Mrs. $\mathcal{P}$ontius's Baked Salmon Charleston

One No. 1 can salmon, 1 teaspoon salt, ⅛ teaspoon pepper, 2 tablespoons prepared mustard, 6 medium-sized potatoes, 3 green peppers (chopped), ¼ lb. cheese (grated), 2 eggs (well-beaten), ¼ cup milk or water, 2 tablespoons butter. Remove all bones from salmon; season with salt, pepper, and mustard. Slice boiled potatoes and peppers. Fill greased baking dish with layers of salmon, potatoes and peppers, covering each layer with grated cheese. Mix beaten eggs with milk; pour over all and dot with butter. Bake in moderate oven until top browns.

–Mrs. Arthur Pontius, 1309 W. 4th St., Apr. 19, 1935.

Mrs. Hawkins's Rice and Salmon Loaf
"A savory Lenten dish."
Two cups of hot boiled rice, 1 cup salmon, 2 eggs (beaten), ¼ teaspoon pepper, juice of ½ lemon, 2 tablespoons melted butter, ½ teaspoon salt. Beat egg yolks (after separating from the whites), and mix with rice, adding seasonings and salmon and juice from the salmon. Beat egg whites stiff and add to mixture. Put into a greased baking dish and set in shallow pan of water. Bake in a moderate oven of 350 degrees F. about 45 minutes. Garnish with parsley and lemon slices, and serve with a tomato sauce. The following is an excellent tomato sauce: 2 cups tomatoes, 1 slice of onion, 3 tablespoons butter, 3 tablespoons flour, salt and pepper. Cook onion with tomatoes 15 minutes, and strain. Brown butter and add flour. When well blended, add tomato and bring to boiling point. Cook three minutes.
–Mrs. V. D. Hawkins, 815 Arkansas St., Feb. 19, 1937.

Mrs. Cadwell's Salmon Roll
Pastry: 2 cups flour, 4 teaspoons baking powder, ½ teaspoon salt, 4 tablespoons shortening, 1 egg, ½ cup milk. Filling: ½ cup milk, 4 tablespoons flour, ½ teaspoon salt, 1½ cups salmon, 2 tablespoons lemon juice, 2 teaspoons chopped onion, 1½ tablespoons chopped parsley. Pastry: Sift flour, baking powder and salt together; cut in shortening. Combine wet and dry ingredients. Roll out on floured board into a sheet 8 inches long and about ¼ inch thick. Spread with filling. Roll up like a jelly roll. Bake in hot oven (400 degrees F.) about 25 minutes. Serve in slices with hot cream sauce. Filling: Mix flour and milk, and heat until thick. Add rest of ingredients.
–Mrs. G. E. Cadwell, 1712 Learnard Ave., Mar. 25, 1938.

Mrs. Sandelius's Salmon Souffle
Remove bone from one can salmon and mash the salmon to a fairly fine consistency with a fork. Add one cup cracker crumbs. Beat 2 eggs, and mix ¾ cup whole milk with beaten eggs. Add to salmon mixture. Add salt and pepper to taste and the juice of one lemon. Two tablespoons chopped pimiento may be added if desired. Dot top of mixture with 3 or 4 pieces of butter. Bake in buttered casserole, set in shallow pan of water, for 45 minutes, in moderate oven, 35 minutes covered and then 10 minutes uncovered. Makes 6 to 8 servings. Any leftover souffle makes a tasty sandwich spread if mixed to a paste with a little mayonnaise and chopped pickle or olives.
–Mrs. W. E. Sandelius, 2325 Massachusetts St., Mar. 10, 1939.

Mrs. Michael's Salmon Croquettes
Three tablespoons Minute Tapioca, 1½ cups flaked salmon, ½ teaspoon salt, dash of cayenne, ⅛ teaspoon paprika, 1 tablespoon lemon juice, 1 tablespoon minced green pepper, 1 tablespoon minced pimiento, sifted bread crumbs or cracker crumbs, 1 cup milk, 1 egg beaten with 3 tablespoons milk and dash of salt. Combine Minute Tapioca, salt, cayenne, paprika, green pepper, pimiento, and milk in top of double

boiler. Place over rapidly boiling water and cook 8 to 10 minutes after water boils again, stirring frequently. Add salmon and lemon juice, and mix thoroughly. Chill; mixture thickens as it cools. Shape into balls, roll in crumbs, dip in egg mixture, then roll again in crumbs. Fry in deep fat (390 degrees F.) 1 minute, or until golden brown. This makes 16 small or 8 medium croquettes.

–Mrs. J. H. Michael,
1029 Kentucky St., Mar. 17, 1939.

Mrs. *W*agner's Salmon Stuffed Potatoes

Six medium-sized baked potatoes, ⅓ cup hot milk, 1 egg (well-beaten), 1 teaspoon salt, pepper, 1 tablespoon lemon juice, 1½ cups cooked salmon (flaked), ⅓ cup minced onion browned in 2 tablespoons butter. While hot, split baked potatoes lengthwise. Scoop out potatoes, taking care not to break the shells. Mash the potatoes and add the milk, egg, salt, pepper, lemon juice, salmon and onions. Mix well and refill potato shells. Sprinkle with buttered crumbs and bake 20 minutes in a moderate oven.

–Mrs. Walter Wagner, 305 E. 19th St., Mar. 1, 1940.

Mrs. *K*eller's Salmon Puff

One pound can salmon (2 cups), 2 tablespoons butter, 2 tablespoons chopped celery, 2 tablespoons chopped parsley, 2 cups seasoned mashed potatoes, 3 eggs, 1 teaspoon salt, 1 teaspoon minced onion, 1 tablespoon lemon juice, few drops tabasco sauce. Drain the fish, flake it with a fork, and remove all bones. Melt the fat, and cook the celery and parsley in it for a few minutes. Then combine with the salmon, mashed potatoes, and seasonings. Add the beaten egg yolks, and beat the mixture until very light. Fold in the well-beaten whites. Pile at once into a well-greased baking dish; bake in a moderate oven (350 degrees F.) for one hour or until set in the center and lightly browned. Serve in the dish. If salmon puff is baked in ramekins or custard cups, it will be especially light and fluffy, and attractive for serving as a luncheon dish.

–Mrs. John L. Keller, 1329 W. 9th St., Apr. 26, 1940.

Heard In Lawrence

There is no salmon shortage in the A. B. Weaver home, thanks to the fishing talent of Mrs. Weaver. Six weeks ago the couple made a trip up the famed Rogue River in Oregon to have a try at big  *salmon and the prize catch was made by Mrs. Weaver who landed a 30-pounder on hook and line. The battling Rogue River salmon cannot be bought or sold, but a sportsman has the right to keep his own legally caught fish. The 30-pounder was too much to consume on the outing party, so it was taken downstream to a cannery where it was carefully preserved for this winter's eating. When the shipment of canned salmon was received a few days ago, the labels bore the legend, "Caught by, and Especially packed for Nell D. Weaver." [LJW, 7-2-46]*

Mrs. *G*rant's Scalloped Salmon
"This is a good nourishing dish, and quickly prepared."

One tall can salmon, 2 cups milk, 2 cups crushed crackers or bread crumbs, 4 eggs, ½ teaspoon salt, and 2 tablespoons melted butter. Beat eggs and add with ½ teaspoon salt and 2 tablespoons melted butter. Combine with salmon. Add 1 cup milk and mix well. Spread a layer in baking dish. Over this sprinkle 1 cup crackers (or bread crumbs), and pour ½ cup milk over these. Add another layer of salmon mixture. Over this, sprinkle the other cup of crackers or bread crumbs. Pour over this the remaining ½ cup milk. Dot top with butter, and bake 25 minutes in moderate oven.

–Mrs. Floyd Grant, Route 1, Aug. 2, 1940.

Mrs. *B*anks's Salmon Souffle

Melt 3 tablespoons butter and add 3 tablespoons flour. Mix well, then add 1½ cups milk; cook slowly, stirring constantly until mixture is thick and creamy. Add 1 teaspoon minced parsley, one teaspoon minced celery, one-fourth teaspoon minced onions, one-fourth teaspoon minced pimientos, one-third teaspoon salt, one- fourth teaspoon paprika, two cups canned salmon, three egg yolks and three beaten egg whites. Mix lightly. Pour into buttered baking dish, and bake 35 minutes in pan of hot water in a 350 degree oven.

–Mrs. John Banks, Route 6, July 18, 1941.

Miss *S*chopper's Salmon and Vegetable Dinner

Turn on gas for slow oven, 325 degrees. Grease six 3-inch muffin tins. Put into mixing bowl 2 cups drained salmon–fresh, cooked or canned. Add 6 tablespoons rolled oats, ¼ cup chopped green peppers, ¾ teaspoon salt, ⅛ teaspoon pepper, ¾ cup of evaporated milk. Mix thoroughly and put into muffin tins. Bake 35 minutes or until firm to touch; loosen sides and let stand about 5 minutes before turning out. Serves 6. Bake 1 hour if in a loaf. Serve with creamed peas or carrots. Note: the rolled oats take the place of eggs.

–Miss Frances Schopper, Eudora, Mar. 6, 1942.

Mrs. *S*ommer's Baked Haddock

Two cups cooked haddock (flaked), 2 egg yolks, 1 tablespoon lemon juice, ½ cup soft bread crumbs, 2 tablespoons melted butter, 1 cup medium white sauce, 1 tablespoon minced onion, ½ cup water, 1 teaspoon minced parsley, salt and pepper. Beat egg yolks slightly. Add white sauce, stirring constantly. Combine with fish, onion, lemon juice, parsley and water. Season to taste with salt and pepper. Pour into well-oiled baking dish. Cover with crumbs. Dot with butter. Bake in hot oven (425 degrees F.) for 20 minutes. Makes 6 servings.

*–Mrs. Albert Sommer, 16*th *and Haskell, Apr. 30, 1943.*

Mrs. *T*ipton's Salmon Patties

Two cups pink salmon (flaked with bones removed), 1 cup of cooked rice or mashed potatoes, 2 tablespoons orange or lemon juice, 2 eggs, salt and pepper, 1 cup bread crumbs, ½ cup milk, 1 tablespoon minced celery. Stir all together and drop by small tablespoons into deep fat. When brown on both sides, put on a platter and garnish with celery leaves.

–Mrs. Eleanor Tipton, 1327 Rhode Island St., Mar. 22, 1946.

*G*ilfillan's Salmon Loaf

One and one-half cups milk, 1 slice bread, 4 tablespoons butter or margarine, 2 cups canned salmon (1 one-lb. can), 2 eggs, ½ teaspoon salt. Mix all together and put into loaf pan. Bake one hour in moderate oven (350 degrees).

–Mrs. P. M. Gilfillan, Waterloo, Iowa, June 11, 1948.

Mrs. *R*oper's Baked Salmon

"This is a tasty and nourishing dish."

One can good salmon (red or pink). Drain off juice, remove bones and skin, and flake fine. Then prepare cream sauce as follows: 1 pint milk, three tablespoons of butter, three tablespoons flour. Scald milk. Mix flour and butter together thoroughly. Add milk and cook until thick. Grease baking dish. Sprinkle a layer of bread crumbs in bottom of dish. Add a layer of salmon, a layer of sauce, etc., until the pan is filled. Cook in oven about 350 degrees until well-browned on top.

–Mrs. Laura Roper, 913 Vermont St., Mar. 11, 1949.

Eggs, Cheese, Noodles, Nuts,
and
Rice

Dinner For William Allen White

A dinner honoring Wm. Allen White, editor of the Emporia Gazette and well known Kansas author, will be given at the Eldridge Hotel Saturday promptly at 12 o'clock. Plates are 75¢ each and reservations may be made by calling the Eldridge Hotel, Phone 807, or 542, the Douglas County Republican. Mr. White will broadcast an address over WREN from 12:45 until 1:00 o'clock. He will speak from the banquet room at the Eldridge. Friends who are interested in helping to honor the distinguished visitor are welcome. Kindly phone in your reservation—you may pay your 75¢ in the lobby of the hotel as you come to the dinner. The women are especially invited to attend. [DCR, 7-31-30]

Cooking Demonstration
Has Audience Laughing, Winning Prizes

Using an assortment of various sizes and kinds of sauce pans such as are found in the average kitchen, E. C. Sorby, a national demonstrator for the George D. Roper corporation, gave a cooking demonstration on a range manufactured by the company at a cooking school held this morning by the local gas company at the Granada theater. A good showman, Mr. Sorby dramatized the process of getting a meal and kept his audience laughing much of the time. About 600 persons were present, including a class of girls from the Junior high school, under the direction of Miss Marie Woodruff. Three of the girls assisted on the stage.

A half bushel of apples was given each of the following persons present: Mrs. N. V. Pyle, the first person in attendance; Mrs. J. N. Neville, 84, the oldest one in attendance; Mrs. Odell Wiley, the most recently married of those present, and Mrs. George Brooks, the youngest married person present.

Those receiving awards of five pounds of Zephyr flour were Mrs. Russell Wager, Mrs. L. E. Blair, Mrs. C. E. Tefft, Mrs. Everett Sperry, Mrs. H. F. DeWolf, Mrs. William L. Hastie, Mrs. James Morris, Mrs. Dora Medhurst, Mrs. R. M. Roberts and Mrs. Allan Shepard.

Those receiving awards of baskets of food were Mrs. Maud Hawk, Mrs. Frank Brown, Mrs. J. C. Harriott and Miss Kathryne Wilson. Mrs. W. S. Lefferd received the food used in the demonstration. [LJW, 10-26-38]

Mrs. *E*dwards's Noodles

Take one-half cup sweet milk or water, three eggs, one-half teaspoon salt, and work into flour until it is as stiff as can be made. (It cannot be too stiff.) Roll out just as thin as possible. Let dry a little while; flour well and roll tightly. Cut across the roll very closely with a sharp knife. Toss up with the fingers until nicely separated. Then drop into boiling soup stock or chicken broth, and boil 20 minutes.

–*Mrs. Burk Edwards,* Route 10, Dec. 30, 1921.

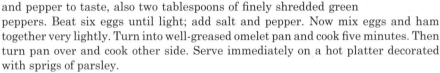

Mrs. *M*arr's Ham Omelet

Grind enough well-cooked ham to make three cupfuls. Add salt and pepper to taste, also two tablespoons of finely shredded green peppers. Beat six eggs until light; add salt and pepper. Now mix eggs and ham together very lightly. Turn into well-greased omelet pan and cook five minutes. Then turn pan over and cook other side. Serve immediately on a hot platter decorated with sprigs of parsley.

–*Mrs. H. W. Marr,* 742 Massachusetts St., Jan. 20, 1922.

Mrs. *M*yers's Cheese Loaf

Two level cups bread crumbs, 1 cup milk, 3 eggs, 1 level cup of grated cheese, 2 tablespoons liquid fat, 1 teaspoon salt, ½ teaspoon pepper, 1 teaspoon Worcestershire sauce, 1 tablespoon pimiento and green peppers, ½ teaspoon baking powder. Cover bread crumbs with milk, and let stand 20 minutes. Separate yolks and whites of eggs. Mix cheese with bread and milk. Add yolks of eggs, fat and seasonings; beat all together for 5 minutes. Whip the egg whites stiff and dry; add baking powder. Cut and fold them into the mixture. (Do not stir or beat.) Bake 35 minutes in well-greased pan or casserole. Serve with a good sauce if desired.

–*Mrs. Carl Myers,* 435 Michigan St., Apr. 7, 1922.

Mrs. *H*unzicker's Italian Spaghetti

One-half package spaghetti, ½ can tomatoes, 3 tablespoonfuls butter, 2 medium size onions, salt and pepper to taste, ½ cup grated cheese, 1 lb. round steak, ½ cup bread crumbs. Break spaghetti into small pieces, and add with it 1 tablespoon butter to plenty of boiling water, and boil 20 minutes, then drain. Put steak through food chopper. Put spaghetti into fireproof dish, then add meat, onions, seasonings, tomatoes, cheese, bread crumbs, and bake in moderate oven one hour.

–*Mrs. C. J. Hunzicker,* 2108 Massachusetts St., June 30, 1922.

Miss *L*ackey's Puffy Rice Omelet

Warm 1 cup cooked rice with 1 tablespoon butter and 1 cup milk. Remove from fire, add yolks of three eggs beaten with one-half teaspoon of salt and one-half teaspoon paprika, and when the mixture has cooled, fold in, lightly and smoothly, the stiffly whipped egg whites. Turn into a frying pan containing 2 tablespoons hot bacon drippings, and when well-raised, turn and finish cooking as for ordinary omelet.

–*Miss Ellen Lackey,* 838 Illinois St., Aug. 25, 1922.

Miss *Z*wick's Creamed Eggs

Boil six eggs until hard. Let stand in cold water a few minutes. Remove from shells and cut the whites into rings. Melt a tablespoon of butter; stir in equal amount of flour, and add one pint of milk. Cook in double boiler until it thickens. Season with salt and pepper, and add the egg rings. Remove from fire and pour over slices of buttered toast. Grate egg yolk and sprinkle over it, and garnish with chopped parsley.

–*Miss Birdie Zwick,*
1236 Connecticut St.,
Mar. 9, 1923.

Mrs. *J*ordan's Easter Nests

Cut as many slices of bread for toast as are required for your family. Toast a light brown, spread with butter and keep warm. Meanwhile, break as many eggs as your family will eat, separating the yolks from the whites. Whip the whites until they will stand alone. Spread thick on each slice of toast. Take a spoon and make a hole in the center of each white, and put a yolk in the center of each piece of toast. Put the toast in a pan or use the broiling part of your oven. Let it brown lightly. Shake salt and pepper on them just before serving. Serve hot with slices of crisp bacon.

–*Mrs. Leroy Jordan,*
Route 4, Eudora,
Apr. 18, 1924.

AUNT HET
BY ROBERT QUILLEN

"The trouble with these new brides is, they know seven ways to make candy an' only two ways to fix eggs."

Publishers Syndicate   LJW, 5-18-27

Mrs. *K*rum's Goldenrod

Four hard-boiled eggs, 2 tablespoons of butter, 2 tablespoons of flour, 1 pint of sweet milk, 6 slices of toast, salt and pepper. Melt butter; add flour, stirring constantly until thoroughly blended and browned. Add milk, salt and pepper. Let boil until the mixture thickens. Add the egg whites, cut in small pieces, and continue cooking until the eggs are heated through. Toast six slices of bread and dip quickly in boiling water to which a little salt has been added. (Care should be taken not to soak.) Place the toast flat on a hot platter and cover with the creamed mixture. Put egg yolks through a potato ricer and cover the top. Garnish with parsley.

–*Mrs. J. W. Krum,* 805 Rhode Island St., Apr. 25, 1924.

Mrs. *K*ennard's Creamed Eggs with Ham

"A splendid Sunday evening dish, as it can be prepared early in the day, reheating just before serving."

Hard boil six eggs, dice the egg whites, and add 1 cup of boiled ham, chopped fine. Season with salt and a dash of cayenne. Make a rich white sauce. Add the egg and ham mixture, and cook slowly until thoroughly heated. Put the egg yolks through a ricer, add 3 tablespoons grated cheese, and mix well. Arrange toast on a large platter for serving. Pour the white sauce mixture over toast, and sprinkle the yolks and cheese over the top. Put in oven under broiler for a few minutes to brown the top very slightly. This amount will serve eight.

–*Mrs. W. E. Kennard,* 411 W. 6th St., Apr. 15, 1927.

Mrs. *W*elch's Baked Spaghetti with Ground Steak

Cook in boiling, salted water one cup of spaghetti, which has been broken into one-inch pieces. When soft, drain and rinse in cold water. Put a tablespoon of butter into a frying pan. When hot, add one pound of ground steak, and stir constantly until all is well-seared. Arrange in a buttered baking dish alternate layers of spaghetti and ground steak. Pour over this two cups of white sauce. Cover with buttered cracker crumbs. Set dish in pan of water and bake in a moderate oven about forty minutes. For the white sauce: Melt four tablespoons butter, add three tablespoons flour, and stir until well blended; then pour on gradually, while stirring constantly, two cups of milk. Bring to boiling point and add one-half teaspoon salt and one-eighth teaspoon pepper.

–*Mrs. L. D. Welch,* 1026 New Jersey St., Feb. 10, 1928.

Mrs. *D*oering's Spanish Rice

One lb. rice, ½ lb. cheese, ⅓ lb. butter, 1 pint sweet milk, 3 green or red sweet peppers, 3 whole tomatoes (or their equivalent in pulp of canned ones), salt, pepper, and cayenne (to taste).

Cook rice in enough water to keep it from sticking or packing together. Do not stir, but simply shake kettle now and then to loosen up the rice until it is about half done, then remove from fire to partly cool. Cut into small bits the tomatoes, cheese, and peppers. With a spatula, spread some of the butter all over the sides and bottom of the pan that you are using to bake this in. Begin with rice, and use alternately in layers all of the previously prepared ingredients, sprinkling each layer lightly with the seasoning mentioned, using the cayenne sparingly, unless you prefer it quite hot. Then, put remaining butter all over the top. Lastly, pour the milk over all and slip in hot oven to bake about ½ hour or more—until nice and brown on top. Then remove from oven and sprinkle liberally with paprika. This will serve 20 with liberal helpings. If a less quantity is desired, reduce the proportions accordingly.

–*Mrs. Ella Doering,* 1214 Tennessee St., Apr. 5, 1929.

Alma *S*abol's Spanish Rice
"This recipe was given to me by a native of Spain in my home town
in Santa Barbara, California, and is a copy of the original.
If directions are followed closely, the result will be a success."

Wash 1 cup of Carolina head rice until water is clear, and dry thoroughly. In a medium-sized aluminum kettle, put 4 tablespoons of pure Italian olive oil, in which fry uncooked rice, stirring constantly until each grain separates and turns white. Add a small onion (chopped fine), ½ can tomato sauce, 1 teaspoon salt and dash of pepper. Cover with boiling water about 1 inch and a half above rice mixture. Cover closely and cook over slow fire until all of liquor is absorbed, when it should be dry and flaky. A half green pepper cooked with the rice adds to its flavor; and fresh green peas, which have been previously cooked, added a few minutes before serving, not only makes an attractive dish, but adds to its taste. Serves from four to six.

–*Alma F. Sabol,* 930 Ohio St., Mar. 28, 1930.

Mrs. *M*cElhiney's Dainty Egg Toast

Butter as many pieces of freshly toasted bread as needed. Dip in milk and arrange on a serving dish which can be set in the oven. Separate the whites and the yolks of the eggs to be used, allowing one for each piece of toast. Beat the egg whites till stiff, and then heap on the toast. Make a depression in the center of each egg white mound with a spoon. Drop an egg yolk in each hollow. Sprinkle lightly with salt and pepper. Place in a hot oven until the eggs are done to your taste.

–*Mrs. R. L. McElhiney,*
1905 Massachusetts St.,
Apr. 3, 1931.

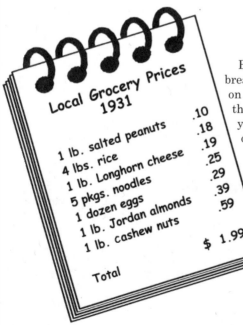

Local Grocery Prices 1931

1 lb. salted peanuts	.10
4 lbs. rice	.18
1 lb. Longhorn cheese	.19
5 pkgs. noodles	.25
1 dozen eggs	.29
1 lb. Jordan almonds	.39
1 lb. cashew nuts	.59
	$ 1.99
Total	

Mrs. *W*ilcox's Vegetarian Nut Loaf

One and one-half cups chopped walnut meats, one tablespoon minced onion, one beaten egg, one teaspoon salt, two tablespoons lemon juice, two tablespoons melted butter, three-fourths cup canned tomato juice, two cups stale bread crumbs. Combine all ingredients well, and pack into a greased loaf pan. Bake in a moderate oven for fifty minutes. Serve hot, with tomato or mushroom sauce, as a main dish in place of meat.

–Mrs. M. N. Wilcox, 726 Arkansas St., Mar. 3, 1933.

Mrs. *B*eal's Eggs a la Goldenrod

Five hard-boiled eggs, 2 tablespoons butter, 2 tablespoons flour, 1 pint sweet milk, 6 slices of toast, salt and pepper. Melt butter; add flour, stirring constantly until thoroughly blended and browned. Add milk, salt and pepper. Let boil until the mixture thickens. Add the egg whites, cut in small pieces. Continue cooking until the eggs are heated through. Toast six slices of bread and dip quickly in boiling water to which a little salt has been added. (Care should be taken not to soak.) Place the toast flat on a hot platter and cover with the creamed mixture. Put egg yolks through a potato ricer and cover the top, then garnish with parsley.

–Mrs. Mary Beal, 828 Mississippi St., Mar. 24, 1933.

Mrs. *S*edore's Spanish Rice

Four tablespoons butter (or substitute); 1 cup rice; 2 teaspoons salt; ¼ teaspoon paprika; ⅛ teaspoon pepper; 1 small onion, chopped; 2 stalks celery, chopped, leaves and all; 2 cups (more if desired) canned tomatoes; 2 cups boiling stock or water; 1 cup leftover meat, cut in small pieces.

Wash and drain rice thoroughly. Heat heavy frying pan, then add butter. Fry the raw rice 5 minutes or until brown, stirring occasionally to keep from burning or sticking. Add salt, paprika and pepper; blend well. Add onions and celery; cook 5 minutes longer. Add tomatoes, leftover meat and stock (or water). Lower heat, cover closely, simmer slowly until rice is tender–about 25 minutes. Stir frequently with a fork to prevent sticking. If you prefer a brown crust, uncover and brown in hot oven. Add water as needed for desired consistency.

–Mrs. George E. Sedore, 1122 Ohio St., Jan. 11, 1935.

Mrs. *F*ey's Codfish Omelet

Soak a piece of codfish, about 3 inches square, overnight. Split 3 crackers and lay them in enough cold water to cover them. Pick the fish into fine pieces and mix well with the crackers. Then add 1 beaten egg, 1 tablespoon of butter, salt, and

pepper to taste. Take 2 cups of milk and 1 teaspoon of cornstarch; boil 5 minutes, and pour it over the other ingredients. Bake 20 minutes. This is fine for lunch, served with toast or with lettuce and raw grated carrots with mayonnaise.
–Mrs. A. P. Fey, 21 Winona St., Feb. 15, 1935.

Mrs. *B*euerman's Noodles and Sauerkraut
Take 2 cups of noodles, uncooked. You can get them already made or make them yourself. One pound of bulk sausage, 3 cups of sauerkraut, salt water. Drop noodles into rapidly boiling water. Allow 1 teaspoon salt to each 4 cups water. Boil rapidly until tender. Pour into sieve. Drain. Boil sauerkraut 30 minutes. Combine noodles, sauerkraut, sausage. Season to taste. Place in well-oiled baking dish. Bake in moderate oven (375 to 400 degrees F.) for 1 hour. Serve warm.
–Mrs. Julius Beuerman, Route 1, Mar. 20, 1936.

Miss *M*cClintock's Cheese Souffle
One cup milk, 3 tablespoons quick-cooking tapioca, 1 teaspoon salt, 1 cup grated American cheese, 3 eggs. Heat the milk to scalding in a double boiler. Add the quick-cooking tapioca and the salt, and cook for 5 minutes, stirring until melted. Remove from the stove and cool slightly. Separate eggs; beat egg yolks, and add to the tapioca mixture. Beat the egg whites stiff and fold into mixture also. Place in a greased baking dish. Set in a pan of hot water and bake in a moderate oven of 350 degrees F. for about 45 minutes.
–Miss Ruth McClintock, Route 2, Mar. 5, 1937.

Mrs. *R*obb's Cheese and Spaghetti Loaf
One and one-half tablespoons butter, 1½ tablespoons flour, 1½ cups milk, 1 cup grated cheese, ¾ teaspoon salt, ⅛ teaspoon pepper, ¼ teaspoon paprika, 1 minced pimiento (optional), 4 cups cooked spaghetti (coarsely chopped), 3 eggs. Melt the butter, add flour and mix to a smooth paste. Gradually add milk; cook until it thickens. Add cheese, seasonings, and pimiento. Cook until cheese

melts. Add spaghetti. Beat eggs until thick and lemon-colored. Fold into spaghetti mixture. Put into a well-oiled pan, and place pan in a pan of water. Bake in a moderate oven for fifty minutes or until loaf is firm. Unmould, and serve plain. Garnish with parsley, stewed tomatoes or tomato sauce.

–*Mrs. Ronald Robb,*
Route 5, Apr. 2, 1937.

Mrs. *R*idgway's Eggs a' la Surprise

Boil eggs for exactly 3½ minutes. Shell very carefully under water without breaking egg, as it is very soft. Let stand in boiling water until ready to use. Have ready circles (about 3 inches in diameter) of fried bread or toast, in the centers of which a hole has been cut. Set each egg upright in center of each piece of toast. Beat up stiff and dry the whites of 2 or 3 eggs (depending upon number served); season with salt. Completely cover eggs with this egg white, putting it on roughly but carefully. Take a narrow strip of Spanish pimiento, and place around the egg about one inch from the top. Place in oven just long enough for the meringue to brown. Serve hot with Hollandaise or other sauce.

–*Mrs. M. Ridgway,* 610 W. 4th St., Apr. 9, 1937.

Mrs. *C*ain's Baked Eggs with Mushroom Sauce

Two tablespoons butter, 2 cups sliced mushrooms, 1½ tablespoons flour, ¾ cup mushroom stock and milk, ½ cup cream, ¾ teaspoon salt, pepper, ½ teaspoon Worcestershire sauce, 6 eggs. Melt butter and cook mushrooms in it about 5 minutes; sprinkle on the flour and blend well. Add the stock (made by cooking together the tougher portions of mushrooms in water, milk and cream), and stir well until thick and smooth. Add seasoning. Break eggs into individual greased baking dishes. Cover with mushroom sauce and bake in a moderate oven (350 degrees) until eggs are firm. A sprinkle of paprika adds to the attractiveness of this dish.

–*Mrs. William Cain,* 411 Elm St., Apr. 1, 1938.

Mrs. *P*fleger's Deviled Eggs On Toast

Four eggs, 3 tablespoons butter, ¼ cup flour, ½ teaspoon salt, ¼ teaspoon paprika, 1 teaspoon meat sauce, 1 cup chopped full-milk cheese, 4 slices toast, 1½ cups milk. Cover the eggs with cold water; bring to a boil, and boil hard ten minutes. In the meantime, make the sauce by melting the butter, stirring in the flour and seasonings, and gradually the milk. Then add the cheese, and finish cooking in a double boiler, stirring occasionally until the cheese is melted. Shell the eggs; cut in halves. Place two halves on each slice of toast, pour cheese sauce over, and dust the eggs with a little paprika.

–Mrs. Fred Pfleger, Linwood, Mar. 8, 1940.

Mrs. *H*oughton's Cheese Souffle
"This is a delicious dish for the whole family."

Three eggs (separated), ½ teaspoon salt, 1 cup grated cheese, 3 tablespoons butter, 3 tablespoons flour, 1 cup milk. Melt butter; add flour and milk slowly. Stir and cook until thick. Pour over beaten egg yolks; add cheese and salt. Fold in stiffly beaten egg whites. Pour into greased casserole. Have oven preheated to 300 degrees F., and bake souffle 50 minutes. Serve immediately. Serves 3 or 4 people.

–Mrs. H. W. Houghton, 940 Louisiana St., Mar. 20, 1942.

Mrs. *S*ullivan's Mushroom Omelet

One tablespoon butter, 1 tablespoon flour, ½ No. 2 can tomatoes, ½ cup sliced mushrooms, ½ cup minced ham or chicken, ⅛ teaspoon salt, ⅛ teaspoon pepper, 4 eggs. Brown the flour in the butter. Add the tomatoes, mushrooms, ham or chicken, salt and pepper. Let simmer for 10 minutes. Beat the eggs, and add them to the mixture, stirring carefully until the eggs are set. Serve on buttered toast. This makes 6 large servings.

–Mrs. E. F. Sullivan, 717 Mississippi St., Apr. 3, 1942.

Mrs. *W*ickey's Noodles

Two cups flour, 3 eggs, 1 teaspoonful butter, 1 teaspoon salt, 2 tablespoons lukewarm water. Sift flour and salt; rub in butter, and add gradually the beaten eggs and water. Knead the paste for ten minutes. Roll out as thin as possible and set aside to dry for fifteen minutes. Cut into strips two inches wide. Shred each strip into narrow match-like pieces. Let dry on board for thirty minutes. When needed, cook noodles twenty minutes in boiling water; drain, and add to soup. The noodles may be cooked in soup, but you will not have as clear a soup.

–Mrs. Emma Wickey, Tonganoxie, Feb. 25, 1944.

Mrs. *L*aCoss's Baked Macaroni with Dried Beef

Three-fourths cup macaroni, 2 cups white sauce (medium), ¼ pound dried beef. Boil macaroni until done; drain. Fry dried beef in three tablespoons butter (or substitute), and when edges begin to curl, add three tablespoons flour and enough milk to make a medium white sauce. Season with pepper and add to macaroni. Pour into a greased baking dish. Sprinkle with grated cheese, and bake at 350 degrees for 30 minutes.

–Mrs. William LaCoss, 1301 Kentucky St., Mar. 23, 1945.

Heard In Lawrence

Mrs. J. H. Saunders, who lives in the Riverside neighborhood, gathers her eggs with a step ladder for she has a hen that lays her eggs in a tree. There is a tree in the yard with a large hollow limb in which Biddy deposits her egg. [DCR, 10-27-27]

Miss *P*arsons's Cheese Souffle (Fondu)

Two cups bread without crusts, broken into pieces; 1 cup milk; ½ teaspoon salt; ¼ teaspoon paprika; ½ lb. cheese; 2 tablespoons melted shortening; 2 or 3 eggs, yolks and whites beaten separately. Beat egg yolks, add milk; pour mixture over bread and let soak. Stir in cheese and seasoning. Fold in stiffly beaten egg whites. Bake in moderate oven until firm, about 45 minutes. Serves six.

–*Miss Margaret W. Parsons,* 1108 Ohio St., Apr. 13, 1945.

Mrs. *M*cMullin's Cheese Souffle

"This is beautiful, stays up, and has a nice crisp crust."

One cup cream sauce made with 3 tablespoons butter, 3 tablespoons flour, 1 cup hot milk. Reduce heat, stir in ½ cup grated cheese. When cheese is melted, add: 3 beaten egg yolks, ¼ teaspoon salt, ⅛ teaspoon paprika, and a few grains cayenne. Cook and stir these ingredients for 1 minute longer to permit the yolks to thicken. Cool these ingredients. Whip until stiff 3 egg whites. Fold them lightly into cheese mixture. Place the souffle in an ungreased 7-inch baking dish in a moderate oven, 325 degrees. After 10 minutes, increase the heat slightly. Bake the souffle until it is firm, for about 30 minutes in all. Makes 4 servings.

–*Mrs. W. B. McMullin,* 637 Indiana St., May 11, 1945.

Mrs. *G*erard's Eggs and Asparagus Casserole

Eight hard-cooked eggs, ½ cup mushrooms, 1 tablespoon butter, ½ teaspoon salt, dash of pepper, 1 cup cut cooked asparagus, 1 cup white sauce. Cut eggs into lengthwise wedges. Brown mushrooms in butter. Add seasonings, asparagus, white sauce, and 7 of the eggs. Turn into baking dish. Garnish with remaining egg wedges. Bake in 350 degree F. oven 20 minutes. Serves 6.

–*Mrs. A. H. Gerard,* 2205 Tennessee St., Apr. 5, 1946.

Mrs. Elizabeth *H*oward's Deviled Eggs

Let six hard-boiled eggs cool in the water they were boiled in, and they will peel smooth. Cut lengthwise, take out yolks and mash fine. Add ½ teaspoon mustard, salt, a little sugar, 2 tablespoons sour cream or salad dressing, 1 tablespoon vinegar. Mix well with the egg yolks and fill whites. One half of a stuffed olive on top of each egg makes a decorative finish. Put halves on a platter with plenty of lettuce.

–*Mrs. Elizabeth Howard,* Route 1, May 10, 1946.

Egg Supper Menu Thursday, M. E. Church, 4ᵗʰ and Elm. Eggs any style, potato salad, egg noodles, baked beans, deviled eggs, hot biscuits, dessert, coffee. Adults 40¢, children 25¢. Everybody come. [LJW, 5-14-29]

Mrs. Paul *H*oward's Deviled Eggs

"Serve as an appetizer, at a picnic lunch, or on lettuce as a salad."

Six eggs, ½ teaspoon salt, ½ teaspoon dry mustard, dash of tabasco, 3 tablespoons mayonnaise, 1 boiled beet (sliced thin), ½ teaspoon scraped onion, 2 tablespoons finely chopped celery, 1 teaspoon finely chopped green pepper. Slip the eggs carefully into boiling water, place over low heat and let simmer 30 minutes. Drain, crack shells slightly, and let stand in cold water 10 to 20 minutes. Remove shells and cut each egg in two, lengthwise. Remove the yolks and set whites aside. Mash yolks thoroughly and mix well with all the ingredients, except the beets. Fill the whites with the mixture, and put a thin half slice of beet on each end of each half egg. Allow 1 egg per person.

–Mrs. Paul Howard, Joplin, Mo., July 4, 1947.

Mrs. *G*regory's Deviled Eggs

Cook 6 eggs about five minutes in boiling water. Let stand in water until nearly cold; they will peel smooth that way. Halve eggs the long way. Turn the yolks into a bowl and mash fine. Add a little mustard, salt, sugar, weak vinegar, and one tablespoon melted oleo. Stir well. Fill the halved whites, and place one half of stuffed olive on each egg. Garnish with parsley.

–Mrs. I. M. Gregory, Route 4, July 9, 1948.

Mrs. *E*berhart's Egg Fondue

One cup milk, 1 cup soft bread crumbs, 1 tablespoon shortening, ½ teaspoon salt, ⅛ teaspoon pepper, 3 egg whites, 3 egg yolks. Heat milk. Add bread crumbs, shortening, salt and pepper. Let cool. Then add the egg yolks, which have been beaten until thick and lemon-colored. Then fold in the stiffly beaten egg whites. Pour into a 2 quart baking dish, and bake 50 minutes at 325 degrees F. or until the tip of a sharp knife comes out clean when inserted carefully into center of fondue. Serves 6.

–Mrs. I. F. Eberhart, 945 Tennessee St., Mar. 25, 1949.

Vegetables, Beans,

and

Savory Sauces

Douglas Co. Corn Husking Champ
Takes Fifth in State Contest

Otto Boerkircher, Douglas county corn husking champion, placed fifth in the state corn husking contest held yesterday near Belle Plaine. Cecil Vining, Franklin county, defending state champion and runner-up in the national contest a year ago, again won the state contest.

Thirty contestants took part in the state contest.

Boerkircher husked 1,350 pounds of corn or 22.5 bushels. Vining husked 1,573 pounds or 26.217 bushels.

Other winners were Orville Peterson, Cloud county, second, 1,464 pounds; William Lutz, Riley county, third, 1,431 pounds; and Roy Johnson, Crawford county, fourth, 1,354 pounds.

Vining and Peterson will compete in the national contest at Sioux Falls, S. D., on Friday, November 4. [LJW, 10-28-38]

Smash Cans; See Movies For Free

Alleys and trash-barrels are being cleaned of tin cans these days as Lawrence youngsters prepared to visit movie houses next week with a bundle of flattened cans serving as an admission ticket.

A package of 25 or more cans will admit children for evening performances at the Jayhawker, Granada and Varsity theaters on Monday, Tuesday and Wednesday. There is no limit to the number of times a child can go to a show during the three day period, and many boys and girls are expected to see a different show each night by assembling three bundles of 25 or more.

All cans must be properly processed: wrappers removed, ends cut out and tucked in, and the cans flattened. The special offer is made by the theaters to aid the tin can salvage program, sponsored by the American Legion. So far, two freight carloads have been shipped to a processing plant and six additional tons are needed to fill a third car.

A special feature will be the awarding of a full year's pass to all Lawrence theaters, to the boy or girl who turns in the greatest number of cans during the three-day event, and a six months' pass to the second place winner. All cans entered in this special contest must be properly labeled with the name of the contestant.

The free admission arrangement is available to all children of grade school or junior high school age, throughout the entire Lawrence trading area. [LJW, 7-27-45]

Mrs. *M*cAuliff's Timbales

Two tablespoons liquid fat, ¼ level cup dry bread crumbs, ¾ cup milk, 1 cup cooked asparagus tips (cut in small pieces), 2 eggs, chopped parsley, salt and pepper. Heat fat, add crumbs and milk, cook five minutes, stirring constantly. Add asparagus tips, slightly beaten eggs, and seasonings. Turn into well-oiled molds, fill two-thirds full, set in pan of hot water, and bake in moderate oven 20 minutes. Turn out on hot plates. Serve at once with white sauce, made by melting 4 tablespoons of butter, 4 tablespoons flour, and ½ teaspoon salt. Stir until smooth (don't let brown), then add 1 cup milk; stir until it thickens.

–Mrs. J. M. McAuliff, 537 Wisconsin St., Mar. 3, 1922.

Miss *L*ackey's Vegetable Pudding

Pare and dice three potatoes, two medium-size carrots, five onions, three medium-sized turnips. Cover with boiling water and cook very slowly until tender; then drain, mash the vegetables and season well with salt, pepper and a little butter. Measure the liquid drained from the vegetables and place in a saucepan. Now dissolve one-half cup of flour in one-half cup of cold water. Stir well to blend and add to the vegetable water in a saucepan. Stir and bring to a boil. Cook for five minutes and then add the prepared vegetables with two well-beaten eggs, one cup of grated cheese, one-quarter cup of finely minced parsley. Beat hard and turn into a baking dish, and bake in a moderate oven for twenty-five minutes.

–Miss Ellen Lackey, 838 Illinois St., May 5, 1922.

Mrs. *M*ettner's Stuffed Tomatoes

Peel and hollow out firm tomatoes, one for each serving. Mix equal quantities of chopped green olives, blanched almonds and crisp tender celery with tomato pulp. Stuff tomatoes with this filling, and cover with French dressing or mayonnaise. Serve on lettuce leaves.

–Mrs. Carl Mettner, 1109 New Hampshire St., Sept. 21, 1923.

Miss *H*artman's Cauliflower in Batter

Wash and cleanse the cauliflower, and half-boil it in salted water. Drain, divide the branches, and shake in a quarter of a pint of vinegar seasoned with salt and pepper. Then fry in a batter. To make the batter, beat up one egg, and sift in one cupful of flour; add half a cupful of milk, a pinch of salt and one tablespoon of olive oil. Mix smooth and stand the mixture in a cool place for one hour. Dip the branches of cauliflower separately, then drop into smoking hot fat and fry to a golden brown. Drain and serve hot, garnished with parsley.

–Miss Wilma Hartman, Route 7, Mar. 7, 1924.

Mrs. *H*ogin's Turnips

"This is by far the best recipe for mashed turnips I have ever used."

Pare and slice turnips, add one or two potatoes, but do not slice, as they cook more readily than the turnips. Cook in salted water (one tablespoon of salt), and when tender, drain and mash. Add one tablespoon of sugar and more salt if desired, a little pepper, some cream and a tablespoon of butter. The potatoes cannot be detected, and if the turnips are a little bitter, they will kill the taste.

–Mrs. John C. Hogin, 1521 New Hampshire St., Mar. 28, 1924.

Miss *H*unter's Scalloped Tomatoes and Corn

One cup of tomatoes, one cup of corn, one-half cup of stewed celery. Mix all together, and season with salt and a sprinkling of pepper. Butter a baking dish, and put half of the vegetables in the pan, then a layer of cracker crumbs, dot with butter, add the remainder of the vegetables, and another layer of crumbs. Save the liquid the celery was boiled in, pour this over the top, and bake slowly.

–Miss Harriet Ruth Hunter, 1217 Rhode Island St., Apr. 4, 1924.

Mrs. *D*eVore's Method of Cooking String Beans

Stem and break as many beans as you desire to cook. My directions will be for 3 pounds. Wash beans and place in kettle. Cover with water. Add 3 slices of bacon and one tablespoon salt. Cook for several hours on a slow fire. Keep plenty of water on them until they are done, then allow the water to cook almost entirely away. Then add one cup of rich milk. Serve as soon as the milk is heated. (Cream makes them better.)

–Mrs. R. E. DeVore, 725 Missouri St., July 4, 1924.

Miss *P*almer's Fried Tomatoes

*"These are much better
than the customary green tomatoes fried in slices."*

Take medium-sized tomatoes, or cut large ones in half. Ripe or half-ripe ones may be used. Wash, dig out core, and cut off a slab of skin on bottom. Roll in flour, letting as much stick as possible. Then lay them, core side down, in a hot pan with

melted lard about ⅛ inch deep. Have fire medium hot. Drop sugar and salt on the open spot where the skin was cut off. Sprinkle some more flour over the tomatoes and in the pan. When you find the first side is brown, turn over and season that side. When the second side has started to brown, loosen from the pan with a glazer. Judge whether more grease is needed or not, and put on lid to let soften and cook out juice, which mixes with flour and makes a good brown gravy. Less sugar will be required if a scant half teaspoonful of soda is added to the amount of flour used with about 8 medium tomatoes.

–Miss Mary M. Palmer, 920 Louisiana St., Aug. 22, 1924.

Mrs. *B*roeker's Potato Dumplings

Boil whole mealy potatoes until almost done, pour water off and let stand until quite cold, then peel and grate. To three parts of grated potato, add 1 part of white bread (a soup plate full), cut in inch squares, fried light brown in butter or drippings. Add also 2 eggs (yolks and whites beaten separately), 2 tablespoons flour, salt, and a little nutmeg. Mix well, form into balls as large as inside of hands, roll in flour, drop into boiling, salted water, and boil till dry inside, about 15 minutes. Drain. Pour browned butter over dumplings, and eat with stewed prunes or any other cooked fruit.

–Mrs. L. Broeker, 834 Massachusetts St., Feb. 20, 1925.

Mrs. *T*ibbetts's Spinach Custard

Prepare half peck of spinach by cutting off the roots and washing thoroughly. Put into a kettle with about a pint of water, adding a tablespoon salt. Boil twenty minutes. Remove from fire and empty into colander to drain. When cool, squeeze dry and chop fine. Add a dash of nutmeg, sugar and pepper. Stir in two well-beaten eggs; add a cup or more milk or cream. Pour into a well buttered baking dish and bake until custard is set. Serve with hard-boiled eggs and vinegar if desired.

–Mrs. Ulalie Tibbetts, 1204 Kentucky St., Apr. 24, 1925.

Mrs. *P*uckett's Cabbage

"This is very delicious and might well be named 'Cabbage in Disguise' as it has altogether a different flavor from other cabbage dishes."

Cut cabbage in halves and let stand in cold water 10 minutes. Drain, shred, boil in salt water until tender. Then place in buttered baking dish. Alternate layers of cabbage and cracker crumbs–leaving a layer of cracker crumbs on top. Add enough sweet milk to moisten the cabbage and crackers. Dot with butter and bake in the oven until the crackers are a rich brown. Serve hot.

–*Mrs. William M. Puckett,* Route 2, McLouth, May 1, 1925.

Mrs. *H*oward's Cauliflower Polonaise

Remove leaves from cauliflower, cut off stalk and soak thirty minutes in cold water to cover. Cook twenty-five minutes, or until tender, in one quart boiling water to which has been added one pint milk and one tablespoon of salt. Drain, place on hot serving dish, sprinkle with yolks of two hard-boiled eggs, forced through a strainer and mixed with one tablespoon finely chopped parsley and one-third cup coarse bread crumbs. Cook in butter until rich brown.

–*Mrs. Chester Howard,* Route 10, May 8, 1925.

Mrs. *D*oering's Mock Fried Oysters

One can corn, 3 whole eggs (beaten lightly), 1 level teaspoon salt, 3 tablespoons rounded full of flour; mix thoroughly. (This should be the consistency of stiff pancake batter.) If the canned corn is soupy, as it sometimes is, the above will be just right; but if the corn is dry and crumbly, as some brands are, enough of sweet milk must be used to make the batter of right consistency.

Have on the fire a skillet with two tablespoons heaping full of fat, piping hot. Drop from a big spoon into the fat, a portion of the dough, at same time shaping the fritter, oyster shape (sort of oblong). Brown nicely on both sides. Place on platter and garnish with parsley. Add more fat, if necessary, as oysters are fried. Do not crowd too many fritters into skillet at one time or you will spoil the shape of the oyster. You will also fail to get the pretty, crisp edges that the fritter should have.

–*Mrs. Ella Doering,* 1214 Tennessee St., May 15, 1925.

Mrs. *H*ill's Lima Beans with Cheese and Tomato Sauce

"This makes a delicious meat substitute."

One quart lima beans (dried), 1 quart tomatoes or 1 dozen fresh tomatoes, ½ lb. cheese. Boil lima beans in unsalted water until done; add salt to taste. Cook tomatoes with salt and pepper to taste, and one teaspoon sugar, thickened with 1 tablespoon flour. Grease baking pan. Place in layer of beans, cover with grated cheese, then cover with tomato sauce. Continue in layers until all is used. Sprinkle top with cheese dotted with butter.

–*Mrs. Arthur A. Hill,* 303 Lincoln St., Sept. 25, 1925.

Mrs. *S*tephenson's Corn Pudding

To a can of sweet corn, add 1½ cups sweet milk, 2 teaspoons sugar, 1 tablespoon flour, 1 egg well beaten, ¼ teaspoon salt, and ¼ scant teaspoon soda. Stir well and put into greased pudding dish or pan, and dot the top of pudding with butter, using a tablespoonful of butter. Bake until firm.

–*Mrs. J. J. Stephenson,* 828 Tennessee St., Oct. 16, 1925.

Mrs. *M*arkley's Potatoes O'Brien

Six raw potatoes, 1 pint milk, 2 tablespoons flour, butter the size of an egg, 1 teaspoon salt, ¼ teaspoon pepper, 1 chopped green pepper, ½ cup grated cheese. Peel and cut potatoes in dice; mix with peppers and put into greased baking dish. Add milk gradually to the flour, add seasonings and pour over the potatoes. Sprinkle the cheese over the top. Bake in a moderate oven 1 hour. Serve hot.

–*Mrs. J. E. Markley,* Route 8, Nov. 6, 1925.

Mrs. *S*nyder's Tomato and Cauliflower en Casserole

One can tomatoes, ¼ lb. cream cheese, 1 good-sized head cauliflower, 1 tablespoon sugar, 1 teaspoon salt, dash cayenne pepper.

Parboil cauliflower whole in salted water till tender, but do not allow to fall to pieces. Lift from water and place in a baking dish or casserole. Cut cheese into small strips and stick into the interstices of the cauliflower. Pour the can of tomatoes, which has been previously seasoned with the salt, pepper and sugar, around cauliflower, and bake in quick oven 20 to 30 minutes.

–*Mrs. Augusta P. Snyder,* 605 Maine St., Nov. 13, 1925.

Mrs. *S*nyder's Beans a la Brazilaro

Two tablespoons olive oil in a sauce pan. Heat and fry in this one medium-sized onion, cut fine, and one tomato, seasoned with salt and red pepper. When these are well done, add ½ cup of water and simmer a few minutes. Drain the liquid from a can of green string beans and add to this. Simmer for a few minutes, until all are seasoned thoroughly, and most of the liquid is boiled away. An equal amount of canned tomatoes can be substituted for the fresh tomatoes, or fresh string beans may be used in season, instead of the canned beans, by adding enough water to allow them to cook from 1½ to 2 hours. Always retain the liquid, and serve.

–*Mrs. Gerrit Snyder,* 605 Maine St., Apr. 23, 1926.

Heard In Lawrence

The warm fall weather has prolonged the growing season in this section to an unusual date. Last Sunday, Nov. 26, to be exact, Ross and James Howe, who live just north of number 6 schoolhouse, gathered a fine bunch of roasting ears. They had noticed that their late patch of sweet corn was staying green and went out Sunday to investigate. They had corn-on-the-cob for dinner—grown on good old Kansas soil in spite of a democratic administration and harvested and eaten on November 26. Can you beat it? [DCR, 10-27-27]

Mrs. *V*an Stratton's Stuffed Cabbage

One medium-sized cabbage, 1 pound beef, 1 slice bacon or salt pork, 1 onion, ½ cup bread crumbs, ½ cup milk, 1 egg, seasoning, 1 green pepper. Select solid cabbage, not too large; remove outside leaves, cut out stalk end, leaving a hollow shell. Chop uncooked beef with bacon and onion. Add crumbs, soaked in milk, beaten egg, salt and pepper. Shape mixture into ball or cakes. Arrange in cabbage. Arrange strips of sweet pepper on top of cabbage. Tie in cheese cloth, then steam or boil until tender. Serve with lemon sauce.

Lemon Sauce: ½ cup sugar, 1 cup boiling water, 1 tablespoon cornstarch, 2 tablespoons butter, 1 ½ tablespoons lemon juice, few gratings of nutmeg, pinch of salt. Mix the sugar and cornstarch. Add the water gradually, stirring constantly. Boil 5 minutes; remove from fire, add the butter, lemon juice and nutmeg. Serve hot.

–Mrs. Ernest Van Stratton, 613 Rhode Island St., Apr. 22, 1927.

Mrs. *S*terling's Baked Squash

Cut squash into individual servings. Do not cut off rind. Scoop out a small depression in each piece. Fill this with butter. Sprinkle a bit of salt and about a teaspoon of sugar on each serving, and bake slowly in a flat baking pan, basting occasionally with melted butter. When the squash is soft, it should have a crisp, candied surface. Serve piping hot in its own shell.

–Mrs. Wilson Sterling, 1129 Louisiana St., Oct. 14, 1927.

Mrs. *S*hirar's New England Baked Beans

One quart of beans, ¾ lb. fat salt pork, 1 tablespoon salt, 1 tablespoon molasses, 3 tablespoons sugar, 1 cup boiling water. Pick over one quart of beans, cover with cold water, let soak over night. In the morning, drain; cover with fresh water, and heat slowly, keeping water below the boiling point. Cook until skins will burst. To determine when this stage has been reached, take a few beans on the tip of a spoon and blow on them. Skins will burst if they have been cooked long enough. Drain the beans. Scald the rind of ¾ lb. of fat salt pork; scrape, remove ¼ inch slice, and put in bottom of bean pot or baking pan. Cut through the rind of the remaining pork, every half inch, making cuts one-half inch deep. Put beans in pot or baking pan. Bury the pork in them. Mix one tablespoon of salt, one tablespoon molasses, three tablespoons sugar, and one cupful boiling water. Pour over the beans, and bake for one and one-half hours.

–Mrs. Charles Shirar, Route 6, Mar. 30, 1928.

Mrs. $\mathcal{H}$ess's Creamed Turnips with Cheese

Wash and peel five or six medium-sized turnips, and cut into one inch slices. Cook in salted, freshly boiling water, enough to cover, until turnips are tender. While the turnips are cooking, prepare a thick white sauce by scalding one and one-third cupfuls of milk, and mixing with two tablespoons butter and three tablespoons flour, which have been rubbed together until free from lumps. Cook the sauce five minutes; add one-fourth teaspoon salt and a few grains of pepper. Cut one quarter pound cream cheese in little pieces. Put a layer of the boiled turnips into a buttered baking dish; cover with the white sauce, sprinkle with cheese, and repeat, putting a layer of buttered crumbs on top. The buttered crumbs are prepared by crumbling stale bread into fine pieces, allowing one tablespoonful melted butter to one-half cup crumbs. Bake only until the white sauce bubbles, and the buttered crumbs are well-browned. Serves six.

–Mrs. John A. Hess, Athens, Ohio, Apr. 27, 1928.

Mrs. $\mathcal{M}$arshall's Italian Asparagus

Two cups of diced cooked asparagus, 4 slices of hot toast, 3 tablespoons of butter, 3 tablespoons of flour, 1 teaspoon of salt, ¼ teaspoon of paprika, ¼ teaspoon of celery salt, 2 cups of sweet milk, ⅔ cup of grated cheese, 2 tablespoons of finely chopped pimientos, 2 eggs. Melt the butter, add the flour, salt, paprika and celery salt. Mix carefully and add the milk. Cook until creamy, then add the cheese, pimientos and eggs, well-beaten, and cook for two minutes. Pour over the asparagus, which has been placed on the hot toast, and serve at once. This amount will serve four people.

–Mrs. D. A. Marshall, 1019 Pennsylvania St., May 18, 1928.

Mrs. $\mathcal{D}$ouglas's Cauliflower au Gratin

Boil one cauliflower in salted water till tender, then take up and drain, and place on dish for serving. Pour over and around the cauliflower two cups of cheese sauce prepared as follows: 2 tablespoons butter, 4 tablespoons flour, 2 cups milk, ½ teaspoon salt, few grains pepper, 1 cup cheese (grated). Melt the butter in saucepan, add flour with seasonings, and stir until well-blended; pour on the milk and stir constantly. Cook until thick. Add the cheese, which has been carefully grated, and cook slowly until the cheese is melted. Sprinkle another tablespoon of cheese over the top, and brown in a very hot oven. Serve very hot.

–Mrs. Lulu Douglas, 1622 New Hampshire St., May 25, 1928.

Mrs. $\mathcal{W}$ilson's Baked Beans

One quart navy beans, ½ lb. fat salt pork, ½ tablespoon mustard, 1 tablespoon salt, 2 tablespoons molasses, 3 tablespoons sugar, 1 cup boiling water. Wash, pick beans over, cover with cold water and let soak over night. In the morning, cover with fresh water, heat slowly, and let cook just below the boiling point until the skins burst, which is best determined by taking a few on the tip of the spoon and blowing over them; if done, the skins will burst. When done, drain the beans, and bury pork in beans. Mix mustard, salt, sugar, molasses and water, and pour over beans, and add enough more water to cover them. Cover pot and bake slowly for about five hours. Uncover the pot for the last hour so that pork will brown and crisp.

–Mrs. Helen Wilson, 1532 Tennessee St., Jan. 4, 1929.

Mrs. *W*ilson's Parsnip Cakes
"These cakes will be found most delicate,
and may be eaten alone or with any other course."

Take one cup of mashed parsnips, half-teaspoonful of salt, one egg, and heaping teaspoonful of good baking powder mixed in one cup of milk. Stir this mixture until it is a smooth batter. Then have some fat in a frying pan half an inch deep. Drop the batter into it by spoonful. Brown nicely on one side, then turn.

–Mrs. J. W. Wilson, 1036 Vermont St., Apr. 19, 1929.

Mrs. *A*rnold's Sweet Potato Balls

Pare and cook sweet potatoes in salted water until done. Mash and season well with butter and sugar. When cool enough to handle, make into balls or croquettes, and dip into corn flakes that have been slightly rolled, covering on all sides. Lay balls in a buttered pan and brown in the oven.

–Mrs. Charles Arnold, 905 Ohio St., Oct. 12, 1929.

1930 General Electric Refrigerator

Mrs. *B*rass's Beets with Cream Sauce

Five or six medium-sized beets, 2 tablespoonfuls vinegar, 2 tablespoonfuls butter (or fat or oil), 3 tablespoonfuls flour, 1 teaspoonful sugar, ¼ teaspoon salt, ⅛ teaspoonful pepper, 1 cupful beet water, ½ cupful cream, 2 tablespoonfuls chopped cress or parsley. Wash the beets thoroughly, being careful not to break the skin. Cook them in boiling, salted water until tender, and drain, saving the water. Rub off the skins and cut the beets in slices. Pour over them the vinegar. Make a sauce in the following manner: Melt the butter, add the flour, sugar, salt and pepper. Stir until well blended, then add the beet water. Cook until it thickens. Then stir in one-half cupful of cream, and cook until smooth and thickened. Pour this sauce over the beets and sprinkle with cress or parsley. Serves six.

–Mrs. Edward Brass,
1919 Rhode Island St., June 27, 1930.

Miss *P*ine's Tomato Stuffed Peppers

Four large green peppers, 1½ cups cooked rice, 1 cup tomatoes, ½ cup cracker crumbs, 1 tablespoon finely chopped green pepper, 1 tablespoon onion, ½ teaspoon salt, ¼ teaspoon paprika, ¼ teaspoon celery salt, 3 tablespoons butter (melted). Clean and prepare peppers by cutting off tops and removing seeds. Mix other ingredients. Fill peppers with this mixture. Set in pan of water. Bake in moderate oven for 30 minutes. Serve hot.

–*Miss Lillian Pine,* 1512 New Hampshire St., Sept. 5, 1930.

Mrs. *C*rim's Eggplant

Wash the eggplant, cut in thin slices–not over ⅛ inch thick, peel if desired, and soak 4 or 5 hours in salted water, using 2 tablespoons of salt to 1 quart of water. Dry the slices between 2 towels. Dip in the batter (recipe follows), and fry until golden brown in deep fat at 400 degrees F., or until a 1-inch cube of bread browns in 1 minute. It is not necessary to add any salt to season. The dried slices may also be dipped in fine bread or cracker crumbs, in slightly-beaten egg, and again in the crumbs, and fried until golden brown in deep fat at the above temperature. This should be done long enough before cooking to set the egg. Batter for the Eggplant: 1 cup flour, sifted before measuring; 1 teaspoon baking powder; 1 teaspoon sugar, if desired; ¼ teaspoon salt; 1 egg; 1 cup sweet milk. Sift and measure the flour; then sift with the other dry ingredients. Beat the egg. Stir the milk into the egg. Pour into the dry ingredients and beat until light.

–*Mrs. E. K. Crim,* 746 Louisiana St., Oct. 3, 1930.

Miss *F*itzsimmons's Cauliflower

Cut the green leaves from the head of cauliflower. Cut in florets or leave whole, as desired, and soak in cold water, head down, an hour to draw out any bugs that might be in the head. Drop in rapidly boiling, salted water, using 1 teaspoon of salt to 1 quart of water, and boil, uncovered, till tender–about ½ hour. This method keeps the cauliflower tender and very white. Drain, and place in a serving dish. Cover with medium thick cream sauce, and sprinkle with grated cheese and paprika. Additional cheese may also be melted in the cream sauce. If preferred, pour melted butter and finely chopped parsley over the cauliflower, and sprinkle with paprika.

Cream Sauce: Melt 1 tablespoon of butter in a sauce pan. Cream into the butter 2 level tablespoons of flour. Add 1 cup of scalded milk, and stir over a low flame until thick. Season with salt and white pepper.

–*Miss Iris Fitzsimmons,* 746 Louisiana St., Oct. 17, 1930.

Mrs. *S*trahl's Stuffed Turnips

Select one dozen medium-sized turnips; peel and boil whole in water slightly salted. When tender, pour off the water, and slice a piece from the end of each turnip. Scrape out the center; mash and season with salt, pepper, butter, and the yolk of an egg. Fill the turnips with the mixture, put back the slice, brush over with butter. Put in a baking dish and place in a hot oven to brown.

–*Mrs. Bertha Strahl,* 118 E. 11th St., Oct. 24, 1930.

Heard In Lawrence

W. H. Schell is displaying in his grocery store, 1001 New Jersey Street, a canteen of the Civil War period, which was uncovered a few days ago when the house at 940 New York Street was torn down. The cork was perfectly sound and the canteen still in good condition. It was probably owned by Martin Conway, first congressman from Kansas, who occupied the house during that war, the house being the first attacked by the Quantrill raiders. Mr. Conway was a great uncle of Mrs. A. W. Cunningham of Lawrence, whose mother was staying with her uncle and aunt the night preceding the attack by Quantrill's men. [LJW,11-16-34]

Mrs. *J*ost's Smothered Rutabagas

Wash, pare and cut into small pieces, a large rutabaga. Place in the skillet a large spoonful of lard. When good and hot, add the rutabagas and brown them a little, then add water and let simmer till tender. Add a little salt and pepper and a teaspoonful of sugar. Thicken with a teaspoonful of flour, moistened with water. Turnips may also be cooked this way. They both make a delicious vegetable dish.

–*Mrs. Frank Jost,* 947 Mississippi St., Jan. 23, 1931.

Mrs. *S*terling's Brussels Sprouts in Lemon Butter

One quart sprouts, 6 tablespoons butter, 1 tablespoon lemon juice, 1 sprig parsley, 1 tablespoon grated lemon rind, salt and pepper to taste. Drain sprouts after cooking in salted boiling water, with cover off cooking vessel, until tender. Add melted butter, minced parsley, and other seasonings. Put sprouts in this seasoning and reheat. Serve hot. Slices of hard-boiled egg may be used as garnish.

–*Mrs. C. W. Sterling,* 920 Indiana St., Feb. 20, 1931.

Mrs. *M*iller's Casserole of Mushrooms

Two and one-half cups of rice, one pound fresh mushrooms, one quart tomatoes, salt, pepper, curry powder, sugar, two slices of bread, one tablespoon of onion juice. Peel and cut up enough firm ripe tomatoes to make one quart, or use one quart of canned tomatoes. Put three tablespoons melted butter into the bottom of the casserole. Stir the mushrooms into it thoroughly and season with salt and black pepper. Season the cooked rice with pepper, salt, nutmeg and curry powder to taste. Spread this over the mushrooms, and dot the rice with two tablespoons of butter. Season tomatoes with pepper, salt, two tablespoons sugar, and one tablespoon of onion juice. Spread tomatoes over the rice. Dot thickly with butter. Spread two medium-sized slices of bread with melted butter; cut into triangles and fit them neatly into a cover for the top of the tomatoes, butter side up. Cook in a moderately hot oven for thirty minutes.

–*Mrs. Mabel B. Miller,* 1205 Rhode Island St., Mar. 13, 1931.

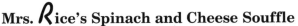

Mrs. *R*ice's Spinach and Cheese Souffle

Two cups cooked spinach, 3 eggs, ⅔ cup of milk, 2 tablespoons of butter, ½ pound American cheese (grated), ½ teaspoon of salt, pepper. Chop spinach very fine. Set aside. Beat egg yolks; add milk, melted butter, grated cheese and seasoning. Stir while heating and boil one minute. Mix half of this cheese sauce with spinach and add stiffly beaten egg whites. Fill buttered casserole; place in pan of hot water and bake in a moderate oven until firm. Turn out on a hot plate, garnish with hard-boiled egg, and pour the remainder of the cheese sauce, hot, around the mould.

–Mrs. Fred Rice, Route 3, May 1, 1931.

Mrs. *E*rwin's Stuffed Summer Squash

*"Squash prepared in this manner
is very tasty."*

Scoop out the centers of two medium-sized round, summer squashes, leaving thin shells. Chop squash fine. Add four tablespoons of melted butter, two teaspoons of salt, one large minced green pepper, ½ cup of milk, one cup soft bread crumbs, and ¼ teaspoon pepper. Refill the shells with the mixture. Place in baking pan with a little water in the bottom, and bake gently for 45 minutes.

–Mrs. E. C. Erwin, Route 1, July 24, 1931.

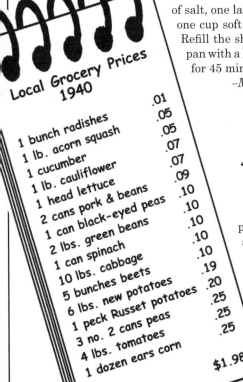

Local Grocery Prices
1940

1 bunch radishes	.01
1 lb. acorn squash	.05
1 cucumber	.05
1 lb. cauliflower	.07
1 head lettuce	.07
2 cans pork & beans	.09
1 can black-eyed peas	.10
2 lbs. green beans	.10
1 can spinach	.10
10 lbs. cabbage	.10
5 bunches beets	.10
6 lbs. new potatoes	.19
1 peck Russet potatoes	.20
3 no. 2 cans peas	.25
4 lbs. tomatoes	.25
1 dozen ears corn	.25
	$1.98
Total	

Alma *S*abol's Eggplant Prepared Differently

*"Eggplant prepared in this way
tastes like escalloped oysters
and is delicious."*

Pare one medium-sized eggplant, cut in pieces, and cook twenty minutes in boiling salt water. Drain off water. Mash and add one slightly beaten egg, 2 tablespoons minced green pepper, 1 tablespoon minced onion, and a dash of pepper. Place in greased baking dish. Sprinkle with fine bread crumbs and dot generously with butter. Bake 20 to 30 minutes, or until nicely browned.

– Alma F. Sabol,
930 Ohio St., Sept. 4, 1931.

Mrs. *S*harp's Stuffed Peppers

For six peppers, remove caps and seeds and fill with one pint of dried bread crumbs or broken and crushed cracker crumbs; ½ to a cup of minced roast or boiled meat, mixed with one medium-sized onion, or less if preferred; one stalk of celery, and any left over vegetables such as green beans, lima beans, and corn—one round tablespoon of each; one medium-sized ripe tomato; salt and pepper to taste, all moistened with stock from pork, beef or chicken, or juices from steak plate. Lacking this, moisten with hot water in which a tablespoon of butter is added. A little grated cheese over the tops of the stuffed peppers adds flavor. After placing in baking dish, add a half-cup of water, or a savory sauce of stewed tomato and meat stock. Bake twenty minutes to half an hour in moderate oven.

–Mrs. Margaret Sharp, 1545 New Hampshire St., Sept. 11, 1931.

Mrs. *H*arwood's Baked Parsnips

Six good-sized parsnips, 1 tablespoon flour, 1 tablespoon butter, ½ teaspoon salt, dash pepper. Wash and scrape the parsnips, cut in halves; put into a sauce pan, cover with boiling water and boil one hour. Drain and put them on a hot dish. Put the butter in a frying pan, add to it the flour; mix until smooth without browning. Add a half pint of the water in which the parsnips were boiled; stir and boil five minutes. Add the salt and pepper, pour over the parsnips, sprinkle over with crumbs enough to cover, and, if liked, a little cheese. Bake in a quick oven for 15 minutes.

–Mrs. Emma Harwood, 841 Maine St., Apr. 1, 1932.

Mrs. *P*eterson's Stuffed Eggplant

One eggplant, butter, one egg (well-beaten), bread crumbs, one-half cup chopped green peppers, salt, pepper and paprika. Boil the eggplant until tender; it takes about an hour for a small one. When done, split in two lengthwise, and scoop out insides. Chop finely and add plenty of butter, then the egg, pepper, and enough bread crumbs to hold together, and season highly. Fill the empty eggplant shells, sprinkle with bread crumbs, and dot with butter. Brown in the oven.

–Mrs. Dora Peterson, 736 New York St., May 6, 1932.

Mrs. *R*iley's Summer Squash

"This makes a delicious dish, either hot or cold."

Peel the squash and either slice or cut into squares. Put a layer of squash into baking pan, then add a little salt, pepper, sugar and butter. Add another layer of squash, and fix the same as first layer until you have the amount needed, then cover with part cream and milk (mixed). Put into a medium-hot oven and bake about 40 minutes, or until it is a rich golden brown.

–Mrs. Charles E. Riley, Route 4, July 8, 1932.

Mrs. *A*nderson's Stuffed Mango Peppers

"These are excellent and will keep indefinitely."

Cut the stem end from 3 dozen mango (sweet bell) peppers, take out the seeds, and place the end that has been removed inside the pepper so that it may be placed back on the pepper from which it was cut, after they have been stuffed. Pack in a stone jar, cover with salt water, and let stand over night. To make the filling, chop very fine 1 or 2 heads of cabbage and 2 bunches of celery. Add some celery seed and mustard seed if desired. Drain the salt water from the peppers, and stuff them with the shredded cabbage and celery. Place the tops back on the peppers and fasten in place with a couple of toothpicks. Place them back in the jar and cover with the following: 1 quart water, 2 quarts vinegar, 1 ½ pints sugar. Boil 30 minutes and pour over the peppers while hot. Drain this off and reheat each morning for 3 mornings. Pour back over the peppers and place a weight on top of them and cover with a cloth. They will be ready for use in a few days. They will not become soft nor form a scum over the top.

–Mrs. William Anderson, Linwood, Aug. 12, 1932.

Mrs. *J*ones's Corn Fritters

"These fritters are good accompanied by a plate
of cold, sliced tomatoes."

Select very tender, fresh sweet corn, and cut from cob a sufficient amount to fill two cups. Add to corn two well-beaten eggs and 1 tablespoon sweet milk. Sift together ¾ cup flour, 2 teaspoons baking powder, 1 scant teaspoon salt, and add to corn and egg mixture. Drop by spoonfuls into deep, hot fat, and fry until brown. Drain on unglazed paper and serve at once. This recipe makes a fritter batter in which corn predominates. Too often corn fritters consist of a flour mixture in which a small amount of corn may be found.

–Mrs. Frank E. Jones, 1140 E. 13th St., Aug. 19, 1932.

Mrs. *K*elsey's Barbecue Sauce

One cup butter, 2 cups water or stock, 1 cup vinegar, ½ tablespoon dry mustard, 2 tablespoons sugar, 2 teaspoons chili powder, 1 teaspoon salt, 1 tablespoon Worcestershire sauce, 1 tablespoon tabasco sauce, 1 teaspoon paprika, 1 clove garlic or 1 onion, 1 cup catsup. Saute the minced garlic (or onion) in part of the butter. Melt the remaining butter in the boiling water (or stock) and vinegar. Add catsup, Worcestershire sauce and the tabasco sauce. Combine the dry ingredients and add to the boiling liquid. Also add the garlic (or onion) mixture. Boil gently for ½ hour. Strain the sauce, and it is then ready to be used in basting the meat.

–Mrs. Jack Kelsey, Route 1, Sept. 30, 1932.

Mrs. *S*impson's Hominy

Put one gallon of shelled white corn in granite pot, and cover with water in which 3 tablespoons of soda have been dissolved. Let soak over night. Next morning, put on hot fire and boil about 3 hours, or until the skins are loose and will slip from grains easily. The baking soda will turn corn yellow. Drain off all soda water and wash corn in several waters, or until skins are all washed out. Put back on stove and boil ten minutes each in 3 or 4 fresh waters, and the hominy will be white and tender.

–Mrs. G. A. Simpson, Route 5, Jan. 6, 1933.

Mrs. *P*ine's Okra with Tomatoes
"This is a popular southern dish."

Two cups sliced okra pods, one cup tomatoes, one tablespoon chopped onions, two tablespoons chopped green peppers, one teaspoon salt, ¼ teaspoon pepper, ½ cup water, three tablespoons butter. Mix all the ingredients, and pour into a buttered baking dish. Bake in a moderate oven for thirty minutes. Serve in dish in which it is baked.

–Mrs. E. B. Pine, Route 5, Aug. 11, 1933.

Miss *C*agle's Baked Eggplant

One good-sized eggplant, cut in middle. Scoop out the inside, and cook in salt water until tender. Have six eggs boiled hard, chop in small pieces, and mix egg plant and eggs with milk and crackers, salt and pepper. Put back in hulls, cover top with cracker crumbs, dot with butter and several strips of bacon, and bake in oven 20 minutes.

–Miss Daisy Cagle, 604 Kentucky St., Sept. 20, 1935.

Miss *A*they's Lima Bean Loaf

Two cups dry lima or canned beans, 1 cup crumbs (bread or crackers), 2 tablespoons grated onion, 1 tablespoon dried celery, 2 teaspoons salt, ¼ teaspoon pepper, 1 cup liquid (potato stock or milk), 1 tablespoon butter or drippings, 4 tablespoons peanut butter–if desired. Wash and soak beans over night, cook until soft, 45 minutes approximately. Drain, and when cool, chop coarsely.

Add crumbs mixed with seasoning. Add peanut butter, liquid and fat. Put into greased bread pan and bake in moderate oven about thirty minutes. Serve with a creamed or stewed vegetable, a tomato, and a fruit salad, for a meatless dinner.
–*Miss Pearl Athey,* Route 1, May 1, 1936.

Mrs. *D*ecker's Eggplant a la Rector

Peel and cut eggplant in half-inch slices; soak in salt water one hour. Drain and cut slices in strips ¾ inch wide. Dip each piece in well-beaten egg, and roll in fine cracker crumbs. Fry in deep fat until golden brown. Drain and serve with cheese sauce, made as follows: Melt 2 tablespoons butter, add 2 tablespoons flour and 1 teaspoon salt; stir until well blended. Add 2 cups milk slowly, stirring constantly until thick and smooth; let boil about 2 minutes. Add ½ cup grated cheese, and stir until cheese is melted.
–*Mrs. C. E. Decker,* 705 Tennessee St., Sept. 25, 1936.

Mrs. *W*ellhausen's Cauliflower with Mushrooms

One medium cauliflower, 1 cup fresh or canned mushrooms, 1 cup mushroom juice, 2 tablespoons butter, ½ cup cream or top milk, 2 tablespoons butter, 2 tablespoons flour, 1 teaspoon salt, ¼ teaspoon pepper, parsley, rounds of hot buttered toast. Break the cauliflower into rather large florets, and cook until tender. Prepare rounds of hot, buttered toast. Place on a hot serving dish, and heap the pieces of cauliflower on them. Pour over these the following sauce, and serve at once with parsley garnish. Sauce: Chop the fresh or canned mushrooms, and put them into a saucepan with a cupful of the juice and two tablespoons butter. If fresh mushrooms are used, add parts of the water in which the cauliflower was cooked. Simmer until the mushrooms are tender. Then add ½ cup of cream or top milk; let come to a boil. Thicken with the remaining two tablespoons of butter and the flour blended together, and add the salt and pepper. Serves 6.
–*Mrs. Edward Wellhausen,* University Dr., Oct. 2, 1936.

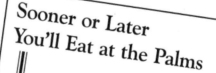

Miss *H*ammond's Carrot Loaf

One and one-half cups carrots, ½ cup bread crumbs, ½ cup chopped nuts, 1 tablespoon sugar, 1 teaspoon salt, dash of pepper, 2 eggs (beaten), 1 cup milk, 1 small cup flour, 1 heaping tablespoon soft butter. Scrape and grate enough raw carrots to make 1½ cups. Add bread crumbs, chopped nuts, sugar, salt, a little pepper, eggs, milk and flour; mix thoroughly. Add butter. Pour into a greased mold. Boil in hot water for 1 hour. Serve with drawn butter.

–Miss Evelyn Hammond, Vinland, Nov. 20, 1936.

Mrs. *H*obson's Spinach Timbales

One-third peck spinach, 2 tablespoons butter, ½ teaspoon salt, 1 tablespoon lemon juice, 2 eggs. Cook spinach 10 minutes, chop, add seasonings and slightly beaten eggs. Put into greased custard cups to cook until firm, about 20 minutes. Unmold and serve with white or cheese sauce, and garnish with slices of hard-cooked egg.

–Mrs. R. W. Hobson, Jr., Route 5, Apr. 30, 1937.

Mrs. *C*anary's Asparagus

Tough lower ends of asparagus should be cut off. Cook in deep sauce pan, standing upright. The steam will cook the tender tips while the hard stalks will be cooked in the boiling water; or break in pieces, cooking stem part fifteen minutes, and adding the tender tips last. Serve on toast with drawn butter or with "Golden Sauce": 3 tablespoons butter, 3 tablespoons flour, 1½ cups milk, ¼ teaspoon salt, ⅛ teaspoon pepper, 2 egg yolks, 1 teaspoon lemon juice or vinegar. Make sauce of first three ingredients, salt and pepper. Beat egg yolks slightly, and just before serving, add egg yolks and heat. Add lemon juice, and serve at once.

–Mrs. Noah Canary, Route 1, Linwood, May 14, 1937.

Mrs. *F*incher's Tahiti Sweet Potatoes

Parboil sweet potatoes in salted water until tender. Peel, cut in halves, and wrap each half in a slice of bacon. Place slices of pineapple in a shallow baking dish, and sprinkle with brown sugar. On each pineapple slice, place a half potato wrapped in bacon. Bake in moderately hot oven (375 degrees F.) for forty-five minutes.

–Mrs. Lena Fincher, 545 N. 8th St., Mar. 26. 1937.

DCR, 4-1-26

? ?

Have you had your beans today?

George's Lunch

DCR, 5-20-26

Beans

Bread
Butter
Coffee

Two-Bits

George's Lunch

DCR, 4-22-26

"x!!-d!h----
?xxz?!!x!!-
zz?x?!x!x!"

Remarks made by a man yesterday noon when he came for lunch, and found the baked beans were all gone.

George's Lunch

Mrs. *S*hultz's Baked Squash

Take the long-necked variety, cut about ½ inch thick; peel, wash and drain. Dredge in a mixture of half each of flour and granulated sugar. Place in a dripping pan with melted fat enough to cover bottom; sprinkle with salt. Bake in hot oven. When brown on the under side, turn and bake until done.

–*Mrs. George J. Shultz,* 746 Indiana St., Nov. 12, 1937.

Mrs. *W*ilcox's Deviled Mushrooms

Chop or break into small pieces one quart of mushrooms; season with pepper and salt. Prepare one pint of bread crumbs. Mix the mashed yolks of two hard-boiled eggs with two raw ones, and stir in a cup of milk or cream. Put a layer of crumbs in the bottom of a baking dish, then a layer of mushrooms. Scatter over bits of butter, then pour on part of the cream and egg mixture; continue until the dish is full, having crumbs with butter as a top layer. Bake for 20 or 30 minutes, closely covered, in a hot oven; then uncover long enough for the top to be well-browned. If preferred, water and lemon juice may be substituted for the milk and cream.

–*Mrs. M. N. Wilcox,* 726 Arkansas St., May 6, 1938.

Mrs. *G*regory's Ambushed Asparagus

Cut into small pieces two bunches of asparagus. Have ready as many stale biscuits as there are persons to be served, from which you have cut a neat top slice. Scoop out the inside, set them in the oven to crisp, laying the tops beside them, that all may dry together. Then take a pint of milk and four well-whipped eggs. Boil the milk first, then beat in the eggs, set over the fire, and stir until it thickens. Add a tablespoon of butter, and season with salt and pepper. Into this custard, put the asparagus that has previously been cooked 20 minutes in salted water. Do not let it boil, but remove from fire as soon as asparagus is fairly in. Fill the biscuits with the mixture. Put on tops fitting carefully, and set in oven three minutes. Arrange on platter and serve hot.

–*Mrs. Fred Gregory,* Route 4, June 3, 1938.

Mrs. *P*iper's Corn Custard

Six medium ears sweet corn, 1 pint milk, 3 eggs, 3 tablespoons butter, 2 tablespoons sugar, salt and pepper. Cut corn from cob. Place in buttered casserole. Beat whole eggs well; add milk, sugar, salt, pepper and butter, which has been melted. Mix well. Pour this mixture over the corn, and bake in moderate oven (375 degrees) for 30 minutes. Do not stir. After 30 minutes, increase heat to 500 degrees for five minutes, to brown. Makes 6 large, or 8 small servings.

–Mrs. Martha Piper, 433 Illinois St., July 29, 1938.

Mrs. *S*mith's Shoestring Eggplant

One eggplant, ⅔ cup cracker crumbs, 1 egg or 2 egg yolks, 2 tablespoons milk. Peel eggplant. Cut into half-inch crosswise slices. Sprinkle each slice with ¼ teaspoon salt, and let stand one hour. Rinse in cold water, and cut into strips ½ inch wide. Dip strips into the egg, mixed with milk and seasoning. Dip in cracker crumbs. Fry in hot fat until browned. Drain on waxed paper.

–Mrs. Cecil E. Smith, Route 4, Sept. 30, 1938.

Mrs. *B*unn's Stuffed Cauliflower

One head cauliflower; 1 cup cold water; 4 slices stale bread; 1 onion, chopped; 2 tablespoons butter; 2 cups baked or fried ham, chopped; ½ teaspoon celery salt; salt and pepper to taste; ¼ cup milk. Place whole head of cauliflower in boiling, salted water and cook 20 minutes, or until nearly tender. Remove to a colander to drain and cool so it can be handled. Pour cold water over bread and let stand. Saute onion in butter until yellow and soft. Add ham and stir until heated through. Squeeze bread dry; add ham, seasonings and milk. Mix well. Place cauliflower in greased casserole. Stuff dressing between florets, packing rest around the outside. Sprinkle with milk and bake in moderate oven (350 degrees) for 30 minutes. The cauliflower should be slightly browned. Serves 6.

–Mrs. E. E. Bunn, 1901 Maine St., Oct. 14, 1938.

Mrs. *C*olbert's Baked Squash

One medium-sized green squash, 2 tablespoons butter, salt and pepper, 1 teaspoon sugar. Wash the squash, cut in half and take out the seeds. Place in a baking dish with a little water in the bottom. Bake in a moderate oven 40 minutes. When done, scrape the squash out of the shell. Mash it, add seasoning and a little cream, then replace mixture in shell. Serve hot.

–Mrs. Eugene R. Colbert, 627 Illinois St., Oct. 28, 1938.

Mrs. *N*icolay's Turnips

Boil a small ham hock or piece of fresh pork until it begins to get tender. Peel and slice the turnips and place with the meat. Add two tablespoons of sugar, and salt to taste. Cook all until tender. Serve with black pepper or pepper sauce.

–Mrs. Bernard Nicolay, 615 W. 9th St., Nov. 4, 1938.

Miss 7errell's Irish Bake

Twelve medium potatoes, 1 can (small) pimientos or 2 large red sweet peppers, 1 cup milk, 1 tablespoon butter, 1 teaspoon salt. Wash the potatoes and bake until tender; cut in halves and remove center. Mash and add the diced pimientos or peppers, milk, butter and salt. Beat until light and fluffy. Return to the shells and serve hot.

–Miss Allis M. Terrell, Eudora, July 21, 1939.

Mrs. Krum's Chili Sauce

Four quarts (peeled and chopped) ripe tomatoes, 2 cups chopped onions, 1 cup chopped sweet red peppers, 1 cup chopped green peppers, 3 or 4 small red hot peppers (ground), 3 tablespoons salt, ½ cup sugar, 1 tablespoon white mustard seed, 1 tablespoon cinnamon (ground), 1 teaspoon allspice (ground), 1 teaspoon nutmeg (ground), ½ teaspoon mustard (ground), ¼ teaspoon mace (ground), ¼ teaspoon cloves (ground). Combine the vegetables, salt, sugar, and seasonings and cook until mixture begins to thicken. Add vinegar [amount not specified] and cook until thick. Part of the juice may be drained from the vegetables before adding the vinegar. This will shorten the cooking period.

–Mrs. J. J. Krum, 432 Elm St., Oct. 11, 1940.

Mrs. *H*oward's Stuffed Peppers

Six green peppers, ½ cup English walnuts, 1 large onion, 1 teaspoon salt, 1 teaspoon melted fat, ⅛ teaspoon pepper, ½ cup bread crumbs, ½ cup milk. Select broad peppers that will stand on end and are easy to serve. Cut top from each pepper. Remove seeds and parboil 15 minutes. Stuff with filling mixed in the order given above. Bake 20 minutes, basting frequently with hot water. Any left over meat can be ground and substituted for the nuts for even greater economy in this inexpensive nourishing main course dish.

–Mrs. Lewis E. Howard, 326 Illinois St., Oct. 25, 1940.

Mrs. *S*turdy's Lenten Dish

Six small potatoes; 6 carrots, sliced; 1 cup of peas; 1 small head of cauliflower, broken in flowerlets. Cook all together, with salt added to taste, until tender. Put into casserole and pour over top 1 package cream cheese, which has been melted in double boiler with ½ cup of milk added gradually. When well-blended, pour over vegetables. Dot with butter. Sprinkle with pepper. Bake about 20 minutes or ½ hour. Garnish with hard-boiled eggs and parsley.

–Mrs. Joe Sturdy, 211 E. 10th St., Mar. 7, 1941.

Mrs. *C*ox's Method of Cooking Okra

Select about 20 okra that are young and tender, wash thoroughly, cut off stem end, then cut across in thin slices. Have nearly an eighth pound of butter hot in a skillet, and turn the okra into this; season with salt, about 1 teaspoonful. Turn the okra frequently with a spoon, and brown slightly. When it begins to thicken, add a little boiling water, and when it is cooked tender (which requires from 20 to 25 minutes), add one medium-sized tomato, cut very fine. Cook five minutes longer, stir well, sprinkle with a little pepper. Serve hot.

–Mrs. M. H. Cox, Eudora, Aug. 15, 1941.

Mrs. *B*owen's Eggplant Sausage Cakes
"The flavor is very 'sausage-like'."

Slice and pare one large eggplant; cut slices into small pieces, and cook in boiling, salted water until tender. Turn into a strainer and mash thoroughly. Then add 1 egg, slightly beaten; 1 medium-sized onion, minced; ½ teaspoon of poultry seasoning; add salt and pepper to taste. Sift in enough flour to bind mixture into a batter stiff enough to form fritters when dropped from a tablespoon. Fry in a small amount of fat; brown on both sides.

–Mrs. Jack Bowen, 734 Mississippi St., Aug. 22, 1941.

Mrs. *B*leakley's Stuffed Peppers

Eight green peppers; 1½ cups corn; 1 small onion, chopped; salt and pepper; 1 pound ground beef; buttered crumbs; 2 tablespoons fat; 4 medium-sized tomatoes (2 cups), chopped. Cut tops from green peppers and remove seeds. Precook peppers 5 minutes in boiling water; invert to drain. Brown onion and beef in fat; add tomatoes, corn, and seasonings. Stuff peppers with mixture, and top with buttered crumbs. Place each stuffed pepper in greased muffin pan, containing 1 tablespoon hot water, or stand stuffed peppers in greased baking dish; add ½-inch hot water. Bake uncovered in moderate oven (325 degrees) for 1 hour.

–Mrs. J. J. Bleakley, 1402 New York St., Sept. 12, 1941.

Mrs. *L*awrence's Sweet Potato Fritters

Two cups mashed sweet potatoes, ½ cup flour, ½ teaspoon salt, 1 teaspoon baking powder, 4 teaspoons melted butter, 2 eggs, 1 cup milk, 1 tablespoon sugar. Combine butter, potatoes, sugar, milk and egg yolks. Beat until smooth. Sift flour, measure, and sift with baking powder and salt. Add to first mixture. Fold in stiffly beaten egg whites. Drop by teaspoon into deep fat (365 degrees F.). Fry until brown.

–Mrs. Roy Lawrence, 1213 Kentucky St., Oct. 3, 1941.

Mrs. *A*llison's Stuffed Peppers

Ingredients: 1½ cups canned tomatoes or six ripe tomatoes (peeled), 1 cup thick sour cream, 8 green peppers, ¼ cup tomato juice, 12 crackers, salt and pepper. Preparation: Chop tomatoes. Add cream and tomato juice. Season to taste. Mix with cracker crumbs until mixture holds its shape. Cut tops from peppers. Remove membrane and seeds. Stuff with tomato mixture. Bake in moderate oven (400 degrees F.) until pepper cases are tender. If desired, peppers may be stuffed with well-seasoned cooked lima beans and corn. Cover with buttered crumbs. Brown in moderate oven. Makes 8 servings.

–Mrs. Morgan K. Allison, 1719 Alabama St., Sept. 4, 1942.

Mrs. *W*ickey's Creamed Turnips

One large-sized turnip, 2 level tablespoons butter, 1 level teaspoon salt, ½ level teaspoon pepper, 1 tablespoon chopped parsley, ½ cup cream. Peel the turnip thickly and cut into dice. Cook till tender in boiling water, then drain and return to the sauce pan. Add the butter, seasoning, parsley and cream. Let the whole boil up once, and serve.

–Mrs. Emma Wickey, Route 1, Tonganoxie, Nov. 13, 1942.

Miss *F*roeliger's Stuffed Whole Cabbage
"A meal in one."

One small firm head of cabbage, 2 cups ground ham (or other leftover meat), 1 cup cooked rice, ½ cup milk, 1 egg (beaten), 1 tablespoon chopped parsley, 1 tablespoon grated onion, ¼ cup grated American cheese. Remove outside leaves of cabbage, and hollow out stem end. Make cavity large enough to contain stuffing. Mix ham, rice and remaining ingredients in order given. Fill cabbage and steam over boiling water until cabbage is tender–about 1½ hours. Six servings.

–Miss Billie Froeliger, 1044 Connecticut St., Mar. 26, 1943.

Mrs. *S*haw's Corn-Stuffed Peppers

Four large peppers (seeds discarded), 1 cup corn, 1 egg (beaten), ½ cup bread or cracker crumbs, 1 tablespoon minced onion, 3 tablespoons cream, ¼ teaspoon salt, ⅛ teaspoon pepper. Stuff peppers with rest of ingredients, mixed. Fit into shallow baking dish. Add ½ inch boiling water. Bake 40 minutes in moderate oven. Baste frequently. Serves four.

–Mrs. Edwin Shaw, Route 4, Oct. 8, 1943.

Mrs. *T*raynor's Sweet Potato Puffs

Combine and mix thoroughly 2 cups cold, cooked, mashed sweet potatoes; 1 egg yolk; ½ teaspoon salt; 2 tablespoons butter, melted. Divide this into six portions. Flatten each portion, and place a marshmallow in center of each. Pull potato up around marshmallow, leaving small opening in top. Crush very finely two cups rice or corn flakes. Combine rice flakes or toasties with 4 tablespoons melted butter. Roll potato balls in mixture. Place on buttered cooky sheet and bake in hot oven 10 to 15 minutes.

–Mrs. B. L. Traynor, 745 Elm St., Oct. 22, 1943.

LJW, 3-20-42

For strength and endurance,
eat wholesome nourishing foods.

Miss *W*ilder's Baked Eggplant

Pare an eggplant, cut in ¼-inch slices, crosswise, and soak in cold water to cover two hours. Drain and cook in boiling, salted water to cover—until soft. Drain and mash; add ¼ cup butter, ½ cup stale bread crumbs, 2 eggs (well-beaten), a few drops onion juice, ½ teaspoon salt, ⅛ teaspoon pepper. Mix thoroughly. Pour into a well-oiled baking dish. Bake in a hot oven fifteen minutes. If desired, ½ cup of minced ham or cold cooked chicken may be added. Or if a Creole flavor is enjoyed, canned pimientos and celery seed may be added.

–Miss Bessie E. Wilder, 1631 Massachusetts St., Oct. 29, 1943.

Mrs. *L*eonard's French Fried Sweet Pepper Rings

Four to six green peppers, 1 egg (beaten), ¾ cup dry bread crumbs, fat. Slice sweet peppers into thin rings. Remove seeds and membrane. Dip rings into egg, then into crumbs, and fry in hot deep fat (370 degrees F.) until browned. Serves 6 to 8.

–Mrs. Clem Leonard, 828 E. 14th St., Sept. 8, 1944.

Mrs. *M*cKinley's Beets Delight

Four cups cooked, diced beets; ½ cup water, or liquid from beets; 2 tablespoons cornstarch; 1 teaspoon sugar (more if desired); 2 tablespoons vinegar; 2 tablespoons butter or margarine; 1 teaspoon celery seed. Combine cornstarch, sugar, butter, vinegar and liquid. Cook mixture until it thickens. Add beets and celery seed, and beat thoroughly. Serves 6 or 8.

–Mrs. H. L. McKinley, 615 Lake St., July 19, 1946.

Mrs. *L*ester's Eggplant Escalloped

One eggplant, ½ teaspoon salt, dash of pepper, 2 eggs, cream, cheese, paprika, 1 tablespoon butter, 1 cup cracker crumbs. Boil the eggplant until tender. Peel and mash thoroughly. Add salt, pepper, and enough cream to moisten. Add the egg yolks; then the beaten egg whites should be folded in. Sprinkle cracker crumbs and cheese on top. Garnish with paprika. Place in oven to brown.

–Mrs. P. P. Lester, 401 Indiana St., Sept. 27, 1946.

Heard In Lawrence

A bean 27 inches long was brought to the Journal-World Saturday by W. G. Deskins, 1114 Mississippi Street. Deskins said that the 27-inch bean is a "midget" for he has grown them 36 inches in length. They're good eating, too, he says. He said he does not know what they are called, but for want of a better name he calls them "The Kansas Pride." The seeds originally came from Texas. [LJW, 8-23-37]

Mrs. *M*esenhimer's Corn Fritters

Two cups corn (fresh or canned), 1 teaspoon salt, ¼ teaspoon pepper, 1 egg, 1 teaspoon melted fat, ½ cup milk, 2 cups flour, 2 teaspoons baking powder. Chop the corn fine; add salt, pepper, well-beaten egg, melted fat, milk, and flour and baking powder sifted together. Fry two or three minutes in deep fat.

–*Mrs. Kenneth Mesenhimer, 635 Rhode Island St., Oct. 4, 1946.*

Mrs. *S*ims's Toasted Carrots Supreme

To serve carrots as a separate vegetable, scrape and wash; leave young carrots whole and cut old carrots in half. Boil until tender (15 to 30 minutes) in water containing 1 teaspoon sugar. Just before cooking is completed, salt the water. Drain, roll in butter or other seasoning, then in crushed cornflakes, and brown in oven at 350 degrees F. Arrange on serving plate with parsley to represent carrot tops.

–*Mrs. S. H. Sims, 901 Maine St., Oct. 11, 1946.*

Mrs. *A*nderson's Stuffed Peppers

Cut tops off 6 peppers, or cut them lengthwise into halves. Remove seeds, and cook in boiling salt water 2 to 3 minutes. Drain, and fill with the following stuffing. Cover with buttered crumbs and bake in moderate oven 25 minutes.

Stuffing: 2 cups minced cooked meat; 1¼ cups crumbs or cooked rice; salt and pepper to taste; 1 tablespoon fat; ½ onion, minced; ¾ cup water or stock. Mix meat with crumbs; add salt, pepper, melted fat and onion. Moisten with water or stock.

–*Mrs. L. F. Anderson, 1712 Kentucky St., Oct. 25, 1946.*

Mrs. *A*nderson's Baked Beans

One pound (2½ cups) beans, 2 tablespoons brown sugar or molasses, 1½ teaspoons salt, 3½ cups hot water, ¾ teaspoon mustard, 3 ounces sliced bacon.

Pick over the beans and wash them; add cold water to cover and let stand several hours. Drain away the water and add the molasses, salt, mustard and hot water to the beans. Heat over a flame to the boiling point and add the sliced meat. Pour into bean pot, or baking dish, and bake slowly for about 6 hours. Serves 12.

–*Mrs. Cordie Anderson, 1712 Kentucky St., Feb. 14, 1947.*

Mrs. *S*andelius's Corn Souffle

One can corn (preferably white, whole grain), 1 cup cracker crumbs, 3 well-beaten eggs, ½ cup milk, salt and pepper, 1 heaping tablespoon butter or margarine. Put eggs and milk into mixing bowl and beat thoroughly. Add finely crushed cracker crumbs and can of corn. (Do not drain off corn liquid.) Salt and pepper to your liking. Put into greased baking dish and dot with little chunks of butter or substitute. Set in pan containing a little boiling water and bake in moderate oven, 350 degrees, for 45 minutes. Keep covered until last 15 minutes of baking.

–Mrs. W. E. Sandelius, 2325 Massachusetts St., Apr. 18, 1947.

Mrs. *S*chermerhorn's Stuffed Peppers

Six medium-sized sweet peppers, 2 cups ham, 3 teaspoons onion juice, 3 tablespoons butter, 2 cups bread crumbs, salt and pepper to taste, 2 cups of tomato sauce, hot water.

Cut out stem end of pepper, remove seeds and wash. Parboil 15 minutes. Mix together ham, crumbs, onion juice, butter and seasoning. Add enough hot water to moisten. Stuff peppers, cover top with buttered crumbs, and pour over tomato sauce. Bake until brown. Chicken, veal or corn may be used instead of ham.

–Mrs. A. E. Schermerhorn, 1429 Kentucky St., Oct. 10, 1947.

Mrs. *W*aggoner's Sweet Potato Puffs

"A surprise in each crispy ball."

Two cups cooked, mashed sweet potatoes; 1 egg, beaten; ½ teaspoon salt; ⅛ teaspoon pepper; 8 marshmallows; ½ cup crushed cornflakes. Method: Add beaten egg to mashed potatoes. Form into 8 balls with a marshmallow inside each. Roll in cornflakes. Deep fry in hot fat. Fry until brown. Drain on absorbant paper.

–Mrs. J. W. Waggoner,
1901 Learnard Ave.,
Oct. 24, 1947.

Mrs. *N*orris's Stuffed Peppers

Six medium-sized green peppers; 1½ cups canned or fresh corn; 1 cup diced, canned or raw tomatoes; ¼ cup finely chopped celery; 1 tablespoon finely chopped onion; 2 tablespoons melted butter; 2 slightly beaten eggs; 1½ teaspoons salt; ⅓ teaspoon pepper; ½ cup soft bread crumbs. Remove tops and seeds from peppers; parboil 5 minutes and drain. Combine remaining ingredients and stuff peppers. Place upright in greased baking dish; add small amount of water. Cover and bake in moderate oven (350 degrees) 1 hour. Serves 6.

–Mrs. Donald Norris, 749 Locust St., Aug. 27, 1948.

Mrs. *W*inchell's French Fried Eggplant
"A good substitute for meat."

One eggplant, salt and pepper, flour, 1 egg (beaten), ¼ cup milk or water, 1 cup cracker or bread crumbs. Peel eggplant and cut in strips as for french fried potoates. Soak in salt water 30 minutes. Roll in flour, then dip in egg and milk mixture, then in crumbs. Fry in deep fat or vegetable oil until brown. Drain on paper towels and serve hot.

–Mrs. T. A. Winchell, 714 New York St., Oct. 8, 1948.

Mrs. *O*'Connor's Corn Pudding
"Canned corn is especially good used in this kind of a dish."

Three eggs, 2 cups canned or fresh corn, 2 tablespoons melted butter, 2 tablespoons sugar, 1 teaspoon salt, pepper, 2 cups milk. Beat eggs and add the other ingredients. Pour into a greased baking dish. Place in a pan of hot water and bake in 350 degree oven for 1 hour, or until set in center.

–Mrs. J. M. O'Connor, Route 1, Oct. 29, 1948.

Mrs. *H*aden's Steamed Cabbage

Shred cabbage and let soak in cold water until very crisp. Drain and put into kettle with about 1 inch of water. Cook over medium flame until tender, stirring frequently and adding a little water when needed. May be cooked almost dry. Just before serving, add salt and pepper, and top with butter.

–Mrs. Jim Haden, 613 W. 4th St., Aug. 5, 1949.

Putting Up
Vegetables
and
Beans

Fine Response to Legion Food Drive

The response of Lawrence citizens to the American Legion food drive last night was most encouraging and today the Dorsey-Liberty Post rooms contained large quantities of foodstuffs donated for the needy.

It was estimated that supplies worth about $800 were given, according to Sgt. William Kollender, director of the drive. Over half the room was filled with all kinds of food "from soup to nuts," as one Legionnaire termed it. In one corner clothing and toys that had been contributed were stacked, and $9.25 in money was turned over to the workers in the drive last night.

The food was collected as a part of a drive staged by Dorsey-Liberty Post of the American Legion and other civic organizations. At a recent meeting the drive was suggested by members of the Americanization Committee and approved by the post.

That isn't all, either. There was more food awaiting the workers but because of lack of numbers they couldn't collect it. Sixty men, with fourteen trucks and nine cars, answered assembly at the Legion rooms at 7 o'clock and after a staff pored over a map of Lawrence, the units were assigned streets, and with the blowing of whistles at 7:30 o'clock, the drive was under way.

A "mop up" squad has been appointed to collect the food which was missed last night. If those persons who were not visited will call the Chamber of Commerce rooms at 485, their names and addresses will be taken and a car sent out in reasonable time to collect the food.

An inventory taken this morning before the food was turned over to the Community Service Committee showed that over 600 jars of home canned fruit and vegetables and 900 store purchased cans of the same type of food, 125 pounds of beans, 20 bushels of potatoes, 150 glasses of jelly and jam, 25 loaves of bread, 80 packages of breakfast food and 50 pounds of sugar were taken in the drive.

The food will be placed in the vaults at the old city hall building, Eighth and Vermont streets, and work of distribution will commence at once, according to H. A. Jetmore, chairman of the Community Service Committee.

It was truly a sharing of bread, the workers said. Some families who had very little gladly gave a share of their portion so that others might not go without. Everywhere there was a spirit of cooperation and the enthusiasm spread quickly from workers to the house owners.

At one place one family had a few crackers, but they offered a share to the workers. At others the family divided the meat secured for the evening meal.

When the shock troops reached the fraternity and sorority house front, they practically found the kitchens deserted, they said, with the exception of a few members who pointed out the supply of food to the raiders and told them to "help themselves." In fact, the raiders had to force the Greek letter organizations to keep some of the food for themselves.

Several orders for food to be given in the future were received from individuals and stores.

The cordial thanks of the Legion is extended to all persons who gave food or signified their intention of doing so and to the city and county authorities who loaned trucks, those citizens who donated cars and to the workers.

As a drive, Dorsey-Liberty Post feels that the work was a success and that several families will have food this winter who might have suffered otherwise, according to Howard Sutherland, post commander. [LJW, 12-13-32]

Mrs. *G*unther's Pickle Relish

Twelve cucumbers, 12 large onions, 12 red peppers (bell), 12 green peppers (bell), 3 tablespoons salt, 2 tablespoons celery seed, 2 tablespoons mustard seed, 2 cups granulated sugar, 1 quart white vinegar. Wash cucumbers, but do not peel them. Remove seeds from peppers and peel onions. Chop all fine in food chopper. Put in cheese cloth bag and drain eight hours. Put in crock, or large pan, and add salt, sugar, spices and vinegar. Mix well, then put in Mason jars and seal. It may be used immediately, or it will keep, when sealed tightly, indefinitely.

–Mrs. John Gunther, 1028 Rhode Island St., Sept. 9, 1921.

Mrs. *M*ortenson's Cucumber Relish

Twelve large cucumbers, 3 large green peppers, 3 large white onions. Chop fine and sprinkle with half cup of salt and let stand one night. In the morning, drain and cover with one quart of vinegar and one cup brown sugar. Pour boiling water over one teaspoon celery seed and one teaspoon white mustard seed. Let stand 15 minutes, drain and add to other ingredients. Let it come to a boil and boil 15 minutes. Pack hot in jars and seal.

–Mrs. A. L. Mortenson, 2011 Ohio St., Aug. 12, 1922.

Miss *M*ichael's Canned Tomatoes
"A No Cooking Method"

1. Scald tomatoes and peel;
2. Sterilize jars;
3. Pack tomatoes into hot jars;
4. Add salt, 1 teaspoon to 1 quart;
5. Fill jars with boiling water;
6. Seal tightly;
7. Place on rack in kettle of boiling water which covers the jars;
8. Turn off fire;
9. Leave tomatoes in water until cool.

–Miss Reva Michael, 1300 Tennessee St., July 27, 1923.

Mrs. *G*lenn's Sweet Tomato Pickle

Four quarts green tomatoes, 4 sliced onions, ½ cup salt, 1 tablespoon each of clove, mustard and cinnamon, 4 cups water, 2 pounds brown sugar, 2 cups vinegar, ¼ teaspoon cayenne. Slice tomatoes, add onions and salt, and let stand twelve hours. Drain; add water and two cups vinegar, and boil one-half hour. Drain tomatoes; add remaining ingredients and cook one-half hour. Keep in stone jar in cool, dry place.

–Mrs. George L. Glenn, Route 2, Lecompton, Oct. 12, 1923.

Mrs. *E*lliott's Green Tomato Pickle

One peck green tomatoes (ground), 1 large cabbage (ground), 4 tablespoons salt. Mix, and drain overnight in a sack. Add 1 dozen green peppers and 1 quart onions (chopped), 1 tablespoon cloves, 1 tablespoon allspice, 1 tablespoon mace, 5 cups light brown sugar, 4 tablespoons celery seed, 4 tablespoons mustard seed, 3 tablespoons tumeric, 3 tablespoons ginger, 2 tablespoons cinnamon, 3 quarts vinegar (diluted to taste). Cook 20 minutes after it begins to boil.

–Mrs. S. S. Elliott, 1416 W. 7th St., Oct. 9, 1925.

Mrs. *T*urner's Piccalilli

Sixty green tomatoes, 5 heads cabbage, 6 onions, 3 peppers, 6 cups sugar, 3 cups vinegar, 3 tablespoons salt, 1 tablespoon cinnamon, 1 tablespoon celery seed. Cut tomatoes and drain overnight. In the morning, put the tomatoes, cabbage, onions and peppers through the food chopper. Mix with the vinegar, sugar, salt, cinnamon and celery seed, and put on the stove. Let it boil 10 minutes and then let it simmer for 1 hour, when it is ready to put in jars and seal.

–Mrs. F. H. Turner, Route 8, Oct. 15, 1926.

Mrs. *H*ughes's Mixed Pickles

One peck green tomatoes, 12 medium-sized onions, 2 heads cauliflower, 2 red and 2 green peppers, 1 bunch celery, ¾ cup salt, 2 quarts vinegar, 2 lbs. sugar, ⅔ cupful whole spices (stick cinnamon, cloves, allspice and bay leaves) tied in small bag. Wash the green tomatoes and slice; peel the onions and slice. Separate the cauliflower into small flowerets. Remove the seeds from the green peppers, and chop. Wash and dice the celery. Place all in a large preserving kettle in layers, sprinkling each layer with salt. Let stand over night. In the morning, drain; add one quart of vinegar and two quarts of water. Bring to a boil and cook fifteen minutes. Drain again. Make a syrup by boiling together for fifteen minutes the other quart of vinegar, the sugar and bag of spices. Add to the pickle; bring to a boil, and can hot. This makes 5 quarts of delicious pickle.

–Mrs. Charles E. Hughes, 2201 New Hampshire St., Oct. 19, 1928.

Mrs. *H*oladay's Bread and Butter Pickles

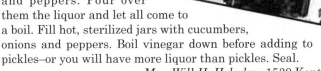

One dozen large cucumbers, ½ dozen white onions, 2 mango (bell) peppers, 1 quart vinegar, 2 cups sugar, 1 teaspoon tumeric, 1 teaspoon white mustard, 1 teaspoon celery seed, 1 half-teaspoon pepper, 1 half-teaspoon powdered alum. Directions: wash, peel and slice cucumbers and onions. Slice peppers into ¼-inch slices. Soak over night in brine made by adding one tablespoon salt to each quart of water. In morning, heat to boiling point the vinegar, sugar, alum and spices. Drain cucumbers, onions and peppers. Pour over them the liquor and let all come to a boil. Fill hot, sterilized jars with cucumbers, onions and peppers. Boil vinegar down before adding to pickles–or you will have more liquor than pickles. Seal.

–*Mrs. Will H. Holaday,* 1530 Kentucky St., Sept. 6, 1929.

Mrs. *L*oomas's Raw Tomato Relish

Peel one peck of ripe tomatoes, chop and let drain in bag over night. In the morning, add 6 medium-sized onions, 2 cups celery, 2 large green mangoes (sweet bell peppers). Grind all together very fine, then add 1½ lbs. of cane sugar, 2 ozs. of white mustard seed, ⅔ cup of salt, 5 cups of vinegar, ½ cup of horseradish. Mix all together thoroughly, then bottle.

–*Mrs. B. E. Loomas,* 723 Massachusetts St., Oct. 18, 1929.

Mrs. *H*atch's Corn Relish
"This is delicious served with meals."

Twelve ears corn, 6 peppers, 2 quarts tomatoes, 1 quart cucumbers, 1 pint onions, ½ cup salt, 2 quarts vinegar, 2 quarts sugar, 1 ounce celery seed, 1 ounce white mustard seed, ½ ounce tumeric, ½ ounce curry powder, 5 tablespoons flour. Cut corn from cob, cut tomatoes into small pieces, and put peppers, cucumbers and onions through coarse food chopper. Add the rest of the ingredients, and boil for 45 minutes. Then rub flour into a paste with a small amount of cold water, and blend well into relish. Boil for 5 or 10 minutes, or until the mixture seems thick enough. This recipe will make 12 pints.

–*Mrs. Frank Hatch,* 800 Pennsylvania St., Aug. 28, 1931.

Mrs. $\mathcal{G}$ann's Canned String Beans
*"I have canned hundreds of quarts of beans by this method
with no spoilage, and the color and flavor of the canned product
has always been excellent."*

Much of the success in canning any vegetable lies in the shortest time possible from garden to jars. For that reason, it is best to have jars and lids tested, washed and sterilized before beginning to work on the vegetables. Gather the beans while young and tender, wash thoroughly, and with a sharp knife, remove ends and cut pods into convenient lengths. One inch is a good size, though some jars may be packed with whole pods to be used in salads. Fill jars with beans, pressing them in firmly. Add one teaspoon of salt to each quart. Put on rubbers, and fill jars to overflowing with boiling water, pouring it in a small stream over the cold beans. This serves to set the color and takes the place of the more lengthy process of blanching. After jars have been filled, adjust lids and process given length of time according to kind of canner used. Green beans require three hours from the time water starts boiling in water bath or steamer, but the time is much shorter with a pressure cooker. When they have cooked the proper time, remove from canner, tighten lids, and turn upside down to test, and cool. Store in cool, dark place.

–Mrs. C. V. Gann, Route 6, July 1, 1932.

Mrs. $\mathcal{J}$ameson's Chili Sauce

Eight quarts ripe tomatoes, 5 or 6 green peppers, 8 medium-sized onions, 3 cups sugar, ¼ cup salt, 3 teaspoonfuls ground cloves, 3 teaspoonfuls cinnamon, 2 teaspoonfuls nutmeg, 2 teaspoonfuls ginger, 1½ quarts vinegar. Peel tomatoes and chop fine. (They will thicken quicker and are of better quality than when run through colander.) Grind peppers and onions. Mix sugar, salt and spices together and add to tomatoes, onions and peppers. Add vinegar as it cooks down. If cooked in the oven, 350 degrees F., it will require less stirring. Boil 3 hours. Seal in jars.

–Mrs. G. E. Jameson, 1113 Connecticut St., Sept. 9, 1932.

Mrs. $\mathcal{H}$arris's Canned Red Peppers
*"These are lovely as garnishes for meats and salads,
or whenever a touch of color is needed."*

Wash one peck of red peppers, cut a slice from stem end of each, and remove seeds; then cut in thin strips by working around and around the peppers, using scissors or a sharp knife. Cover with boiling water; let stand two minutes, then drain and plunge into ice water. Let stand ten minutes; again drain, and pack solidly into glass jars. Boil one quart of vinegar and two cups sugar fifteen minutes. Pour over peppers to overflow jars; seal and keep in a cool place.

–Mrs. J. F. Harris, 1422 New York St., Oct. 7, 1932.

Mrs. $\mathcal{V}$iets's Piccalilli
"A Family Favorite"

Eight cups chopped green tomatoes, 8 cups chopped green peppers (sweet), 8 cups chopped cabbage, 2 cups chopped celery, ⅔ cup salt, 6 cups vinegar, 2 cups sugar, 1¼ cups dark brown sugar, ½ cup cinnamon bark, ⅓ cup whole cloves, 1 tablespoon whole allspice berries. Wash tomatoes, cut out blossom ends. Do not peel. Wash peppers, cut in halves and remove all pulp and seeds and rinse well. Chop tomatoes and peppers. Add cabbage, celery and salt and let stand over night. Pour into a colander and let drain thoroughly. Add vinegar and sugar. Loosely tie spices in muslin bag. Add vegetable mixture. Boil gently and stir frequently until relish thickens. Pour into stone jar, cover with a plate and store in cool, dry place.

–Mrs. I. D. Viets, 714 Arkansas St., Oct. 14, 1932.

Mrs. $\mathcal{H}$oley's Dill Pickles

Put four quarts water, one quart vinegar, and one-half pint salt into granite kettle and let come to boiling point. Remove from fire and cool. While above mixture is cooling, carefully wash and wipe cucumbers. Those about six inches long are preferable. Pack into sterilized jars with two or three six-inch stalks of dill, two or three wild grape leaves, and two or three cherry leaves. Fill jars with the cooled liquid. Place rubbers, and turn on sterilized lids only as tight as the thumb and little finger will turn them. Put in cool, dark place and when fermentation stops, which will take from 15 to 21 days, seal tight. Note: the cherry and grape leaves may be omitted.

–Mrs. W. E. Holey, Route 3, July 21, 1933.

Mrs. $\mathcal{S}$timpson's Bread and Butter Pickles

Seven quarts cucumbers, 3 pints vinegar, 3 cups sugar, 9 small onions, 1 tablespoon tumeric powder, 1 tablespoon celery seed. Select good, firm medium-sized cucumbers. Wash the cucumbers, but do not peel. Slice enough to make 7 quarts. Make a salt solution of 1 cup of salt in 5 quarts of water, and soak the cucumbers in this over night. In the morning, drain and add the sliced onions and the other ingredients. Bring all to the boiling point, and can in sterile jars. Seal at once.

–Mrs. Ted Stimpson, 926 Indiana St., Aug. 25, 1933.

Mrs. $\mathcal{W}$right's Red Chili Sauce

Chop 30 large ripe tomatoes, 6 red peppers (seeds removed), and 8 medium-sized onions. Mix with 5 tablespoons salt and boil until fine and thick. Add 10 tablespoons sugar and 4 cups vinegar. Cook a few minutes and seal. This keeps its color.

–Mrs. Jennie C. Wright, 707 Missouri St., Oct. 13, 1933.

Heard In Lawrence

A cucumber that would almost pass for a watermelon, grown by J. D. Fincher, 545 North Eighth street in North Lawrence, was brought to the Journal-World today. The giant potential pickle was 16 inches long and weighed 2 pounds 5 ½ ounces. According to a conservative estimate, it would provide the pickle part of the pickles and onions for 728 hamburgers. [LJW, 7-30-37]

Mrs. ℬ all's Bread and Butter Pickles

Five quarts of sliced cucumbers, 1 quart of sliced onions, 1 quart of vinegar, ½ quart of water, 3 teaspoons of white mustard seeds, 1 teaspoon of celery seeds, 6 cups of sugar, 2 teaspoons of salt. Slice pickles and onions, soak in weak salt water over night, and drain well in the morning. Mix vinegar, water, salt and sugar, celery and white mustard seeds to taste. Bring to a boil, add sliced cucumbers and onions, and boil until tender. Pack in jars and seal.

–Mrs. Maggie Ball, 506 N. 8ᵗʰ St., Aug. 17, 1934.

Mrs. ℋ enry's Sweet Pepper Hash

Twelve red sweet peppers, 12 green peppers, 12 onions (medium), 2 cups chopped celery, 1 pint vinegar, 1 pint water, 1 tablespoon salt, 1 pint light brown sugar. Chop peppers and pour on boiling water. Cover and let steam 5 minutes. Drain and repeat process three times. Bring to a boil vinegar, salt, water, and sugar. Add chopped peppers, onions and celery. Cook 15 minutes and seal.

–Mrs. Frank Henry, 223 N. 4ᵗʰ St., Nov. 16, 1934.

Miss 𝒫 iper's Cauliflower for Winter Use

Remove outside leaves, wash and soak for two hours in a cold brine, using 2 teaspoons salt to 1 quart of water. Blanch for 3 minutes, then dip in cold water. Pack in hot jars, adding 1 teaspoon salt to each quart. Fill the jars with boiling hot water. Place caps on jars and tighten, then release one-half turn. Process as preferred, using the following table: Hot water bath: 150 minutes; Oven: 180 minutes at 250 degrees; Pressure cooker: 40 minutes at 10 pounds. Remove from canner and tighten cap.

–Miss Aimee Piper, 433 Illinois St., July 19, 1935.

Mrs. ℬ radley's Sauerkraut

"This keeps for several years, has a nice light color and delicious flavor."

Select solid heads of cabbage. Shred on cutter as for slaw. Allow 1 teaspoon of salt and 1 teaspoon of sugar to a quart of cabbage. Press or stomp in large stone jar. Weight down to form brine. Next day, put kraut in quart jars. Heat brine to boiling point. If not enough liquid, add boiled water to fill jars. Then place rubbers and caps on jars. Seal loosely until fermented. Keep liquid over kraut at all times, so it will not turn dark and soft.

–Mrs. Bradley [first name and address unavailable], Oct. 25, 1935.

Mrs. *S*mith's Chunk Pickles

Wash cucumbers (large ones are best) and place in stone jar. Do not cut. Pour on salt water strong enough to bear up an egg. Cover and weight down; let stand three days. On fourth day, drain and put on clear water. On the sixth day, change water again; also on the seventh day. On the eighth day, cut in uniform pieces, put back into stone jar, and cover with the following solution: One heaping tablespoon powdered alum, one pint vinegar, five pints water. Let come to a boil; pour on while boiling, weight down. Be sure liquid covers all; let stand three days; drain. Throw away liquid and make a syrup of the following solution: 3 lbs. white sugar, 2 pints vinegar, cinnamon bark to taste, and one tablespoon whole allspice (to each gallon pickles). Heat to boiling; pour on hot and let stand through the day. The second and third days: reheat, and while the liquid is heating the third day, place in quart jars, cover with liquid and seal while hot.

–Mrs. H. W. Smith, 2235 Tennessee St., Aug. 21, 1936.

Mrs. *N*eis's Canned Green or Wax Beans
"Hot water bath method."

Select fresh, sound, firm snappy beans. Wash thoroughly and remove strings. Cover with boiling water and boil 5 minutes. Pack into clean, hot jars, adding 1 teaspoon salt to each quart. Fill with the boiling water in which beans have been cooked; partly seal and process for 3 hours in a hot water bath. Points in canning: 1. Pack beans loosely enough so they will retain their shape; 2. Fill jars with the boiling water to within one-half inch of top of jar; 3. Have water in canner hot, place jars in slowly, and cover and keep at least one inch of water over tops of jars; 4. Begin counting time when water is in a hard boil; 5. Keep water boiling steadily during the entire processing period, always adding boiling water–not cold; 6. When processing time is over, remove jars from canner and seal immediately; 7. Keep jars out of a cool draft after filling; 8. Place cloth or paper over metal-top table which holds the hot jars; 9. Store in a cool, dry place.

–Mrs. C. P. Neis, 1012 Illinois St., June 25, 1937.

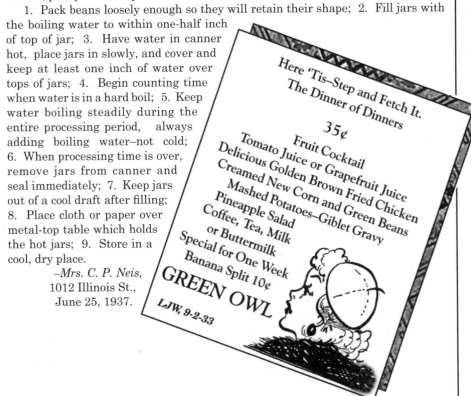

Here 'Tis–Step and Fetch It.
The Dinner of Dinners

35¢

Tomato Juice or Grapefruit Juice
Fruit Cocktail
Delicious Golden Brown Fried Chicken
Creamed New Corn and Green Beans
Mashed Potatoes–Giblet Gravy
Pineapple Salad
Coffee, Tea, Milk
or Buttermilk

Special for One Week
Banana Split 10¢

GREEN OWL

LJW, 9-2-33

Mrs. *R*ockhold's Carrot Relish

"This relish is easy to make and is excellent."

Two medium heads of cabbage, 8 green mango peppers, 3 red mango peppers, 12 good-sized carrots, 12 onions. Put all through food chopper and add ⅓ cup of salt. Let stand 3 hours and drain 1 hour. Heat, until sugar is dissolved, 6 small cups of sugar, 3 pints vinegar, 2 teaspoons celery seed, 2 teaspoons mustard. Let cool and pour over relish. Seal in fruit jars cold.

–Mrs. A. T. Rockhold, Route 3, Baldwin, July 23, 1937.

Mrs. *D*reher's Canned String Beans

"This method has been used for a number of years with no spoilage, and they are excellent."

Have jars and lids tested, washed and sterilized before beginning work on the vegetables. Gather the beans while young and tender, wash thoroughly, remove ends and break pods into convenient lengths. Fill jars with beans, pressing them in firmly. Add one teaspoon of salt to each quart. Put on rubbers and fill jars to overflowing with boiling water. This sets the color and takes the place of blanching. After jars have been filled, screw lids on loosely and boil three hours in water bath–from the time water starts boiling. Remove from canner, tighten lids and turn upside down to test and cool. Store in a cool, dark place.

–Mrs. Otto Dreher, Route 2, July 8, 1938.

Mrs. *F*erguson's Tomato Catsup

Use red tomatoes that are thoroughly ripe. Cook rapidly–as long cooking time darkens them. When soft, rub through sieve. To each gallon of liquid, add 3 tablespoons salt, ¼ tablespoon red pepper, 2 tablespoons whole allspice, 4 tablespoons white or yellow mustard seed, 1 tablespoon whole cloves, 2 tablespoons whole celery seed, 1 ounce stick cinnamon, 3 ounces green ginger root. Put spices into bags, and add 2 large whole onions to the gallon. Stir frequently while the catsup cooks, as it will scorch easily. When it has thickened, add 2 cups of vinegar to the gallon and 3 tablespoons sugar. Continue boiling hard until when a little is put on a plate, the liquid will not run from it. Remove onions and spices. Pour into bottles or jars and seal tightly.

–Mrs. D. W. Ferguson, Route 2, Sept. 16, 1938.

Mr. *G*urss's 14-Day Sweet Pickles

Seventy-five medium-sized cucumbers. To one gallon of water, add one pint salt. Let stand one week. Drain off and place the pickles in the following solution: 1 gallon boiling water and 1 tablespoon powdered alum. Let stand 24 hours. Drain off. Place pickles in one gallon clear boiling water; let stand 24 hours. Drain and split pickles and put in the following solution: 5 pints of vinegar, 6 cups sugar, and whole spices–allspice, cinnamon bark, celery seeds (or use mixed spices without the red pepper). Put on pickles while solution is hot. Let stand 24 hours. Drain off and add one cup sugar. Heat again to boiling point; pour over pickles. Repeat this three mornings. Then three mornings, drain off and heat without adding sugar. Then seal if you wish, or they will keep in open jars, if the pickling vinegar covers them.

–Mr. Roy O. Gurss, 1007 W. 6th St., Aug. 4, 1939.

Mrs. *W*iggins's Tomato Preserves

Select good, firm (not over-ripe) tomatoes. Scald slightly, peel and scoop out the seeds, being careful to have good-sized pieces of the fruit. Place tomatoes in a crock or enameled bowl. Add sugar and let stand over night. To 5 pounds of tomatoes, add 8 cups sugar. In the morning, drain off the juice and boil it rapidly until it threads. Add the tomatoes and 2 lemons, sliced thin, and cook until the mixture is thick and clear. Pack into hot sterilized jars and seal immediately. The preserves should be a rich, red color.

–Mrs. James Wiggins, Route 1, Sept. 8, 1939.

Mrs. *H*unter's Tomato Catsup
"The secret of the fine flavor is the peach leaves"

Take a half bushel of firm, ripe tomatoes. Wipe them off with a damp cloth and place in porcelain-lined or aluminum kettle. Place over fire and add 2 large handfuls of peach leaves, if possible–this is the secret of the fine flavor of this catsup. Add 10 to 12 large onions, sliced fine. Boil until tomatoes are thoroughly done. Remove from fire, strain through coarse mesh sieve, pour the liquid into kettle and add 1 quart strong vinegar. Have ready 1 ounce ground allspice, 1 ounce black pepper, 1 ounce mustard (ground or in seed, as preferred), ½ ounce ground cloves, 1 grated nutmeg, 1 pound light brown sugar, and ½ pint salt. Mix these ingredients well before adding to tomato liquid, then boil 1 hour, stirring frequently to prevent burning. If desired "hot," add cayenne to suit taste. When cool, bottle for use, sealing with paraffin or wax. Quantities may be lessened to convenience.

–Mrs. J. W. Hunter, Route 1, Linwood, Oct. 6, 1939.

Mrs. *W*iedemann's String Beans To Put Up
"This is a quick, easy way to can string beans."

String, wash, and cut beans in small pieces. Cover with hot water. Add one teaspoon salt for each quart of beans. Boil until tender, about one hour. Keep beans covered with water while boiling. Scald jars, fill with beans and the water in which they were cooked–to within one-half inch of top of jar. Add two tablespoons of boiling vinegar, and seal tight. When ready to serve, pour all water off beans, cover with fresh boiling water, and let stand on back of stove for ten minutes. (This draws out vinegar taste.) Pour water off and repeat, this time leaving water on only a few minutes. Prepare in favorite way.

–Mrs. F. Wiedemann, 1947 Vermont St., July 5, 1940.

Mrs. *M*edhurst's Bread and Butter Pickles

One gallon (sliced measure) rather large cucumbers, 1 quart (sliced measure) onions, 2 or 3 large sweet peppers (chopped fine). Combine. Add ½ cup salt stirred well through the mixture. Let stand 3 or 4 hours, then drain well. Bring to a boil pickle mixture of 1½ quarts cider vinegar, 4 cups brown sugar, 2 tablespoons mustard seed, 1 tablespoon celery seed, 1 teaspoon turmeric, 1 teaspoon ground ginger. Add cucumbers and stand in hot liquid 30 minutes, but do not let them boil. Seal in sterilized jars. Makes about 7 pints. Mixed pickling spices may be used instead, but these do not give the same flavor.

–Mrs. Dora Medhurst, 929 Connecticut St., July 26, 1940.

Mrs. *S*eiwald's India Relish

Twelve green tomatoes, 1 red pepper, 1 green pepper, 4 large onions, 1 cup sugar, 1 tablespoon salt, 2 cups vinegar, 1 tablespoon celery seed, 1 tablespoon mustard seed. Chop vegetables, using coarse knife of food chopper. Drain. Combine vegetables and remaining ingredients. Mix thoroughly. Cook slowly, stirring frequently. Cook about 30 minutes. Pour into sterilized glasses or jars, and seal.

–Mrs. William Seiwald, 227 N. 6th St., Oct. 17, 1941.

To Blend Your Own Pickling Spices

Spices should be bought fresh for each year's pickling. A mixture of spices commonly known as "pickling spice" may be obtained loose or in packages, or they may be blended at home. They should include whole cloves, peppercorns, stick cinnamon, mace, tiny red peppers, mustard seed, allspice, bay leaves and root ginger. Spices are usually tied in a square of cheesecloth and cooked with the pickles.

[The Ball Blue Book, c. 1943]

Mrs. $\mathcal{G}$lenn's Sweet Gherkins

Two quarts small green cucumbers (1 to 2 inches long), 2 quarts boiling vinegar, 4 cups sugar, 2 tablespoons whole allspice, 1 tablespoon celery seed, 2 tablespoons stick cinnamon, 2 tablespoons whole cloves, ½ cup white mustard seed. Cover the fresh cucumbers with boiling hot brine made by dissolving 2 cups of salt in 2½ quarts boiling water. Soak the cucumbers in this brine for twenty-four hours; drain. Heat the vinegar to the boiling point and pour it over the cucumbers. Let the mixture stand twenty-four hours; drain. Save the vinegar and add the sugar and spices. Boil the mixture five minutes. Pack the pickles into clean, sterile, hot jars. Cover cucumbers with the boiling syrup and seal the jars.

–*Mrs. Viola Glenn,* Lecompton, July 24, 1942.

Gardening and Canning were never so important to our family and national welfare as today

Bernardin Home Canning Guide, 1943

Mrs. $\mathcal{S}$elichnow's Tomato Catsup
"The tart apples make the catsup thick."

One gallon tomato pulp, 12 tart apples (pulp), 1 teaspoon red pepper, 4 teaspoons paprika, 1 heaping teaspoon cinnamon, 5 green peppers, 1 cup to one pint sugar, 1 teaspoon black pepper, 1 teaspoon cloves, 3 tablespoons salt (or to taste), 1 bulb of garlic, 10 to 15 onions. Cook onions and garlic till well-done. Run through sieve. Add this to the tomato and apple pulp. Put all of the spices into a bag or a clean cloth and boil all this together until as thick as desired. Then, last of all, add 1 cup to 1 ½ cups of vinegar and let cook 5 to 10 minutes longer.

–*Mrs. Marvin Selichnow,* 622 Alabama St., Sept. 18, 1942.

Mrs. $\mathcal{M}$iller's Tomato Preserves

Two and one-half pounds of ripe tomatoes, 2 pounds of sugar, ½ lemon or to suit taste, ½ teaspoon salt. Scald tomatoes and slip off skins. Place tomatoes in crock or enamel bowl. Add sugar and allow to stand over night. Cook lemon–in just enough water to cover–until tender and transparent. Drain juice from tomatoes and boil it rapidly until it threads from spoon. Add tomatoes, cut in small pieces, lemon and salt. Boil until thick.

–*Mrs. Ralph Miller,* 536 Tennessee St., Aug. 27, 1943.

Mrs. *J*ohns's Bread and Butter Pickles

"These pickles are delicious and very simple to make."

Six quarts sliced cucumbers; 6 onions, sliced medium; 1 cup salt. Combine and allow to stand 3 hours. Drain. Combine and boil the following: 1½ quarts vinegar, 4 cups sugar, ½ cup mustard seed, 1 tablespoon celery seed. Add cucumbers and onions. Heat to simmering, and pack. Be careful to avoid boiling after adding cucumbers and onions, as boiling will make pickles soft. Pack in sterilized hot jars and seal immediately.

–Mrs. Walter Johns, 1846 Barker Ave., Sept. 3, 1943.

Mrs. *C*raig's Tomato Catsup

Three large sweet red peppers, 10 pounds ripe tomatoes, 3 medium-sized onions, 1 bud garlic, 1 bay leaf, 1 tablespoon salt, 1½ cups vinegar, ¾ cup sugar, 2 teaspoons paprika, 2 teaspoons celery seed, 1 teaspoon whole cloves, 1 tablespoon whole allspice, 3 inches stick cinnamon. Wash vegetables and remove seed cores from peppers. Slice peppers, tomatoes, onions and garlic. Add bay leaf and salt. Cook slowly in large preserving kettle 30 minutes, until tomatoes are soft, stirring frequently. Remove bay leaf. Sieve tomato mixture into large saucepan; add vinegar, sugar, and paprika. Mix well. Add remaining spices tied in a bag. Cook slowly until thickened and volume is reduced about one-half, stirring frequently. Remove spice bag. Pour immediately into hot sterilized fruit jars or bottles; fill to top and seal. Makes about 4 pints.

–Mrs. George Craig, Baldwin, Sept. 10, 1943.

Mrs. *R*obertson's Old-Fashioned Chow-Chow

Grind separately 2 large heads of cabbage, ½ peck green tomatoes, 6 large onions, 9 large red sweet peppers, 1 hot pepper. Mix the ground ingredients with 1 cup salt, and let stand 3 hours in colander to drain. Add 1 oz. white mustard seed, 1 oz. black mustard seed, 2 ozs. celery seed and 3 pounds brown sugar. Pour over the mixture enough hot vinegar to moisten thoroughly. Heat thoroughly and seal. (The hot pepper may be omitted if desired. One large ripe cucumber and 1 coffee cup grated horseradish may be added if one desires a spicier relish.)

–Mrs. Leslie Robertson, 2121 New Hampshire St., Sept. 24, 1943.

Mrs. *B*lakely's Carrot Marmalade

Four cups chopped or ground carrots, 3 cups sugar, 3 lemons (sliced), 1 teaspoon cinnamon, ½ teaspoon cloves. Combine ingredients. Simmer slowly, stirring constantly until thick.

–Mrs. Harry Blakely, 1229 New York St., Oct. 1, 1943.

Mrs. *Hunt's* Tomato Preserves

Six pounds ripe tomatoes and five pounds sugar. Scald and peel ripe tomatoes. Cut in half crosswise. Scoop out seeds and juice. Cover tomatoes with diluted vinegar. (Use ½ cup vinegar to each cup of water needed.) Let stand 3 hours. Drain well. Add sugar. Bring to a rolling boil and continue boiling rapidly until clear and thick. Stir occasionally with a fork to prevent sticking. Pour into sterilized jars and seal.

–Mrs. Ira E. Hunt, 414 Forest Ave., Sept. 22, 1944.

Miss *Rayhill's* Green Tomato Relish

Run through a food grinder, then measure: 4 quarts green tomatoes, 2 quarts ripe tomatoes, 2 cups cabbage, ½ dozen green peppers (sweet), ½ dozen red peppers, 1 cup onion. Add ½ cup salt to the above and let it stand over night. In the morning, drain off the liquor and discard. Add 2 quarts vinegar, 6 cups brown sugar, 2 tablespoons white mustard, 2 tablespoons celery seed, 2 teaspoons cinnamon, 2 teaspoons cloves, 2 teaspoons allspice. Boil until tender. Place in glasses or jars (sterilized) and seal or top with paraffin.

–Miss Martha Rayhill, 2042 Massachusetts St., Oct. 20, 1944.

Mrs. *Beurman's* Chili Sauce

One-half gallon chopped ripe tomatoes, ¼ cup chopped white onions, ¼ cup chopped sweet green peppers, ¼ cup chopped sweet red peppers, ¼ cup brown sugar, 1 tablespoon ginger, 1½ teaspoons cinnamon, 1½ teaspoons mustard, ½ teaspoon nutmeg, 2½ teaspoons salt, 1 pint vinegar, ¼ teaspoon cayenne pepper. Peel tomatoes and onions. Chop onions and peppers fine. Boil all the ingredients, except the vinegar, together for two hours, or until soft and broken. Add vinegar and simmer for one hour. Stir frequently. Fill into sterilized jars and process at simmering temperature (180 degrees) for 15 minutes.

–Mrs. J. C. Beurman, Route 1, Oct. 27, 1944.

Mrs. *Skinner's* Canned Green Beans

"For perfectly tender beans, pick them young, before the bean starts to mature, and waste no time from bush to jar."

Wash and remove any strings and tips, and cut or break into small pieces. Cover with boiling water and boil 5 minutes. Pack hot into jars, adding 1 teaspoon salt to each quart. Fill to 1 inch of top of jar with boiling water–the water in which the beans were boiled. Seal and process 35 minutes at 10 lbs. pressure or 3 hours in a hot water bath.

–Mrs. Harold Skinner, 227 Mississippi St., June 29, 1945.

Mrs. *B*arnes's Sugar-Saving Sweet Pickles

"Makes eight quarts of pickles that will keep well and remain crisp."

Take freshly picked cucumbers, any size you can pack in jars, and cut off stems, but do not cut the skins. Wash well and pack into jars. Mix 1 gallon vinegar, ½ cup salt, 1 teaspoon ground mustard, 1 dram saccharin, 3 teaspoons ground cloves, 3 teaspoons ground cinnamon, 3 teaspoons allspice. Bring this mixture to a boil and pour over cucumbers. Fill jars to brim and seal. These should stand about 2 months before using.

–*Mrs. Jaff Barnes,* Route 3, Sept. 14, 1945.

Mrs. *A*uchard's Carrot Relish

Twelve carrots, 2 medium-sized heads cabbage, 8 medium-sized onions, 4 green peppers, 4 red peppers, 8 green tomatoes. Grind together all these ingredients and add ½ teaspoon salt. Mix thoroughly and let stand 2 hours. Put into a clean muslin sack and squeeze out all the juice. Then add 8 to 10 red Jonathan apples and a stalk of celery, chopped fine. Leave skins on the apples when chopping them, for the red skins add to the appearance of the relish. Cover the mixture with the following spiced vinegar. One pint vinegar, 1 pint water, 6 cups sugar (part honey may be used), 1 teaspoon celery seed, 1 teaspoon white mustard seed. Mix well and let stand 2 hours. It is now ready to put into containers. Needs no cooking. Yields about 6½ pints.

–*Mrs. V. M. Auchard,* 1405 New York St., Sept. 28, 1945.

Mrs. *D*eWitt's Chili Sauce

Four quarts chopped ripe tomatoes, ½ cup chopped white onions, ½ cup chopped sweet green peppers, ½ cup chopped sweet red peppers, ½ cup brown sugar, 2 tablespoons ginger, 1 tablespoon cinnamon, 1 tablespoon mustard, 1 teaspoon nutmeg, 1 quart vinegar, 5 tablespoons salt, ½ teaspoon cayenne pepper. Peel the tomatoes and onions. Chop the onions and peppers fine. Boil all ingredients together, except the vinegar, for two hours, or until soft. Add vinegar and seasonings and simmer for one hour. Stir frequently. Put into hot glass jars and seal.

–*Mrs. Alda DeWitt,*
820½ Massachusetts St.,
Oct. 5, 1945.

Local Grocery Prices 1943

1 (2 oz.) pickling spices	.10
1 pair wire jar tongs	.10
1 quart vinegar	.12
1 lb. green beans	.14
1 lb. cucumbers	.14
1 lb. tomatoes	.15
2 boxes Morton's salt	.17
4 doz. jar rings	.19
4 lbs. onions	.23
1 doz. Mason quart jars	.69
Total	$ 2.03

Mrs. *P*earson's Piccalilli Relish

Two quarts well-chopped ripe or semi-ripe tomatoes, 2 quarts well-chopped green tomatoes, 3 cups well-chopped green peppers, 2 cups well-chopped red pepper, 1 cup well-chopped onions, ¼ cup salt, 4 cups sugar, 4 cups vinegar, 2 tablespoons mustard seed, 2 tablespoons celery seed, ¼ cup bark cinnamon, 2 whole cloves. Method: Pour boiling water over the chopped vegetables. Drain; add salt and let stand over night. The next morning, drain well. Add sugar to vinegar and boil three minutes. Add spices tied in a cloth bag, then add vegetables and boil gently. Fill jars and seal.

–Mrs. George M. Pearson, Route 2, Oct. 18, 1946.

Mrs. *D*unkley's Tomato Catsup

Six quarts tomato pulp (from about ½ bushel tomatoes), 3 onions, 2½ cups vinegar, 1¼ cups sugar, 3 tablespoons salt, 1 teaspoon paprika, about 2 teaspoons red cayenne pepper (to taste hot), 1 tablespoon dry mustard mixed with 3 tablespoons cold water, 2 teaspoons whole cloves, 4 (2-inch) sticks cinnamon, 2 teaspoons whole allspice, 2 or 3 red hot peppers (either fresh or dried), 2 teaspoons celery seed. Tie cloves, cinnamon, allspice, peppers, and celery seed in cheesecloth sack. Wash, remove core, and split tomatoes, which should be very ripe and red. Add diced onion. Boil in aluminum or enameled kettles till mushy. Rub through sieve to remove skins and seeds. Boil down rapidly, stirring often, till reduced to about half, then add vinegar, sugar, salt, paprika, red pepper, mustard mixture and the sack of spices. Boil till quite thick, and during this period of boiling, it will be necessary to stir very often. Remove sack (which may be rinsed off, wrapped in waxed paper and stored in refrigerator to be used over and over). Seal in hot, sterilized jars or bottles.

The secret of having bright red catsup is in not allowing the least bit of scorching, and in never allowing the tomatoes to come into contact with iron. Do not use any chipped enamel utensils. Use stainless steel knives and boil in either aluminum or enamel kettles. Cook quickly. Slow cooking causes loss of color. Scorching causes loss of both color and flavor. Store in the dark. Yields 8 pints.

–Mrs. George B. Dunkley, 628 Maine St., Sept. 24, 1948.

Mrs. *J*ames's Tomato Preserves

One pint ripe tomatoes, 1 lemon, ¼ cup water, 1¼ cups sugar. Peel and dice enough red tomatoes to fill a pint cup. To this add ¼ cup water, a small pinch of salt, and bring to a hard boil. Then add 1¼ cups of sugar and a lemon that has been thinly sliced. Boil until thick. Seal while hot.

–Mrs. Cora James, 941 Vermont St., Sept. 9, 1949.

Mrs. *O*lson's Piccalilli
"This makes a very good relish."

Four quarts chopped green tomatoes, 4 cups chopped green peppers, 1 cup chopped red peppers, 1 cup chopped onions, 2 cups chopped cabbage, 2 cups chopped celery, 2⅔ cups salt. Mix all vegetables, add salt, and let stand over night. In the morning, drain well. Vinegar mixture: 2 quarts vinegar, 3 cups sugar, 2 tablespoons white mustard seed, 2 tablespoons yellow mustard seed, 2 teaspoons cinnamon, 1 teaspoon cloves. Mix ingredients. Add drained vegetables, and let cook slowly until mixture thickens, stirring frequently. Pour into sterilized jars and seal.

–Mrs. H. F. Olson, 702 Rhode Island St., Oct. 7, 1949.

Appendix

$\mathcal{C}$ooking Terms

Oven Temperatures:

Slow: 250° to 300° F.
Moderate: 325° to 375° F.
Hot, brisk, or quick: 400° to 450° F.
Very Hot: 450° and above

Can Sizes:

No. 300 = 1¾ cups
No. 1 Tall = 2 cups
No. 303 = 2 cups
No. 2 = 2½ cups
No. 2 ½ = 3½ cups
No. 10 = 12 to 13 cups

Equivalent Measurements:

Dash = less than an eighth teaspoon
60 drops = 1 teaspoon
3 teaspoons = 1 tablespoon
4 tablespoons = ¼ cup
4 tablespoons = 1 wine glass
16 tablespoons = 1 cup
2 gills = 1 cup
2 cups = 1 pint
2 pints = 1 quart
4 quarts = 1 gallon
8 quarts (solid) = 1 peck
4 pecks = 1 bushel
16 ounces = 1 pound
4 cups of flour = 1 pound
2 cups of granulated sugar = 1 pound
10 unbroken hen's eggs = 1 pound
Butter the size of an egg = 2 ounces

Aitch Bone: Hip bone

Catsup: Ketchup

Double Boiler: A cooking system comprised of two nested saucepans, the bottom containing boiling water, and the top containing food, such as delicate sauces, to be heated and cooked slowly.

Dover Beater: Rotary egg beater

Drawn Butter: Drawn butter is made by melting butter and then allowing the salt and curd to settle. The clear oil is then carefully poured off into small hot cups to be served with fish and seafood, among other foods.

Fat: When fat is called for, use butter, margarine, oleo, lard, or vegetable shortening. Vegetable oil–such as for frying–may also be used.

Flour: The all-purpose flour sold on the market today usually comes pre-sifted, eliminating the need to sift (as many as three times) as directed in some of the older recipes. When self-rising flour is called for, all-purpose flour can be substituted by adding 1½ teaspoons baking powder and ½ teaspoon salt for each cup of all-purpose flour.

French Dressing: The bottled French dressing sold in supermarkets today is a tomato-based product, unlike the true French dressing (originating in France), which consists of oil, vinegar and seasonings. A good all-purpose true French dressing can be made by combining and thoroughly beating the following: 1 cup olive oil, ¼ cup vinegar, ½ teaspoon salt, a few grains cayenne pepper, ¼ teaspoon white pepper and 2 tablespoons chopped parsley. (Yield: 1¼ cups)

Ice Box: Refrigerator

Mango Peppers:

Sweet bell peppers

Pimiento:

Sweet red pepper

Refrigerator Trays:

Aluminum ice cube trays, with their cube release mechanisms removed, served as shallow, narrow vessels for chilled or frozen salads and desserts. Some older model refrigerator manufacturers provided trays twice the depth of the ordinary ice cube tray.

Salt Pork:

Salted side pork, that area of fat on the outside of the spare ribs. Often used for larding and for seasoning beans.

Sweet Milk, Sour Milk:

Sweet Milk is milk that has not turned sour. When sour milk is called for, and none is on hand, add 2 teaspoons of lemon juice or vinegar to 1 cup of milk.

To "Try Out":

To "try out" means to fry bits of solid fat or fatty meat until fat is separated from the membrane.

The Food Chopper was an essential kitchen tool during the 1920s, '30s, and '40s. Constructed of cast iron and equipped with various blades, the food chopper could turn beef steak into hamburger and whole vegetables into fine dice.

Toast Points:

Toast points are made by cutting each slice of toast diagonally from one corner to the opposite corner.

Top Milk:

Cream

White Sauce:

A basic sauce made of equal amounts of butter and flour, cooked to make a roux, then combined with milk and cooked further until thickened, then seasoned with salt and white pepper.

Yeast:

When "a cake" or "a cake of compressed" yeast is called for, substitute a quarter-ounce packet of granular yeast.

The Baking Powder Can was a common mold used for making Boston Brown Bread. The cans were filled half to two-thirds full with batter; then, with lids on, the filled cans were steamed in a kettle of boiling water for approximately 3 hours.

Index

*I*ndex
of Persons, Businesses, Organizations, and Enterprises

Holmes (Drake &) Baking Co., 80
Holmes, Hallie, 87
Holt, Alberta, 63
Hoover, Mrs. Elva M., 53
Hornberger, Mrs. Henry, 131
Horr, Mrs. W. H., 156
Hotel Wood, 16
Houghton, Mrs. H. W., 194
Houk, Mrs. H. A., 29, 98
Houk, Mrs. Harry, 11, 14, 138
Houser, Mrs. E. P., 158
Houser, Winifred, 51
Howard, Elizabeth, 195
Howard, Mrs. Chester, 177, 202
Howard, Mrs. Fred, 28
Howard, Mrs. Lewis E., 218
Howard, Mrs. Paul, 196
Howe, James, 204
Howe, Ross, 204
Hughes, Mrs. Charles E., 228
Hull, Maggie V., 56
Humphrey, Cecile, 105
Humphries, Mrs. Clyde, 42
Hunsinger, Lucy, 113
Hunt, Mrs. Ira E., 239
Hunter, Harriet Ruth, 200
Hunter, Mrs. Alfred, 40
Hunter, Mrs. J. W., 235
Hunzicker, Mrs. C. J., 187
Hunzicker, Mrs. Otto, 80-81
Husted, Mrs. Charles, 73
Hyde, Arthur, Secretary and Mrs., 66
Ice, Mrs. LaVern, 100
Ince, Mary E., 64
Ince, Mrs. J. W., 177
Indian Village, 155
Ingalls, Harry, 174
Ingalls, Maurine, 81, 137
Ingham, Mrs. H. G., 111
Isaacs, Dr. Fred, 7
James, Cora, 241
James, Helen, 133
James, Mrs. J. F., 101
Jameson, Mrs. G. E., 230
Jayhawk Café, 48
Jayhawker (Theater), 198
Jennings, Mrs. George, 71, 79-80
Jetmore, H. A., 226
Johanning, Mrs. D. W., 129
Johns, Mrs. Walter, 238
Johnson, Mrs. Dan, 32
Johnson, Mrs. R. E., 94
Johnson, Mrs. Vic, 158-59

Johnson, Roy, 198
Jones, Frank E., 138
Jones, Marie, 97
Jones, Mrs. C. A., 49
Jones, Mrs. Eli, 68
Jones, Mrs. Frank E., 211
Jones, Mrs. I. J., 49
Jordan, Mrs. Leroy, 188
Jost, Mrs. Frank, 208
Kansas Electric Power Co., 23, 36, 64
Kapfer, Mrs. George L., 67
Kasson, Mrs. W. O., 91
Kaw Flour Mills, 70
Keefe, Mrs. E. F., 92-93
Keefe, Mrs. Ed, 161
Keiffer, Mrs. F. H., 125
Keller, Mrs. John L., 181
Kelsey, Mrs. Jack, 212
Kemp, Sarah, 93
Kennard, Mrs. W. E., 189
Kennedy, Mrs. A. R., 162
Kennedy, Mrs. L. W., 74
Key, Mrs. Richard, 37
Kieffer, Mrs. F. H., 87
King, Mr. & Mrs., 20
Kirchhoff, Mrs. G. G., 46
Kirchhoff, Mrs. George Jr., 110
Kline, Mrs. William V., 119
Klock's (Grocery), 125
Knox, Mrs. William F., 49
Koerner, Wilma, 48
Kollender, Sgt. William, 226
Krum, Lillian, 25
Krum, Mrs. J. J., 217
Krum, Mrs. J. W., 189
Krum, Mrs. Jessie J., 124
Lackey, Ellen, 123, 188, 199
Lackey, Hattie R., 11
Lackey, Mildred, 21
Lackey, Mrs. F. B., 106
Lackey, Mrs. Roy B., 105
LaCoss, Mrs. William, 43, 194
Lacy, H. B., 134
Laird, Mrs. John R., 16
LaMont, Ethel, 111
Lanning, Mrs. George B., 56
Large's Café, 178
Lawrence, Mrs. Roy, 219
Lawrence Choral Union, 96
Lawrence Journal-World, 5, 8, 222, 232
Lawrence Memorial Hospital, 7
Lawrence Public Library, 5, 8
Lawrence Recreation Parlors, 131
Lawrence Sanitary Milk and Ice Cream Co., 86

Shaw, Mrs. Edwin, 220
Shepard, Mrs. Allan, 186
Sherfy, Luella C., 12
Shimmons, Fred, 134
Shirar, Mrs. Charles, 204
"Shorty," 7
Shultz, Mrs. George J., 5, 215
Simpson, Mrs. G. A., 212
Sims, Mrs. S. H., 222
Skeet, Anna M., 58
Skinner, Mrs. Harold, 51, 239
Skinner, Rody, 112
Skyline (The New), 142
Simons, Dolph Jr., 8
Smith, Marie J., 138
Smith, Marjorie, 98
Smith, Mrs. Albert C., 83
Smith, Mrs. Cecil E., 216
Smith, Mrs. Gilbert L., 23
Smith, Mrs. H. W., 233
Smith, Mrs. R. A. Jr., 17
Smoots, Mrs. J. A., 157
Snyder, Augusta P., 203
Snyder, Mrs. Gerrit, 203
Sommer, Mrs. Albert, 183
Sorby, E. C., 186
Spalsbury, Margaret, 124
Spear, Mrs. Roy D., 99
Sperry, Mrs. Everett, 186
Stable (The), 163
Stanwix, May Marie, 140-41
Stanwix, Mrs. C. E., 64
Starkweather, Mrs. Charles, 86
Stemmerman, Mrs. A. W., 76
Stephenson, Mrs. J. J., 203
Sterling, Mrs. C. M., 96, 153
Sterling, Mrs. C. W., 208
Sterling, Mrs. M. W., 44
Sterling, Mrs. Wilson, 204
Stevens, Mrs. R. B., 136
Stevenson, Ruth, 157
Stimpson, Mrs. E. C., 73
Stimpson, Mrs. Ted, 231
Stocks, Ruth, 114
Stowit, H. W., 133
Strahl, Bertha, 207
Stringham, Mrs. R. P., 56
Strong, Mrs. C. B., 66
Strong-Pringle (see West End Grocery)
Sturdy, Mrs. Joe, 218
Suiter, Mrs. Maurice, 128, 175-76
Sullivan, Mrs. E. F., 194
Sunflower Café, 223
Sunflower Grill, 167
Supreme Café, 210
Sutherland, Howard, 226
Sutton, Elizabeth, 150
Taylor, Bessie, 47
Tefft, Mrs. C. E., 186
Teich, Pauline, 112
Terrace Tea Room, 127
Terrell, Allis M., 217
Thimble Tea Room, 10
Thompson, Marion, 107, 154
Thornton, H. C., 10
Thudium Bros. Market, 115
Tibbetts, Ulalie, 201
Tipton, Eleanor, 183
Towne, Louise, 72
Towne, Mrs. Roy, 84
Traynor, Mrs. B. L., 220
Turner, Mrs. F. H., 228
Ulrich, Mrs. Robert, 126
Van Deusen, Mrs. C. A., 26
Van Stratton, Mrs. Ernest, 204
Varner, Mrs. Warren, 89-90
Varsity (Theater), 198
Victory Lunch, 217
Viets, Mrs. I. D., 33, 112, 231
Viets, Mrs. Ivan, 177
Vining, Cecil, 198
Virginia Inn (The), 93
Waffle Shoppe (The), 34
Wager, Mrs. Russell, 186
Waggoner, Mrs. J. W., 223
Wagner, Mrs. Walter, 181
Wamego, Eli, 96
Watkins, Mrs. J. E., 155
Watts, Mrs. H. G., 127
Watts, Mrs. William, 149
Weaver, A. B., 182
Weaver, Mrs. A. B. (Nell D.), 182
Webster's Grocery, 52
Welch, Mrs. L. D., 189
Wellhausen, Mrs. Edward, 213
Werner, Henry, 96
West End Grocery, 41
West End Meat Market, 154
Westheffer, Mrs. Don, 135
White, Bertha, 7
White, Harold, 7
White, Kathe, 7
White, Mrs. T. H., 30
White, William Allen, 186
White, Wilma, 7
Whitelaw, Bertha, 27